# Facilitative Leadership
# in Local Government

James H. Svara
and Associates

# Facilitative Leadership in Local Government

*Lessons from Successful Mayors and Chairpersons*

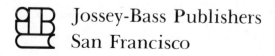

Jossey-Bass Publishers
San Francisco

Substantial discounts on bulk quantities of Jossey-Bass books
are available to corporations, professional associations, and other
organizations. For details and discount information, contact the
special sales department at Jossey-Bass Inc., Publishers.
(415) 433-1740; Fax (415) 433-0499.

For international orders, please contact your local Paramount Publishing
International office.

Manufactured in the United States of America. Nearly all Jossey-Bass
books and jackets are printed on recycled paper that contains at least
50 percent recycled waste, including 10 percent postconsumer waste.
Many of our materials are also printed with vegetable-based ink; during
the printing process these inks emit fewer volatile organic compounds
(VOCs) than petroleum-based inks. VOCs contribute to the formation of
smog.

**Library of Congress Cataloging-in-Publication Data**
Svara, James H.
    Facilitative leadership in local government : lessons from
successful mayors and chairpersons / James H. Svara and associates.
— 1st ed.
      p.    cm.—(The Jossey-Bass public administration series)
    Includes bibliographical references and index.
    ISBN 0-7879-0007-9
    1. Municipal government by city manager—United States.
2. Mayors—United States.  3. Municipal officials and employees—
United States.  4. Political leadership—United States.  I. Title.
II. Series.
JS344.C5S84     1994
306.2—dc20
                                                94-11408
                                                  CIP

FIRST EDITION
*HB Printing*    10 9 8 7 6 5 4 3 2 1                      *Code 9485*

# The Jossey-Bass
# Public Administration Series

# *Contents*

## Contents

*To my parents,*
*Herman and Esther Svara*

# *Preface*

The mayoralty in the council-manager form of government has been a poorly understood leadership position. On the surface, there is little that this official can do. The mayor lacks executive powers, which are vested in the manager, and shares responsibility for "political" leadership with the entire council, of which the mayor is simply one member. Anecdotal evidence suggests that leadership from a mayor is possible, although the general perception is that such leadership is rarely found. Henry Cisneros, former mayor of San Antonio and now Secretary of the U.S. Department of Housing and Urban Development, was widely recognized for his leadership in city government, as Erik Jonsson of Dallas and Murray Seasongood of Cincinnati were earlier. Such leadership is appreciated when it is present, but the nature of the mayor's contributions has not been clearly specified. Neither is there good understanding of what resources and attributes support effective leadership, nor of how common it is for council-manager cities to have extensive and effective leadership from the mayor. Our knowledge of a comparable official—the chairperson of the county commission in a county that uses the county administrator form—is even more scant.

In the early decades of the council-manager form, the mayor was intended to have a limited role. The mayor, as head of the council, played a limited role as presiding officer, spokesperson, official representative, and performer of ceremonial functions. As councils have become more diverse in their membership in recent decades, the need for the mayor to provide a focal point for elected leadership has become evident. Despite the increasing importance of the mayor's office, our understanding of the nature of the leadership has remained limited. The mayor is still often dismissed as a figurehead.

### Purpose of the Book

*Facilitative Leadership in Local Government* seeks to fill the vacuum of knowledge about the chief elected official in council-manager governments. Throughout, we try to answer a number of key questions:

- Can mayors and chairpersons be leaders in their governments?
- What kind of leadership do they provide?
- What difference do they make in their communities?
- What are the bases of their leadership?
- What attributes do successful leaders demonstrate, and what are their leadership skills?

These are not academic questions, although they are questions that scholars have puzzled over with little success. They indicate gaps in the knowledge of public officials, the media, and the public. Officials who hold the office of mayor or chairperson (or consider seeking the office) and people who work with them need to know what the office is and can be. Incumbents typically figure out the office as best they can through trial and error. Frequently (but not usually), new mayors and chairpersons are sources of conflict and tension with other officials because they overstep the appropriate boundaries of the office. Others fail to provide needed leadership activities. The fact that they do too much of the wrong things and not enough of the right things indicates that we do not know enough about which is which.

Reporters and editors who cover and analyze local government often do not understand the office of mayor or chairperson. They need to be more perceptive in their coverage and to assess mayors and chairpersons in terms of criteria appropriate to the council-manager form, rather than criteria derived from cities in which the mayor or county executive is the true executive officer. For example, if the mayor or chairperson is not a highly visible leader who appears to be in charge, the media often portray the official as deficient. On the other hand, success may be treated as an aberration—achieved despite the features of the office rather than because of them.

Citizens, too, should have a better appreciation of what kinds of leadership they can expect from the mayor or chairperson and of the qualities that contribute to effective performance. Otherwise, they will make inappropriate requests or have unrealistic expectations of what the chief elected official can do. For example, when citizens look to the mayor to "fix" a problem by issuing orders to the responsible department, they ignore that the mayor and the council collectively provide direction for a city manager.

Questions about the leadership of the mayor or chairperson also have some bearing on assessments of the form of government itself and of whether it should be retained. Finding ways to enhance the role of the mayor, without weakening the council or the city manager, has become a key issue in many jurisdictions. Increased diversity in cities and counties, particularly large ones, and splintered councils add to the need for effective leadership. The issue is whether the strong mayor or county executive form is required to meet this need.

The debate about the best way to enhance leadership in local government is limited by lack of both understanding and information about the nature of mayoral leadership in council-manager cities and counties. I believe that *Facilitative Leadership in Local Government* will make an important contribution to this debate.

## Case Studies

To clarify the effects of structure on mayoral leadership and the nature of facilitative leadership, nine case studies are presented in this book. These studies examine not only leadership by chief elected officers in cities and counties with the council-manager form but also a government that underwent a transition from the commission form to the mayor-council form. These cases were selected from papers presented at a symposium held in North Carolina in April 1991, and they were revised for this book. In response to a national call for papers, the authors identified examples of successful mayors and chairpersons who offered significant leadership to their cities and counties. The case studies cover these areas:

- Governmental and community context
- Official's background
- Leadership style and roles
- Areas in which the official has made a positive impact
- Nature and sources of leadership

The subjects, arranged by type and size of jurisdiction, are as follows:

### *Cities*

Mayors in San Diego, California, 1971–1991 (1,015,190)

E. S. "Jim" Melvin, mayor, 1973–1981, Greensboro, North Carolina (180,000)

Gene Roberts, mayor, 1981–present, Chattanooga, Tennessee (175,000) (transformation from commission form to strong-mayor–council form of government)

Noel C. Taylor, mayor, 1975–1992, Roanoke, Virginia (101,250)

Gary Halter, mayor, 1980–1986, College Station, Texas (60,000)

Betty Jo Rhea, mayor, 1986–present, Rock Hill, South Carolina (35,327)

Michael Mears, mayor, 1985–1993, Decatur, Georgia (17,400)

*Counties*

Paula MacIlwaine, chairperson and commissioner, 1976–1991, Montgomery County, Ohio (571,000)
Carla DuPuy, chairperson, 1985–1990, Mecklenburg County, North Carolina (500,000)

## Overview of the Contents

The existing literature relies heavily on case studies of single cities. One case study may not provide generalizations that apply to all council-manager cities. Here, we combine analysis of survey data with in-depth examination of officials in nine cities.

In Chapter One, I examine leadership by the mayor or chairperson in theory and practice and present the facilitative model of leadership, which guided the preparation of the case studies. I ask how common it is to find effective chief elected officials in council-manager governments and what impact, if any, effective leaders have.

The three cases in Part One discuss examples of comprehensive leadership by mayors and chairpersons in the sense of their having fully developed all aspects of the office. Because of the scope and extent of their activities, these officials are perceived as leaders by the public and the media. Mayor Michael Mears (Chapter Two, by Dan W. Durning) of Decatur, Georgia, was a leader in the successful effort to build a hotel and convention center as the anchor for downtown development, resolving disputes between developers and neighborhood interests. Commission Chairperson Paula MacIlwaine (Chapter Three, by Mary Ellen Mazey) of Montgomery County, Ohio, was an advocate for women and minority rights and initiated a tax-sharing program among local jurisdictions. In Chapter Four, I discuss Mayor Jim Melvin of Greensboro, North Carolina, who helped secure the acceptance of expanded municipal involvement to influence the timing of highway construction projects. He also developed and maintained support—throughout a decade of opposition, repeated studies, and rising costs—for a regional sewage-treatment plant.

In these examples, it is often hard to distinguish what the

mayor or chairperson wanted to accomplish from the preferences of the council as a whole and those developed by the manager and the staff. Indeed, this is the mark of a facilitative leader. Nevertheless, these leaders were recognized for their special contributions in crystallizing an issue, developing a solution, securing broad support, and winning acceptance.

Part Two explores the cases of two mayors and a chairperson who have been highly effective at developing a sense of cohesion and purpose in local government. The spirit of cooperation they helped foster did not exist before they assumed office. Part of their leadership was to focus the policy-making process and make it more effective. This is not to say that these officials are not without issues that they have raised or policies that they have advanced. For example, Mecklenburg County Chairperson Carla Dupuy (Chapter Five, by Timothy D. Mead) helped define and organize support for a new superregional organization that brought jurisdictions together in several regional councils from North and South Carolina. In Chapter Six, Linda C. Winner shows how Mayor Noel C. Taylor fostered urban revitalization in Roanoke, Virginia. Mayor Betty Jo Rhea (Chapter Seven, by Craig M. Wheeland) promoted the use of strategic planning in Rock Hill, South Carolina. Still, these leaders are more process-oriented than policy-oriented.

The three cases in Part Three raise questions about the impact of change on the viability of facilitative leadership. Gary Halter, the author and subject of the case in Chapter Eight, describes from first-person and academic perspectives what the mayor's office entails and examines the changing council composition and new leadership challenges in College Station, Texas.

Glen W. Sparrow's assessment of San Diego, California, in Chapter Nine presents an alternative to the view of leadership presented in other chapters. He argues that in large, diverse cities experiencing rapid growth, leadership of an executive type is needed from the mayor. Although former mayor Pete Wilson achieved the executive model informally, his successors have not been able to sustain it. Charter change, in Sparrow's opinion, is now required.

In Chapter Ten, Edward Thompson III and David M. Brodsky analyze a case that is different in two respects from the rest of the cases. The mayor, Gene Roberts, began his tenure under the commission form of government in Chattanooga, Tennessee, and later became the first mayor elected under the mayor-council form. This case demonstrates how the model of facilitative leadership was applicable to a mayor in a commission city. Furthermore, once he had established the facilitative style, Roberts sustained it through the change in the new form of government, even though he played certain roles differently under the two forms of government.

In the final chapter, I consider the future of leadership in local government, especially council-manager government. I examine the following questions:

- How are the mayor's and the chairperson's office and council-manager government generally changing in the 1990s?
- Will officials be able to meet the leadership challenge within the council-manager form of government, or will that form have to be altered substantially or replaced?
- If there is not structural change, how can the effectiveness of leaders be increased?

The analyses and case studies presented in this book indicate that effective chief elected officers and effective managers are not incompatible; strong leadership from a mayor or chairperson does not produce conflict with a manager or diminish the manager's position. Rather, it strengthens relationships and promotes a constructive balance between the contributions of the council and the manager. The challenge is to expand our understanding of the office of mayor and chairperson and promote effective performance by incumbents. The qualities illustrated by these case studies need to become the norm in American cities and counties; the vitality of local government depends on it.

### Acknowledgments

The conference for which these case histories were originally drafted met April 12-13, 1991, in Raleigh, North Carolina. The conference was sponsored in part by grants from the Murray & Agnes Seasongood Good Government Foundation in Cincinnati, and the encouragement and support of the foundation is greatly appreciated.

Additional support was provided by the Samuel J. Ervin, Jr., Fund of the Department of Political Science and Public Administration, the college of Humanities and Social Sciences, and the Office of Research Administration, North Carolina State University.

Several graduate students in the Master of Public Administration Program at North Carolina State University provided assistance at various stages in the project. They include Tom Elkins, Susan Fleetwood, and Elizabeth Kurzer. Genie French, graduate secretary, helped in many ways and kept the Public Administration Program running smoothly while I was absorbed in this book.

*Raleigh, North Carolina*                                   JAMES H. SVARA
*June 1994*

# Note on Forms of Local Government

Most city and county governments in the United States use of one of two models for organizing offices and assigning authority to them.[1] The terms used to refer to the officials in these forms vary widely across the country, but the most common ones associated with each approach are the following:

- Model 1: Elected executive, with separation of powers
  The separation of powers, or system of checks and balances, is between the executive (mayor or county executive) and the legislative body (council, board of aldermen, or board of commissioners in cities; county commission, board of commissioners, or board of supervisors in counties). Examples are the strong- and weak-mayor–council and county executive forms.
- Model 2: Appointed executive, with no separation of powers
  The governing board, headed by the mayor or chairperson, appoints the executive (city manager in cities; county man-

ager, county administrator, or in rare cases, county executive in counties). (The governing board is called the council or board of commissioners in cities; in counties, the county commission, the board of commissioners, or the board of supervisors.) The appointed executive serves at the pleasure of the governing board, and there are no formal powers that the executive can use to check the governing board. Examples are the council-manager and county administrator forms.

Failure to distinguish between the two models leads to confusion in classifying the forms and offices in local government, particularly in cities. The term *mayor* refers to vastly different offices, depending on the form, by contrast with the clear distinction between the offices denoted by the titles *county executive* and *county chairperson*.

The terms *strong* and *weak* should be used only to refer to variations in the mayor-council form, where mayors have formal powers over other participants in the governmental process but vary in the extent of these powers. The terms are often used inappropriately to distinguish between the mayor-council mayor and the council-manager mayor, who does not have such formal powers. Their use is inappropriate because mayors cannot be measured on a single scale that extends from strong to weak. The characteristics of each model are briefly discussed here, to provide a background for understanding the unique qualities of the mayor and the chairperson in the council-manager form of government.

### Elected Executive

The mayor-council governments are the most commonly used form in very large and small cities (population over 500,000 and under 5,000). Smaller cities are more likely to have a *weak* mayor, whereas larger cities are somewhat more likely to have a *strong* mayor. Approximately 12 percent of counties have an elected executive with powers similar to those of a strong mayor.

The *weak-mayor–council* form of government is characterized by extensive fragmentation of authority. This form divides power up into many small parcels, has many instances of shared authority, and allows for direct election of many officials (for example, independently elected boards and commissions with authoritative jurisdiction over such local governmental functions as libraries or water and sewers). The weaknesses of these mayors stem from (1) their limited powers to appoint staff, some of whom are directly elected, some of whom are appointed by the council, and some of whom are appointed (or removed) by the mayor, but only with approval of the council; and from (2) their inability to develop the budget as an executive proposal that reflects overall policy. A committee of the council, or composed of the council, the mayor, and other elected officials, typically drafts the budget. Therefore, the council has both legislative and administrative responsibilities, since it passes laws and creates programs but also appoints staff and shares in the supervision of administrative departments. Because of weakness with respect to personnel and budgeting, the mayor lacks integrated administrative control over the staff and operations of city government. Still, this mayor has powers not found in the council-manager form, and some "weak" mayors have been able to augment their influence through skillful use of these powers.

The *strong-mayor–council* or *county executive* forms of government also have separation of powers, but the separation is between, on the one hand, a mayor with extensive power and integrated administrative control over staff and, on the other, the elected legislative body. This form was patterned after the strong executive in the national government and incorporated the goal of the reform movement, to consolidate influence in the hands of the executive and thus eliminate the power vacuum that had been exploited by the political machine. Typically, in strong-mayor cities, the mayor and council members are the only elected officials. The mayor has the authority to appoint and dismiss certain department heads, often without the consent of the council. Other department heads may be covered by civil service provisions or, once appointed, may not be removable by the mayor except for cause (demonstrated failure to perform official duties adequately). The mayor prepares the budget and controls its administration and is responsible for directing the efforts of the departments of city government. Therefore, the mayor has the integrated administrative control that the weak mayor lacks. The lines of authority for all or most departments of city government lead to the mayor's office.

In some cities, the mayor may appoint a chief administrative officer (CAO), who handles whatever tasks the mayor assigns. These usually involve extensive delegated authority over program implementation, operational concerns, and budget formulation, as well as advisory roles in developing other policy recommendations. The CAO augments the capacity of the mayor to attend to broad-ranging demands for political and organizational leadership.

The council is confined to a more limited role. Even in policy making, the council is heavily dependent on the mayor for proposals and information, and it can be checked by the mayor's veto power and the mayor's favorable position for mobilizing public opinion in support of proposals. The council must approve policies, however, and it can override vetoes; thus there is the potential for deadlock between the executive and the legislature.

Because the mayor and the council exercise offsetting powers, there are times when each party perceives that its powers and prerogatives are being challenged by the other. For example, the mayor may assert the authority to sign contracts below a certain dollar amount without the council's review, whereas the council may insist on approving all contracts. Furthermore, the administrative staff can be caught in the middle, as when the council adopts a new program and wants to see it put into effect but the mayor orders the staff to delay implementation. Learning to prevent and manage the conflicts that can arise over separation of powers is part of being an elected official in mayor-council government (Svara, 1990).

### Appointed Executive

The *council-manager* form of government provides, in effect, for specialization of roles. The council and the mayor occupy the overtly political roles in government, set policy, and select the city manager. The manager provides policy advice and recommendations to the council and directs the administrative apparatus. The council-manager form is used in the majority of cities with populations of between 10,000 and 250,000. The mayor and council members are the only elected officials in city government. The council possesses all governmental authority except as it delegates authority to the manager; thus there is no separation of powers or system of checks and balances. The mayor is typically the presiding officer of the council and has no formal powers different from those of other council members (except for veto power in 12 percent of council-manager cities; see DeSantis and Renner, 1993). Mayors, directly elected in 62 percent of these cities (Adrian, 1988), can be an important source of policy guidance and coordination of participants, although they rarely exercise any administrative authority.

The relationship between the commission and the manager is the same in the 25 percent of counties that use the county administrator form of government. The differences are that the chairperson is usually selected from within the commission and that there are other elected line officers (such as the sheriff) in county government.

In these cities and counties, the manager is the executive officer, with extensive authority for directing staff, drafting and (after approval by council) expending the budget, and controlling operations. Given the great scope of the manager's influence and authority, some feel that the form weakens public control. Others contend that democratic government is not jeopardized: "In this system, executive authority can safely be great, because limits on the executive are even larger, and they may be exercised swiftly and decisively" (Newland, 1985, p. 8).

The manager is appointed by the council and serves at the pleasure of the council, without term. The manager is typically the only staff member hired by the city council (in some cities, however, the city attorney, the clerk, or both are also selected by the council), and all other employees are hired under the authority of the manager. In some cities, direct communication between council members and any staff member except the manager and attorney is prohibited, and even if it is not explicitly proscribed, the norm of the system is for elected officials to respect the insulation of staff from "political" interference. In counties, it is common to have some agency heads directly elected by the voters (for example, the sheriff).

The council-manager form of government has always sought to mark off the appropriate spheres of responsibility for the council and the manager. The division of roles is intended to keep the council out of excessive involvement in administrative affairs and to maintain democratic control of the manager. The shorthand guide to separation of spheres has been the advice that the council "handles policy" and the manager "takes care of administration." In actuality, the theoreticians of the council-manager plan did not intend that, and most city and county managers themselves do not adhere to a fundamental dichotomy between policy and administration. The commentary that accompanied the second Model Charter, published in 1919, did not advance the policy-administration dichotomy in the new council-manager form of government; it argued that the manager must "show himself to be a leader, formulating policies and urging their adoption by the council" (Woodruff, 1919, p. 130). Thus the founders of the plan intended the manager to provide leadership and advice to the council in its enactment of legislation. A narrowing of the definition of the manager's position began in the 1920s and continued for twenty years. Perhaps to allay suspicions that managerial government would lead to administrative dominance, popularizers of the plan stressed the idea that the manager should be simply an administrative technician.

Every empirical study of the manager's roles before and since the assertion of this narrow view, however, has found policy involvement. Recent examples are Ammons and Newell (1988), Svara (1989), and Nalbandian (1991). The policy role of the manager has important implications for the roles of elected officials. They can assume that the manager not only will keep them informed about developments in the city or county but also will provide recommendations about actions that are needed. In fact, the potential influence of the manager is such that the performance and integrity of council-manager government is affected by the ability of the council to determine the overall mission and policy priorities for the government and clearly communicate them to the manager. The performance of the mayor or chairperson is important to goal setting by the council and smooth coordination with the manager.

The structure of council-manager government promotes cooperative relationships among officials. Because the ultimate control over city government lies with the council, there is less likelihood of power struggles between the council and the manager. The council and the manager do not compete for the same rewards from public service. Elected officials seek public support and re-election, whereas managers are concerned about how the council assesses their work and about their standing and respect within their profession. Furthermore, the city manager has a professional commitment to helping the council accomplish its goals; if the manager does not, he or she can be replaced. To be sure, tensions can emerge among elected officials, or between them and the staff. An important function of the mayor or chairperson is to promote effective working relationships and alleviate tensions if they develop. With no separation of powers, officials do not have to deal with structural impediments to cooperation.

This book focuses on council-manager government, but there are some similarities in the commission form of city government regarding the nature of the mayor's position. As in the council-manager form, there is no separation of powers between the executive and the legislative body because the commissioners serve a dual role, as directors of departments and as members of the governing board. The mayor does not have powers over other commissioners. There is a tendency toward mutual accommodation among commissioners; each one is likely to operate in accord with the principle "I won't interfere in your area of responsibility if you don't interfere in mine." There is the potential, in this situation, for the mayor to promote more active cooperation, depending on the nature of the leadership he or she provides.

## Implications of Form for Elected Leaders

Mayors in cities with and without separation of powers differ dramatically, even though they have the same title.[2] The mayor in a city with the mayor-council form of government is an executive with administrative authority for hiring, budgeting, and directing governmental departments.[3] The mayor in a council-manager city does not have any executive powers but is head of the governing board. These differences do not imply, however, that one variety of mayor is better or more complete than the other. Each can make substantial contributions and has distinct roles to play. These roles are determined by the requirements of the form of government and by the patterns of interaction that characterize the governmental process.

In a mayor-council city, the mayor is the key initiator of action. This form, to function beyond the level of maintaining current operations, depends on certain kinds of leadership from the mayor. By establishing direction, forging coalitions, and galvanizing the bureaucracy, the executive mayor becomes the driving force in this form of government. The effective mayor in this form sets goals, builds coalitions, and influences the council, the bureaucracy, and the public to act according to his or her preferences. It is normally expected that these mayors will use their formal powers of office and their informal resources to gain leverage over other actors in local government.

The mayor in a council-manager government need not take on the same roles but makes a different kind of contribution. This office is important to the city government's operation, but what the mayor can do beyond filling ceremonial roles has often been overlooked. To be sure, policy making is shared by the entire council; the manager draws on professional expertise and staff support to generate proposals, and executive powers are vested in the manager. An active and effective mayor, however, can elevate the level of performance of the other officials and of the governmental system as a whole.

What is different about council-manager mayors and chairpersons is that, rather than executing and controlling, these mayors *facilitate*—that is, they accomplish objectives by enhancing the efforts of others. This distinction is essential to the orientation of these chief elected officials. Rather than seeking power as the way to accomplish tasks, facilitative mayors and chairpersons seek to empower others. Their roles are to foster communication and promote effective interaction among other officials and to provide a greater sense of purpose to city government. In this sense, the mayor is a guiding force in city government who helps ensure that all other officials are performing as well as possible and that all are moving in the right direction. The same leadership possibilities exist for mayors in commission cities and for chairpersons of county commissions.

The difference between executive and nonexecutive chief

elected officers is clear, but a similarity should also be noted: like the elected executive, the mayor or chairperson in a council-manager government provides political leadership, as opposed to the professional leadership offered by the city or county manager. The mayor or chairperson, as an elected official, has issues, arguments, audiences, and contacts that the manager does not have.

Take the example of former mayor John Crowley of Pasadena, California.[4] Between 1985 and 1988, the city faced severe financial problems. Because of his professional background in finance, Crowley was able to help develop a solution to the problem, and his political leadership was critical to its adoption. He was highly effective at framing the issue and communicating the solution to the public. For one part of this solution, he won the backing of other council members, secured media support, and led a campaign that resulted in a referendum that secured the 66 percent voter approval needed for a general-obligation bond issue. For the second part, which required state legislative action, he worked with the legislature, forged a diverse alliance of groups in the city to support the bill, negotiated with other local government officials to overcome their opposition, bargained with a local housing-advocacy support group over future funding for housing, and lined up support from political allies of the governor to secure his approval. Mayor Crowley relied heavily on city staff and received extensive assistance from them, but he was able to operate publicly and privately in a political realm where the professional staff lacked the background and contacts to be as effective. Furthermore, although professional staff often engage in negotiating and brokering solutions, they could not legitimately have bargained with the same resources or made the same commitments. A politician like Crowley could promise to help the housing-advocacy groups find creative techniques to raise $10 million in new city funds; a manager could not make such a commitment independently. Articulating issues and selling proposals with simple rhetoric, making commitments with political support as collateral, and winning support with trade-offs are actions better taken by a political leader than by an appointed professional leader in local government.

The case studies presented in this book contain other examples of mayors or chairpersons taking on the tasks of articulating an issue, shaping the agenda, mobilizing support, forming coalitions, and enlisting the commitment of important groups. Their accomplishments, like Mayor Crowley's, show that it is more useful to distinguish levels of effectiveness than to use such terms as *strong* and *weak* in assessing mayors. Chief elected officials in cities and counties—mayors, chairpersons, and county executives—may differ in using power-oriented or facilitative styles of leadership, but are all potentially important political leaders.

## Notes

1. The exceptions among cities are the commission form (a plural-executive form, in which the members of the commission head departments in city government and collectively serve as the legislative body) and the town-meeting form in New England. In counties, the traditional commission form has a plural executive (the commission), and elected heads of certain departments (such as the sheriff), but no single executive.

2. In counties, there is less confusion about the authority of the chief elected official because of different titles. The term *commission chairperson* obviously refers to the head of the governing board, whereas the term *county executive* indicates executive authority.

3. The generalizations about differences are most appropriate in contrasting the strong-mayor–council form with the council-manager form. In the weak-mayor–council form, which is common in small cities, the mayor shares executive powers with the council and may be a member of the council (DeSantis and Renner, 1993).

4. This example is taken from a case study that was presented at the symposium on mayoral leadership described earlier. It was written by Donald McIntyre, former city manager, City of Pasadena, and Paul Heller, former intern in Pasadena and administrative assistant in the town manager's office, Apple Valley, California.

## References

Adrian, C. R. "Forms of City Government in American History." In *Municipal Yearbook, 1988*. Washington, D.C.: International City Management Association, 1988.

Ammons, D. N., and Newell, C. " 'City Managers Don't Make Policy': A Lie; Let's Face It." *National Civic Review*, 1988, *57*, 124–132.

DeSantis, V., and Renner, T. "Contemporary Patterns and Trends in Municipal Government Structures." In *Municipal Yearbook, 1993*. Washington, D.C.: International City Management Association, 1993.

Nalbandian, J. *Professionalism in Local Government*. San Francisco: Jossey-Bass, 1991.

Newland, C. A. "Council-Manager Governance: Positive Alternative to Separation of Powers." *Public Management*, 1985, *67*, 7–9.

Svara, J. H. "Policy and Administration: Managers As Comprehensive Professional Leaders." In H. G. Frederickson (ed.), *Ideal and Practice in City Management*. Washington, D.C.: International City Management Association, 1989.

Svara, J. H. *Official Leadership in the City: Patterns of Conflict and Cooperation*. New York: Oxford University Press, 1990.

Woodruff, C. R. (ed.). *A New Municipal Program*. East Norwalk, Conn.: Appleton & Lange, 1919.

# The Authors

JAMES H. SVARA is director of the Public Administration Program at North Carolina State University. He received his B.A. degree (1965) in history from the University of Kentucky and his Ph.D. degree (1972) in political science from Yale University. Before arriving at North Carolina State University in 1989, he was a member of the faculty at the University of North Carolina, Greensboro.

Svara's teaching and research deal with local government management and urban politics. He has given special emphasis to the roles and relationships of city government officials—mayors, council members, and administrators. Recent publications include *Official Leadership in the City: Patterns of Conflict and Cooperation* (1990) and *A Survey of America's City Councils: Continuity and Change* (1991). He is a regular contributor to programs of the International City Management Association, the National League of Cities, the North Carolina League of Municipalities, and the North Carolina Association of County Commissioners.

*David M. Brodsky* is UC Foundation Professor of Political Science at the University of Tennessee, Chattanooga, where he is also coordinator of the master's degree program in public administration. His teaching and research areas are methodology and public administration. He received his Ph.D. degree (1973) in political science from Emory University.

*Dan W. Durning* is research associate in the University of Georgia's Carl Vinson Institute of Government and adjunct professor in the university's Department of Political Science, where he teaches public policy analysis. He is on the editorial board of the *Journal of Public Administration Research and Theory* and is book review editor of the *State and Local Government Review*. He received his Ph.D. degree (1986) in public policy from the Graduate School of Public Policy at the University of California, Berkeley.

*Gary Halter* is professor of political science at Texas A&M University, where he also serves as director of undergraduate programs. He received his Ph.D. degree (1970) in political science from the University of Maryland. He served as a member of the College Station City Council from 1975 to 1980 and as mayor from 1980 to 1986.

*Mary Ellen Mazey* went to Wright State University in 1979 as assistant professor of geography. She received her Ph.D. degree (1977) in geography from the University of Cincinnati. In 1986, she initiated the development of the university's Center for Urban and Public Affairs. She also worked with the university administration to create the Department of Urban Affairs in 1988. She currently serves as director of the Center for Urban and Public Affairs and as chair of the Department of Urban Affairs.

*Timothy D. Mead* is professor of political science at the University of North Carolina, Charlotte. He received his Ph.D. degree (1969) in political science from George Washington University. For most of the period covered by his case study in this volume, Mead was a member of the Charlotte-Mecklenburg Planning Commission.

*Glen W. Sparrow* is professor in the School of Public Administration and Urban Studies at San Diego State University. He received his Ph.D. degree (1976) in government from Claremont Graduate School.

*Edward Thompson III* is associate professor of political science at California State University, San Marcos. His teaching and research areas are urban and African American politics and public administration. He received his Ph.D. degree (1981) in urban and public administration from Howard University.

*Craig M. Wheeland* is assistant professor of political science at Villanova University, where he is also coordinator of the public administration concentration in the Human Organization Science Program. He received his Ph.D. degree (1989) in political science from Pennsylvania State University.

*Linda C. Winner* is director of enrichment at the alumni association of the University of North Carolina, Chapel Hill. She formerly served as professor of organizational behavior and public policy at the Federal Executive Institute, Charlottesville, Virginia, and as director of leadership development at the University of Virginia's Center for Public Service. She received her Ph.D. degree (1986) in education administration from the University of North Carolina, Chapel Hill.

# Facilitative Leadership
# in Local Government

# 1

*James H. Svara*

# Redefining Leadership in Local Government: The Facilitative Model

Understanding the kind of leadership that the chief elected official in council-manager and commission governments can provide requires a rethinking of standard assumptions and models. Americans are accustomed to looking for strong executives to lead in Washington and state capitols and to direct city or county governments. The president or the governor is expected to put his or her stamp on government. Aren't all mayors supposed to do the same? Similar thinking is reflected in the dominant leadership model for mayors in the political science literature, in which the concept of leadership is based on the acquisition and use of power. The innovator or entrepreneur—as the prototype of leadership is labeled in this model—is characterized by the ability to pyramid the limited assets of the mayor's office in order to initiate policy and implement change. With augmented power and resources, the mayor can use inducement and threat to forge coalitions of officials and citizens and

1

to galvanize reluctant bureaucratic agencies. This model emphasizes power as the essential means of achieving effective leadership.

The characteristics of council-manager and commission government both permit and require a different kind of leadership on the part of that chief elected official who is not the executive officer in the government. Power is not a precondition of effective leadership in this setting. The council-manager form supports a model of mayoral leadership that stands in contrast to the standard power-based model.

The alternative found in council-manager governments is based on a facilitative model of leadership. That alternative model is described in this chapter, after a review of the literature on mayoral leadership. Next, the dimensions of the model are used to measure the proportion of mayors in council-manager cities that can be considered effective. This estimate is based on responses given in surveys of city managers in North Carolina and Ohio. These data are also used to analyze the impact of differing levels of mayoral leadership. The critical question is whether effective facilitative leadership, as we are defining it, improves the performance of local government. In subsequent chapters, case studies offer vivid portraits of men and women who have given significant leadership to their communities as mayors or county commission chairpersons. From these sources, the new model of leadership is refined.

### Review of Previous Research

The *innovator* or *entrepreneur* type of mayoral leadership emerges from studies conducted in mayor-council cities as the norm for mayoral leadership (Dahl, 1961; George, 1968; Cunningham, 1970).[1] The innovator sets goals, builds coalitions, and influences the council, the bureaucracy, and the public to act according to his or her preferences. Although formal resources are of some help in establishing this type of leadership, mayors must also accumulate resources from informal sources in order to gain leverage over other actors. Because of the conflict common in city government, mayors face obstacles in establishing their position and must contend with challengers, including the council and entrenched department heads inside government. In this model of mayoral leadership, it is necessary for the mayor to overcome the "considerable fragmentation of authority and dispersal of power characteristic of the formal governmental structure" of American cities (George, 1968, p. 1196). To this end, Ferman argues, "formal tools and informal resources must be manipulated in such a way that the mayor establishes the conditions for increasing executive power" (1985, p. 10).

Some discussions of the mayor in council-manager cities are based on the same premises, despite the fact that the structure and process of government are very different in these cities.[2] Two previously published case studies of individual mayors examine the office from the "strong executive" perspective. They share the assumption that the so-called normal council-manager form does not provide the opportunity for mayoral leadership. Pressman's study (1972) of a reluctant mayor in one city—Mayor Redding of Oakland—has strongly colored perceptions of the office. Pressman argues that when the mayor's leadership is displayed, it will be largely "hortatory in nature," given the characteristics of the form (p. 523). Following this lead, Lineberry and Sharkansky (1978), in their urban-politics text, assert that the "ribbon cutter" type of leadership is "the common role in council-manager cities" (p. 194). In the second study, Sparrow (1984, p. 5), who charts the creation of a "new municipal chief executive model" by Mayor Pete Wilson of San Diego, demonstrates that broader leadership is possible but argues that basic precepts of the form of government must be altered in order for it to be achieved.[3]

These studies are based on a standard political-science interpretation of the mayor's office and the council-manager form of city government. There are four shortcomings to this approach:

1. Ignoring the significance of structure
2. Overstating the centrality of the mayor and distrust of the manager
3. The presumption of conflict
4. Excessive reliance on the use of power to fashion leadership in comparison to other resources

As for the first shortcoming, authority is formally concentrated and centralized in council-manager governments (see the

Preface, this volume). Little notice is taken, however, of the potential for direction by the mayor and other elected officials, based on exercise of this authority rather than on an accumulated informal power base.

As for the second, it is assumed that the mayor must activate the lethargic city government and give it direction, if any elected official is to do so. The manager, as Pressman (1972) and Sparrow (1984) both suggest, will manipulate the council, pursue a personal or professional agenda, and take cues from influential outsiders but will not provide leadership responsive to elected officials or supportive of their exercise of democratic control. Only the mayor is presumed capable of curtailing the manager, by limiting his or her scope of responsibility and by expanding the mayor's own activities. Thus mayoral leadership is seen as essential to providing direction and to curtailing the power of staff. This view of the mayor and the manager ignores the possibility of collective leadership, either exercised by the mayor and the manager together or by the council as a whole. It also ignores the fact that managers are responsive to the mayor and the council, as other studies have shown. For example, Boynton and Wright (1971) characterize the interaction between the mayor and the manager in large cities as indicative of "collaborative or team relationships" (p. 33). Wikstrom (1979) also concludes that council-manager government has evolved into "teamwork governance; mayors and managers need and depend upon each other" (p. 275). Cooperative relationships between elected and appointed officials are common in council-manager cities (Svara, 1990).

As for the third shortcoming of standard interpretations, there may be a presumption of conflict within the governmental process because of competition for power. As mentioned in the Preface, the appearance of "strong" mayors is often assumed to produce problems for city managers. Sparrow (1984) has noted that many in San Diego viewed power as a hydraulic system "whereby decrease in the manager's power would result in increased mayoral power" (p. 6), and Pressman's analysis of Oakland (1972) also rests on a zero-sum conception of power. When participants in the governmental process view the payoffs of interaction in this way, conflict is indeed likely. When the mayor's winning depends on the manager's losing, there is distrust between the two, and each views the other's goals as incompatible with his or her own. Each must seek to block the other while seeking to advance his or her own goals.[4]

Where the fourth shortcoming is concerned, the emphasis on power as the mayor's key resource has Pressman (1972) and Sparrow (1984) arguing that all mayors must increase their resources, in order to acquire leverage over other participants or induce support: "Without governmental jurisdiction, staff, and financial resources, it is hard for any mayor to direct, or even influence, the actions of others" (Pressman, 1972, p. 522). Sparrow also stresses the need for informally pyramiding power. According to Sparrow, Mayor Pete Wilson's leadership was based on his "adroit accumulation of political, policy making, and administrative power" (pp. 5-6), culminating in de facto control over selection of the manager. The power assumed to be needed for leadership is assumed in turn to come only through resources outside the formal structure, or through alteration of the form. Thus, even without separation of powers, conflict may be present, and so mayors should be prepared to use power-oriented approaches to leadership. The defect in this approach is that the behavior appropriate for an executive mayor may be unnecessary in council-manager and commission government. Moreover, it may produce conditions that would otherwise not be present. Conflict may be introduced when the mayor takes actions that advance his or her own interests and block those of others. If a mayor uses power tactics, on the assumption that a manager will resist mayoral control (as opposed to control by the entire council), these tactics are likely to provoke the very resistance that the mayor anticipates. Thus anticipation of resistance becomes a self-fulfilling prophecy. When a cooperative relationship is present among officials, the mayor does not need to be an autonomous power wielder who activates and checks other officials. Rather, the mayor can be seen as an agent of cooperation in relations among officials.

The roles and types of leadership provided by the mayors in the two forms of government are distinct. The council-manager mayor is not limited in his or her leadership. He or she is not merely a "weak" mayor. Rather, he or she is different in the kind of leadership provided. All mayors potentially offer political leadership, regardless of the form of government. The same is true of county executives and the chairperson of the county commission. In the council-manager form of government, such leadership depends on an understanding of the kind of leadership that the chief elected official should provide and on full use of the potential inherent in the office in this form. Formal or informal power resources are not essential to leadership.

What is different about the council-manager mayor is that this mayor does not execute (or directly promote the accomplishment of tasks). Rather, the mayor is a *facilitator*. The facilitative mayor leads by empowering others—in particular, the council and the manager—rather than by seeking power for himself or herself; this mayor accomplishes objectives by enhancing the performance of others (Svara, 1990). The distinction makes a great difference in the orientation of the mayor. Rather than seeking power resources in order to gain leverage over other participants in the governmental process, the facilitative mayor seeks to empower others. The mayor leads by enhancing and influencing the performance of other officials; promoting information exchange among the council members, the manager, the public, and other organizations; and providing a sense of purpose and direction.

In the facilitative model, the fully effective mayor provides leadership in two dimensions. First, the mayor contributes to the coordination of efforts among officials and raises the level of communication among them and with the public. Second, the mayor provides guidance in the formation of policy. Thus the mayor attends both to the process of interaction and to the purposes toward which efforts are directed.

### The Facilitative Model in the Private Sector

This view of the mayor's office is consistent with a number of recent studies of leadership in the private sector, which emphasize facilitation rather than power or control as the basis for leadership. These include Bennis (1985, 1989), Gilmore (1988), and Kouzes and Posner (1988). The key leadership attributes identified in these studies are creating a vision and securing broad commitment and participation from organizational members. The two dimensions identified in the mayor's leadership—coordination and direction setting—parallel dimensions in the "seven habits" identified by Covey (1989) in his assessment of the qualities that are associated with effectiveness. Effective leaders stress empathetic communication, think in "win-win" terms rather than seeing their interests in conflict with those of others, and use synergism to make the whole greater than the sum of the parts. Furthermore, effective leaders are proactive, have a clear sense of the ends they wish to achieve, and prioritize tasks to achieve long-term goals. Thus effective leaders improve process and sharpen the sense of purpose.

These elements are also found in the leadership traits of facilitative team managers, described by Rees (1991). Leaders improve the process of interaction by empowering participation and by developing consensus and focus on the purpose toward which a group is working.

Two styles of leadership and two types of organizations are posited in these writings. One is an authoritarian style, with one-way or top-down communication. The leader seeks to use powers of the office to manipulate people and resources in order to establish control. The counterstyle stresses the following skills: helping groups solve problems, listening, communicating, developing team capacity, coaching, motivating, and inspiring (Rees, 1991, pp. 14–15), and the roles of the facilitative leader are to "listen, ask questions, direct group process, coach, teach, build consensus, share in goal setting, share in decision making, [and] empower others to get things done" (p. 21). When people are not in charge, they are "primarily in the business of supporting other people in the accomplishment of their own goals" (Bellman, 1992, p. 6), and consequently they must "lead from the middle" to be effective (p. 20). A strong advocate of viewing leadership in terms of service rather than power is Richard Greenleaf, whose concept of servant leadership is finding support in the business world (Kiechel, 1992). The servant-leader is one who "wants to serve, to serve *first*"; in time, "conscious choice brings one to aspire to lead," and this leader is "sharply different from one who is a *leader* first" (Greenleaf, 1977, p. 13; emphasis in original).

The organization that matches the control- or power-oriented style is hierarchical in nature. Increasingly, organizations are flatter and loosely knit. This counterview sees organizations as networks with fluid authority, ambiguous limits, and overlapping domains. Bryson and Crosby (1992) argue that the world is characterized by shared power. Leaders in this setting "inspire and motivate followers through persuasion, example, and empowerment, not through command and control. Such leaders foster dialogue with their followers and the situations in which they find themselves, and they encourage collective action to address real problems" (Bryson and Crosby, 1992, p. 13). They cannot rely on formal authority or positional power to get things done.

To conclude this overview of how the facilitative model is described, primarily in studies of private sector organizations, it is useful to look at the summary of the practices and "commandments" of "leaders at their best" presented by Kouzes and Posner (1988, p. 14):

I.   Challenging the Process
    1.   Search for opportunities
    2.   Experiment and take risks
II.  Inspiring a Shared Vision
    3.   Envision the future
    4.   Enlist others
III. Enabling Others to Act
    5.   Foster collaboration
    6.   Strengthen others
IV.  Modeling the Way
    7.   Set the example
    8.   Plan small wins
V.   Encouraging the Heart
    9.   Recognize individual contribution
    10.  Celebrate accomplishments

This kind of leadership presumes an inclusive approach and work with others, rather than the achievement of power over them or the manipulation of resources to secure their support. As Covey (1989) puts it, leaders must inspire "creative cooperation" (p. 262). Together, all these writers articulate a distinct paradigm of leadership. The paradigm appears to be a startling departure from what we expect to find in the corporate world, and it may seem completely alien to the political process.

## *The Facilitative Model in Council-Manager Government*

The emphasis on cooperation in this alternate paradigm matches well the formal power position of the mayor or chairperson in council-manager governments. The difference is that the private sector manager can choose to use positional power to support a leader-centered style; the mayor or chairperson cannot, because formal authority over other officials is absent. Therefore, it is imperative that officials become adept practitioners of the facilitative style. As Bryson and Crosby (1992) observe, to be able to "marshal the legitimacy, power, authority, and knowledge required to tackle any major public issue, organizations and institutions must join forces in a 'shared-power' world" (p. 4). This is an apt description of the situation facing elected officials in council-manager governments.

The alternative leadership model—the leader-centered, power-oriented style—is not viable in the council-manager form, as we can see by examining each of the ten practices identified by Kouzes and Posner (1988). Seeking opportunities for change and risk taking—the first and second of the listed practices—is common to all leaders, but the styles of power-oriented and facilitative political leaders deviate from the third practice on. Leaders whose approach is based on power develop their own plans rather than a shared vision. They line up supporters, rather than enlisting others. What is most critical, they seek to maintain control, rather than fostering collaboration and strengthening others. Power-oriented leaders often find it necessary to conceal their intentions, limit the knowledge that even their allies have of their plans, and play one group off against another in order to move the political process toward achieving the goals that the leaders want to accomplish. They may "set the example" but are more likely to use dramatic forms of presenting and promoting their agendas, and they prefer big wins (with extensive media coverage) to small ones. Power-oriented leaders are limited in their ability to "encourage the heart" because they must emphasize their own contributions and celebrate their own accomplishments in order to remain in the limelight.

The contrast pointed out here between power-oriented and facilitative leadership is not meant to portray executive mayors or county executives as power-hungry or egomaniacal. It is important to remember that they are typically operating in conflictual settings, where other actors will exploit the situation for their own benefit, if the elected executives do not act likewise. As one study concludes (Feiock and Clingermayer, 1986), executive mayors are strongly inclined to engage in "credit claiming" activities; they have an "incentive to provide some form of visible—if only symbolic—benefits to a great array of potential supporters" (p. 224). It is hard to reconcile "credit claiming" with the attributes of facilitative leadership, since it drives out the trust, collaboration, and sharing on which facilitative leadership is based. In the words of Mayor Noel Taylor of Roanoke, the subject of one of the case studies in this volume, "I believe you can accomplish anything if you don't care who gets the credit." The case studies illuminate the key features of the facilitative leadership style—collaborating and fostering the creation of a shared vision. In various ways, all the cases stress the cooperative nature of relationships between the mayor or chairperson and the other actors in the political process. To mention just two examples, a central feature of Michael Mears's leadership in Decatur was helping others contribute to the governmental process, while Carla DuPuy of Mecklenburg County created a family atmosphere among officials. Mutual support and trust between the mayor and the manager is common to all the cases. Gary Halter (Chapter Eight, this volume), the former mayor of College Station, is typical when he characterizes his leadership as collaborative. These leaders sought to "envision the future" with their ideas for change. Some actively fashioned that vision by drawing on the resource of other participants; others established formal or informal processes to arrive at a collective vision. For the time being, we shall focus on the broad process and purpose dimensions of the facilitative model. It will be possible to develop a more detailed specification of the facilitative model in the concluding chapter, after the cases.

One potential weakness of the leadership provided by a facilitative mayor should be noted at this point. Durning (Chapter Two), in his case study of Michael Mears of Decatur, suggests that there may be an inherent limitation in facilitative leadership. He argues that the mayor or chairperson relies on the support of the governing coalition in the community, as well as on the permission of the council, in order to be effective.[5] Mead (Chapter Five) notes that DuPuy's influence increased when, through persistent contact and consistently sound performance, she secured the support of business leaders. In Chapter Two, however, Durning warns that if the mayor or chairperson tries to lead the government toward goals other than those supported by consensus, he or she risks loss of effectiveness. In some respects, Halter agrees (Chapter Eight), pointing out the difficulty of getting the council to act on agreed-upon planning goals when they are opposed by neighborhood groups, a key element in the governing coalition in College Station. Other cases (for example, in Chapters Three and Four) suggest that the mayor or chairperson can help forge the governing coalition or generate goals for it. Still, there is an important question that we will explore further in Chapter Eleven: Does a leadership approach that is not based on power entail a limited capacity to foster change?

In sum, a new style of leadership—or, more precisely, a style that has not been adequately recognized before—is available to mayors and chairpersons in the council-manager form of government. The resources required to adopt facilitative leadership are available as well.

### Resources for Leadership

The formal powers assigned to the mayor are limited in a council-manager city. The mayor usually does not appoint any staff, develop the budget, or control the manager. Rather than emphasizing the mayor's powers in order to understand the bases of mayoral leadership, it is more appropriate for us to examine the range of the mayor's interactions and the quality of his or her ideas.

Kotter and Lawrence (1974) have analyzed mayoral behavior in terms of processes: agenda setting, network building, and task accomplishing. They argue that the "scope of the mayor's domain"—those areas in which the mayor "behaves *as if* he has some responsibility" (p. 61)—is determined more by the nature of the mayor's agenda-setting activities than by the assignment of formal responsibility. Mayors can also establish broad networks of relationships, regardless of their formal powers. Inherent in this form is a potential for mayors to promote communication and cooperation, starting with the close relationship to the city manager. Tasks are accomplished through coordinating the efforts of other officials.

Additional resources that support facilitative leadership in council-manager cities have received only scant attention. Wikstrom (1979) identifies leadership roles that draw on essential features of the council-manager form and the tasks assigned to the mayor: presiding over the council, representing the city, and promoting constructive interaction between the council and the manager. The mayor may be able to provide leadership to the council, offer political leadership, and help realize goals. Boynton and Wright (1971) identify three significant spheres of activity in city government: the legislative, the public, and the bureaucratic. The mayor's significance derives from the dominant role typically played in the first two spheres, given the nature of the position, and from the mayor's unusually close relationship to the bureaucratic sphere, given the extensive interactions with the city manager.

The mayor has broad opportunities for facilitative leadership, by virtue of the attributes and duties of the position. As ceremonial head and spokesperson for the council, the mayor has much more extensive public and media contact than other council members do. As presiding officer, the mayor can guide the conduct of meetings and have some impact on the flow of debate and the timing of resolutions. As liaison with the city manager, the mayor links the two major components of the system—the legislative body and the administrative apparatus—and can foster communication and understanding between elected and appointed officials. As official representative, the mayor has wide dealings with officials in other governments and may serve as a key participant in formulating agreements with state or federal officials, local governments, developers, and others who seek joint ventures with the city government.

In performing these activities, the mayor occupies a *strategic location*, shaped by his or her special and close relationship with the council, the manager, and the public. The mayor's distinctive interactions with these participants provide a network that is readily available if the mayor chooses to use it. All the major interactional channels pass through the mayor. Because of this favored position, the mayor is able to tap into various communication networks among elected officials, governmental staff, and community leaders. All these actors can and do interact with one another independently, but the mayor can transmit messages better than anyone else in the government because of the breadth of knowledge and range of contacts he or she is likely to have. The mayor is a "broker"—not trading power but information and ideas. In so doing, the mayor has the unique potential to expand understanding and improve coordination among participants in the governmental process. The mayor can be the linchpin between elected and administrative officials and between officials and the public in council-manager governments.

To be sure, the mayor must recognize the strategic potential of his or her position and seek to maintain and expand the network. Eberts and Kelly (1985) have found that mayors differ in the importance they assign to facilitating citizen participation, as well as in their desire to establish links at the state and national level. When mayors are active locally and extralocally, however, they "perform a central coordinative role" not found in "any other community position" (pp. 41-42).

The mayor's opportunity for policy leadership is based on relationships formed through providing coordination. It also derives from the mayor's superior knowledge, gained through extensive contacts with the council, the manager, and the public, and from the ability to insert his or her own ideas while transmitting the messages of others.

The mayor's performance is also affected by his or her individual characteristics: experience; personal or occupational financial and staff support; such attributes as charisma, reputation, and wisdom; commitment to the job, in terms of time, resources, and energy; and his or her relationship with the media. These factors determine how well and how fully the mayor fills the position, whatever the scope of the office. Individual traits may explain why one mayor is generally perceived to make a significant difference in the way the city operates, whereas another is merely a figurehead.

### Leadership Roles and Types

My own research on the mayors of the five large cities in North Carolina has identified roles that mayors can play in four dimensions of the position (Svara, 1987; see also the case study in Chapter Six of this volume). The roles and illustrative activities are as follows:

### Traditional Roles

1.  Ceremonial figure: giving speeches, offering greetings, cutting ribbons
2.  Spokesperson: announcing and explaining positions taken by the council
3.  Presiding officer: facilitating discussion and resolution of business in council meetings

### Coordination and Communication

4.  Educator: providing information to the council, manager, or public, beyond announcing positions taken by the council; promoting awareness and understanding of problems
5.  Liaison with manager: increasing communication and understanding between the council and the manager
6.  Team builder: lining up a majority on the council; consensus building; unifying the council

### Policy and Organizing Roles

7.  Goal setter: setting goals and objectives; identifying problems; establishing a tone for the council
8.  Delegator/organizer: helping the council and the manager maintain their roles; helping council members recognize their responsibilities; defining and adjusting relationships with the manager
9.  Policy advocate: advocating programs; developing proposals for action; lining up support for proposals

### External Relations

10. Promoting the city or the county: creating a positive image; attracting development
11. Intergovernmental relations: serving as a liaison with local, state, and federal governments; promoting intergovernmental cooperation

As ceremonial leader, the mayor is presiding officer, spokesperson for the council, and official representative at ceremonial functions. The activities associated with these roles may seem inconsequential, but they provide extensive contact with the public and give the mayor the opportunity to set the tone for city government in its meetings, its orientation to staff, and its relations with the public. Furthermore, the mayor in these roles can shape supportive public attitudes. An important early example of the "moral leadership" that a mayor can provide was Murray Seasongood, a leader in the effort to adopt the council-manager plan in Cincinnati in 1925 and mayor for four years after the change.[6] Through his eloquence and his actions, he was instrumental in securing acceptance for the values and institutions of the new form. He provided a political buffer for the city manager, shielding him from political attack, and thereby helped ensure the establishment of professional management and public support for the institution. (Many of the cases presented in later chapters of this volume demonstrate how important it is for the mayor to be supportive of professional management, indicating that the ceremonial dimension should be expanded to include the creation and maintenance of the public understanding and support that are important in order for the council-manager form to function well.) As coordinator, the mayor can be an educator, a liaison between the council and the manager, and a team builder. In these roles, the mayor contributes to higher levels of communication and facilitates action by officials. As organizer and guide, the mayor is a goal setter and a delegator who monitors and adjusts working relationships, as well as distributing tasks to members of the council and others. The mayor is also a policy advocate, with activities that range from proposing specific solutions to developing a comprehensive agenda of action for the city. As representative and ambassador, the mayor promotes the advancement of the city and links the city to other governments.

The kind of mayoral leadership provided by an incumbent depends on which roles the mayor performs and how well he or she handles them. Some general types have emerged from observations of how mayors combine the four dimensions of leadership. The mayor who fills traditional roles but few others can be called the *symbolic head* of government.

If the next set of roles is performed as well, the mayor becomes a *coordinator*. The coordinator is a team leader, keeping the manager and the council in touch and interacting with the public and outside agencies, all of which roles contribute to improved communication. Coordinators help achieve high levels of shared information, but since they are weak in policy guidance, they contribute little to policy formulation (at least, no more than other members of the council).

*Activists* or *reformers* emphasize policy guidance and advocacy but neglect coordinative activities, especially team building. Essentially, they go it alone. They want to get things accomplished quickly and may succeed by force of personality alone but may also become isolated if council members view them as abrasive and exclusionary in their leadership.

The *director* is a complete type of mayor, who not only contributes to the smooth functioning of government but also provides a general sense of direction. A primary responsibility of the council is to determine the mission of city government and its broad goals. Directors contribute significantly to the consideration of broad questions of purpose. These mayors stand out as leaders in the eyes of their councils, the press, and the public, and they use that recognition as a basis for guidance rather than control. A director enhances the influence of elected officials by unifying the council, filling the policy vacuum that can exist on the council, and guiding policy toward goals that meet the needs of the community. Furthermore, the director is actively involved in monitoring and adjusting relationships within city government to maintain balance, cooperation, and high standards. The director does not supplant the manager's prerogatives or diminish his or her leadership. This type of leader avoids trying to take over the manager's responsibilities. Performance of the delegator/organizer role is oriented toward enhancing the ability of the manager to function as the chief executive officer. In sum, although the director does not become the driving force (as an executive mayor may), he or she is the guiding force in city government.

Some argue that there is an additional kind of leader, the *chief executive;* Sparrow presents this argument in Chapter Nine of this volume. Nevertheless, the logic of the council-manager form indicates that this type of leadership either is a temporary deviation or represents the transition to a different form of government. This kind of mayor acquires the de facto ability or formal authority to nominate or even hire the city manager.[7] This feature produces separation of powers because the manager's relationship to the entire council is altered. Such a change calls into question whether the government still corresponds to the council-manager form.[8]

Facilitative mayors in council-manager government utilize the characteristics of the form to foster communication and improve interaction among officials. Although it is possible for the rare council-manager mayor to take on executive prerogatives, this type of leadership either will be unstable or will lead to change in the form of government; it should not be viewed as the ideal, as some studies have suggested. Coordinators and directors represent the types of active leadership that are consistent with the values and characteristics of this form of government. How common are such leaders in American cities? What impact do they have? How do they relate to city managers? How do they affect council's involvement in decision making? These questions are addressed in the remainder of this chapter.

## Evidence from Surveys

An alternative view that presents a positive model of mayoral leadership has been developed in the discussion up to this point. Because of the criteria for selection of the cases to be examined, it is obvious that the case studies in subsequent chapters will offer portraits of successful leadership in council-manager cities and counties. Is such a high level of facilitative leadership a fluke that is rarely found in city governments? Furthermore, does leadership (as we have described it) make a difference when exercised? In this section, we will assess the level of mayoral leadership by examining two sources of survey data: a survey of city managers in North Carolina and of city managers in Ohio, and a national survey of city council members. In the next section, we will assess whether the level of leadership makes any difference in the performance of city government. We can then turn to the case studies with greater awareness of how these specific examples compare to mayors (and, by extrapolation, chairpersons) generally.

The performance of mayors can be measured by an examination of how they fill certain key roles. For each of the ten roles already discussed, an indicator of performance was included in a survey that was distributed to city managers in North Carolina in 1987 and in Ohio in 1988. Together, the ten indicators represent an inventory of the mayor's performance and a profile of the mayor's relative strengths and weaknesses (see Table 1.1). Respondents were asked to rate separately the *extent* to which the mayor engaged in a particular activity and his or her *effectiveness* at it. In scaling the responses, greater weight has been given to the latter.

The roles that the mayors were judged to perform best are ceremonial figure, presider, and promoter. They do a good job as spokespersons for councils. The roles that involve active communication and unifying a city council (liaison, team builder, and organizer or delegator) and that involve advocating policy are performed moderately well. Mayors do least well at providing information (as educators) and at helping to formulate goals (as opposed to advocating policies).

These averages are a useful indicator of relative strengths and weaknesses, but they mask wide variations in performance among individual mayors. To measure these variations, it is useful to combine the roles into broader categories. Of particular interest are the roles that make up the two dimensions of leadership in the facilitative model—coordination and policy guidance. These are the most important ones for influencing how governmental affairs are conducted. When the ratings for the roles in these two facets of the job are combined and grouped into four categories, we find that mayors vary widely in their performance: 27 and 28 percent of the mayors fell into the *low* and *moderate* leadership categories, respectively, as indicated in Table 1.2. These mayors may handle the ceremonial and traditional aspects of the position well, but they do not get very involved in and are not very effective at coordination and policy leadership. Approximately 20 percent were ranked *moderately high* in leadership. One-quarter were highly active in and effective at bringing council members together, promoting communication and strong working relationships, monitoring and ad-

Table 1.1. Ratings of Mayors' Role Performance by City Managers.

|     |                | Average | Rank |
|-----|----------------|---------|------|
| 1.  | Ceremonial figure | 4.08 | 1  |
| 2.  | Spokesperson   | 2.99    | 4    |
| 3.  | Presider       | 3.71    | 2    |
| 4.  | Educator       | 2.38    | 11   |
| 5.  | Liaison        | 2.86    | 5    |
| 6.  | Team builder   | 2.83    | 6    |
| 7.  | Goal setter    | 2.49    | 10   |
| 8.  | Organizer      | 2.68    | 9    |
| 9.  | Policy advocate | 2.75   | 7    |
| 10. | Promoter       | 3.21    | 3    |
| 11. | Ambassador     | 2.70    | 8    |

$N$ = 131 city managers in North Carolina and 56 city managers in Ohio.

*Note:* The scale for each role was calculated by adding separate ratings for the extent of involvement and the effectiveness of the mayor at handling each activity. Ratings of *low, medium,* and *high* were combined to create a 5-point scale. The coding of involvement ratings was low = 0, medium = 1, and high = 2. The coding of effectiveness ratings was low = 0, medium = 2, and high = 3. The questions used were based on the activities discussed in the preceding section of this chapter.

Table 1.2. Variations in Mayoral Leadership in Council-Manager Cities.

|                                        | %     | N   |
|----------------------------------------|-------|-----|
| Low coordinative/policy leadership     | 26.5  | 48  |
| Moderate                               | 28.2  | 51  |
| Moderately high                        | 19.9  | 36  |
| High coordinative/policy leadership    | 25.4  | 46  |
| Total                                  | 100.0 | 181 |

*Note:* The measures of extent and effectiveness were combined, giving greater weight to effectiveness. The scale was calculated by adding separate ratings for the extent of involvement and the effectiveness of the mayor in each activity. Ratings were combined to create a 5-point scale. The ratings of involvement were scored low = 0, medium = 1, and high = 2. The ratings of effectiveness were scored low = 0, medium = 2, and high = 3. The leadership index adds the scores for the coordination and policy guidance areas (six roles). The highest combined score was 30. The range of scores is 0–11 for *low,* 12–18 for *moderate,* 19–24 for *moderately high,* and 25 and above for *high.*

justing the division of responsibility within the council and between
the council and the manager, setting goals, and providing direction.
As we shall see in the next section, moderately high and high levels
of leadership make a difference in the attitudes, relationships, and
performance of city council members and the city manager.

A national survey of city council members in cities over
25,000 in population, conducted in 1989, provides another source of
data for measuring the level of mayoral leadership. This survey
approached the measurement of mayoral leadership in an entirely
different way, but the results were similar to those obtained from the
survey of managers in the two states. Respondents rated the level of
importance of officials as policy initiators in their governments
(Svara, 1991). Overall, 45 percent of the council members in council-
manager cities consider the mayor to be a very important source of
policy initiation (not even one in six feels that the mayor is not very
important).[9] Asked to identify the *one* official who was the *most* important policy initiator, only 7 percent of respondents chose the
mayor as an individual, although the council (including the mayor)
was rated most important in 42 percent of the council-manager cities.

Thus it appears that a rather large minority of mayors provides moderately high to extensive leadership in council-manager
cities. (Information about the performance of the chairperson of the
county commission is limited to data from one state. The North
Carolina county managers gave the chairperson essentially the same
rating as the city managers gave the mayor in the ceremonial and
coordinative roles, but the chairperson received lower ratings in the
policy-guidance dimension of the position; see Svara, 1988.[10]) The
widespread perception that all council-manager mayors and chairpersons are merely figureheads appears not to be substantiated. Nevertheless, there are shortcomings in the leadership provided by the
mayors in over half of the council-manager cities, and policy (as
opposed to coordinative) leadership is probably even less common
in council-manager counties than in cities.

## Impact of Effective Leadership

When effective leadership is present, the performance of local government officials improves. The managers surveyed in Ohio and

North Carolina were asked to assess relationships among officials and the performance of the city council as a whole in handling its policy-making responsibilities. The results are presented in Table 1.3. When mayors provide greater leadership, council members are more likely to work well together, to provide direction to city government, and to understand their role in administration. When leadership is weak, councils are more likely to have difficulty making decisions, to focus on immediate concerns and neglect long-term planning, to react rather than initiating, to seek special services and benefits for their constituents, to dabble in administrative matters, and to make poor use of their time.

On some mayoral attributes and activities, there is little difference between the impact of high and moderately high levels of leadership but a substantial difference between the mayors in both those categories and the mayors in the low and moderate categories. On other items, there is a continuous difference across the full scale of leadership. For example, in an assessment of the overall working relationship among city officials, the results presented in Table 1.4 emerged. Mayors who could be labeled coordinators (moderately high leadership) and directors (high leadership) are both highly associated with a positive climate for conducting the city government's business, whereas this condition is much less common for those who are moderate or low in leadership. Among the items in Table 1.3, there is also little difference between high and moderately high leadership with regard to the process of decision making, understanding the role of the council in administration and service delivery, and overall leadership. But, when it comes to focusing on long-term concerns, making clear decisions, expediting action, and involving the council in determining the goals and purposes of city government, the performance of cities with high-leadership mayors is clearly stronger than that of cities with mayors at the other three levels of leadership. The mayor classified as a director on the basis of role performance is more likely to provide a sense of purpose and direction than a mayor classified as a coordinator. Both improve the general performance of the council, enhance the quality of working relationships, and promote an understanding of the council's roles.

When mayors are uninvolved and ineffective, the performance of city government suffers. Officials do not work as well

Table 1.3. Mayoral Leadership, Relationships,
and Performance of Officials in Council-Manager Cities.

| Mayoral Leadership:[b] | Percentage of Respondents Agreeing with Statement[a] | | | | |
| | Low | 2 | 3 | High | Gamma |
|---|---|---|---|---|---|
| *Relationships* | | | | | |
| The council members have a good working relationship with each other. | 58 | 80 | 80 | 96 | -.55[c] |
| The mayor and council have a good working relationship. | 65 | 78 | 81 | 98 | -.53[c] |
| *Council Performance* | | | | | |
| Council members try to get special services and benefits for their constituents. | 38 | 47 | 28 | 24 | -.21 |
| The council provides sufficient direction and overall leadership to government. | 50 | 58 | 80 | 84 | -.46[c] |
| The council focuses too much on short-term problems and gives too little attention to long-term concerns. | 85 | 76 | 63 | 42 | .52[c] |
| The council is more a reviewing and vetoing agency than a leader in policy making. | 83 | 72 | 46 | 47 | .47[c] |
| The council has difficulty making clear decisions. | 52 | 50 | 49 | 22 | .31[d] |
| The council does not have enough time to deal effectively with important policy issues. | 46 | 48 | 31 | 29 | .23 |
| The council deals with too many administrative matters and not enough policy issues. | 48 | 45 | 28 | 27 | .28 |
| The council understands its role in administration. | 60 | 56 | 77 | 89 | -.41[c] |
| The council is too involved in administrative activities. | 42 | 32 | 17 | 18 | .36[d] |

$N$ = 131 managers in North Carolina and 56 managers in Ohio; 6 respondents were dropped from the leadership index because one or more items was not answered. The number of managers in each group was 48, 51, 36, and 46, from low to high, respectively.

Table 1.3. Mayoral Leadership, Relationships,
and Performance of Officials in Council-Manager Cities, Cont'd.

[a] As a function of the respondents' judgments of mayoral leadership.
[b] The mayors were divided into four groups, based on combined ratings of the extent and effectiveness of their performance of activities related to coordination and policy guidance; 2 = moderate, 3 = moderately high.
[c] Significance <.05, measured by chi square.
[d] Significance <.01, measured by chi square.

Table 1.4. Mayoral Leadership and Relationships Among Officials.

|  | Level of Mayoral Leadership | | | |
| --- | --- | --- | --- | --- |
|  | Low | Moderate | Moderately High | High |
| Percentage of city managers who rate relationships as: |  |  |  |  |
| Very positive or good | 56 | 58 | 80 | 85 |
| OK or poor | 43 | 41 | 20 | 15 |

*Note:* This table uses the same categories developed for Table 1.2.

together. The council is reactive, focuses on short-term problems, and is relegated to the position of reviewing and commenting on the manager's proposals, with little capacity for independent initiative. Members do not use their time well and are more likely to have difficulty making decisions. The council is more likely to focus on administrative details than on policy issues, to seek special benefits for constituents, and to get involved in administrative activities.

Thus mayors do make a difference in the performance of their governments. Whether the difference is positive or negative depends on the strength of the leadership that mayors provide.

## Mayor-Manager Relations

It has been argued by some and assumed by others that a high level of leadership from the mayor (or county commission chairperson) diminishes the position of the city manager, even if no powers are given to the chief elected official. There is a long-standing presumption, based on limited empirical studies, that conflict will develop between the mayor (and presumably the chairperson) and the manager if the chief elected official is directly elected and "strong" (Kammerer, 1964).[11] An emerging issue is whether a more highly competitive political environment will cause the mayor to engage in more self-promoting activities that will strain relations with the manager (and the council).

Effective mayors need not supplant the city manager, however. Strong facilitative leadership can be provided by the mayor, along with that provided by the city manager. In studies noted earlier, Boynton and Wright (1971), who examined mayor-manager relations in forty-five large cities, and Wikstrom (1979), in a study of forty-one cities in Virginia, concluded that mayors and managers offer team leadership rather than competing with each other.

The surveys of city managers in North Carolina and Ohio offer direct evidence about the relationship between level of mayoral leadership and quality of interaction among officials (see Table 1.5). The working relationship grows better as mayoral leadership improves, particularly the relationship between the mayor and the manager. With an effective mayor, the council makes better use of the professional staff and is less likely to make excessive demands. The high-leadership mayor is inclined to take an active interest in administrative matters, as are other mayors, but is no more likely to direct the manager, give orders to the staff, or seek to correct staff performance independently of the rest of the council. The mayors who provide higher leadership are less likely to be viewed as too involved in administration but are more likely to expedite action by staff and to improve governmental performance. This impact presumably results from enunciating priorities and helping all officials keep track of goals and objectives—one of the indicators of a directorial mayor. The higher-leadership mayor is also strongly associated with doing a good job of evaluating the performance of the manager. Therefore, extensive and effective leadership does not necessarily mean that the mayor interferes with the administrative process in the city, but high-leadership mayors do have an impact on governmental administration.

The high-leadership mayor does not get enmeshed in operational details or displace the manager; it is the mayor who is

Table 1.5. Mayoral Leadership and Mayor, Council,
and City Manager Interaction.

| | Percentage of Respondents Agreeing with Statement[a] | | | | |
|---|---|---|---|---|---|
| Mayoral Leadership:[b] | Low | 2 | 3 | High | Gamma |
| *Relationships/Working Arrangements* | | | | | |
| The council and the manager have a good working relationship. | 87 | 92 | 94 | 98 | -.42[c] |
| The mayor and the manager have a good working relationship. | 81 | 84 | 100 | 100 | -.70[c] |
| The council effectively draws on the expertise of professional staff. | 71 | 76 | 91 | 96 | -.52[c] |
| The council makes excessive demands for reports and information. | 25 | 26 | 20 | 9 | .28 |
| *Administrative Involvement by Mayor* | | | | | |
| The mayor takes an active interest in administrative matters. | 55 | 65 | 67 | 69 | -.16 |
| The mayor directs the manager and/or gives orders to staff. | 19 | 24 | 36 | 22 | -.10 |
| The mayor monitors and seeks to correct staff performance independently of the entire council. | 23 | 39 | 31 | 31 | -.06 |
| The mayor is too involved in administrative activities. | 28 | 39 | 19 | 13 | .26[d] |
| The mayor expedites action by staff and improves governmental performance. | 10 | 32 | 50 | 62 | -.59[c] |
| *Evaluation of Manager* | | | | | |
| The council's appraisal of the manager's performance is satisfactory in depth and frequency. | 31 | 53 | 69 | 67 | -.41[c] |

N = 131 managers in North Carolina and 56 managers in Ohio; 6 respondents were dropped from the leadership index because one or more items was not answered. The number of managers in each group was 48, 51, 36, and 40, from low to high, respectively.

[a] As a function of the respondents' judgments of mayoral leadership.

[b] The mayors were divided into four groups, based on combined ratings of the extent and effectiveness of their performance of activities related to coordination and policy guidance; 2 = moderate, 3 = moderately high.

[c] Significance <.05, measured by chi square.

[d] Significance <.01, measured by chi square.

ranked low or moderate in leadership who is also perceived to be too involved in administrative activities. This may be a case of the difference between a leader who instills a sense of purpose and a mayor with limited horizons, who is inclined to meddle in administrative details. There is no evidence to support the presumption that a high level of leadership necessarily causes the mayor to take over executive functions or leads to conflict with the manager. Indeed, all the mayors who provide moderately high to high levels of leadership have good working relationships with managers.

### The Council's and the Manager's Involvement in Decisions

The mayor has a substantial impact on the level of the council's involvement in goal setting and policy making. As we have seen, high mayoral leadership increases the council's attention to long-range concerns, makes it more proactive, and improves the council's ability to make decisions. Table 1.6 contains measures of the extent to which the council and the manager take part in decisions regarding mission (goals and purpose), policy (middle-range decisions about plans, programs, and allocation of resources), administration (delivery of services and implementation of programs), and management (control of the human and material resources of city government, including hiring and contracting). As one would expect in the council-manager form, the council's involvement is highest in mission and recedes across the other dimensions (Svara, 1985.) City managers display the opposite pattern, although as professional leaders they are expected to be involved in all aspects of city government.

The ratings of the manager's performance in Table 1.6 reflect the high level of involvement that city managers have in all types of decisions in city government (Svara, 1989). Higher ratings for managers than for councils indicate that the manager frequently provides the initiative in developing proposals, which the council reviews and then accepts or rejects.[12]

Ratings of councils by city managers indicate that as the mayor's leadership expands, councils are more actively engaged in the formation of mission and the setting of policy. A rating of 3.6

Table 1.6. Mayoral Leadership and Contributions of Council
and Manager to the Governmental Process.

|  | Mayoral Leadership[a] | | | | |
|---|---|---|---|---|---|
|  | Low | 2 | 3 | High | Correlation |
| Council's involvement[b] | | | | | |
| Mission | 2.9 | 3.1 | 3.2 | 3.6 | .33[c] |
| Policy | 2.9 | 3.1 | 3.1 | 3.3 | .18[c] |
| Administration | 2.7 | 2.8 | 2.9 | 2.9 | .11 |
| Management | 2.0 | 2.4 | 2.4 | 2.4 | .14[d] |
| Manager's involvement | | | | | |
| Mission | 3.7 | 3.7 | 3.5 | 3.6 | -.10 |
| Policy | 4.0 | 3.9 | 3.9 | 3.8 | -.08 |
| Administration | 4.0 | 4.0 | 3.9 | 4.0 | -.04 |
| Management | 4.3 | 4.1 | 4.0 | 4.2 | -.10 |

[a]See note to Table 1.1.

[b]Involvement was measured on a 5-point scale, with 1 as *very low*. For an explanation of the measurement of involvement and the activities included in each dimension, see Svara (1990, appendix B).

[c]Significance <.01 for Pearson correlation.

[d]Significance <.05 for Pearson correlation.

(on a five-point scale) for mission decisions by a council whose mayor provides high leadership indicates a council that frequently initiates proposals, raises issues, and actively reviews the recommendations of the manager. A 2.9 rating for a council in a city with low mayoral leadership indicates a council that is essentially reactive and merely reviews proposals that come from the manager. In all dimensions, the relationship of involvement to level of leadership is positive. Still, the councils with active mayors are not substantially more involved in administrative or management decisions than the other councils are.

The manager's involvement is not significantly related to the level of the mayor's leadership. There is a slight tendency for the manager to have a higher rating when the mayor's leadership is lower. If these differences mean anything (it is not clear that they do, since the relationships are weak and not statistically significant), they would seem to mean that, to some extent, managers fill a leadership vacuum in the dimensions of mission and policy. There is no indication that a vigorous mayor (as we are defining the high level of leadership) suppresses the manager. In a separate set of questions not included in Table 1.6, managers were asked to indicate what they thought their involvement in policy initiation should be, as opposed to what it actually was. Their preferred level of involvement was not significantly related to the level of mayoral leadership. In other words, managers with active mayors are no more likely than those with weak mayors to feel that they should have more latitude. Another indicator suggests just the opposite. The managers with mayors who provide the highest leadership are also the most likely to feel that they should consult with the council on the budget before it is drafted. This finding is consistent with the general picture of a higher level of positive interaction when elected leadership is stronger.

In sum, greater activity by the mayor improves the council's performance. The differences across cities indicate that when mayoral leadership is high, councils are actively involved in setting direction. The lower the level of mayoral leadership, the more reactive and less involved the council is. Higher involvement on the part of elected officials will not diminish the involvement of managers if elected officials' involvement is channelled into certain activities: determination of goals for the city or county, careful review of managerial recommendations and policy decisions, oversight of program accomplishment, and systematic appraisal of the performance of the manager and the local governmental organization. The survey data reported here indicate that the mayor as facilitator focuses the council's attention on these activities and leads the council and the manager to accomplish them. Thus the mayor can strengthen representative democracy while reinforcing the contributions of professional staff.

## Conclusion

Council-manager mayors and chairpersons can contribute substantially to the performance of their governments and to the betterment of their communities. The position of mayor in this form of government is not a pale imitation of the elected executive's office in mayor-council cities or in counties with county executives. Rather, it is a unique leadership position that requires distinctive qualities.

On the basis of surveys conducted in cities, we can estimate that perhaps 40 to 50 percent of mayors are more or less effective as leaders. Our information about counties is more limited, but it appears that the chairperson is somewhat less likely than the mayor to be an effective leader.

The resources and skills needed for effective performance can be derived from the form of government itself, from personal resourcefulness and drive, from the ability to articulate or help fashion a vision, and, at the same time, from self-restraint, from a commitment to enhancing the position of other participants in the governmental process, and from personal flexibility. The lesson for mayors and chairpersons that can be taken from the survey data, as well as from some of the previous research, is that mayors build effective leadership by strengthening the other participants in the governing process, rather than controlling or supplanting them. This attitude, along with an emphasis on developing a shared commitment to goals, is the essence of the facilitative leadership model.

The logic of this approach applies equally well to chairs of school boards and agency boards of directors. The leaders of most governing boards at the local level are understood more appropriately in terms of a model of facilitative leadership than in terms of the power-oriented model appropriate for elected executives. Furthermore, with such changes as diffusion of information and increasing interdependency among governments and private organizations, fewer leaders are "in charge," even if they are executives within their governments. The facilitative leadership model has applicability to these settings as well.

## Notes

1.  For a complete review, see Svara (1987, 1990).
2.  It appears that there are no published studies of the mayor in commission cities or the chairperson in county government. Consequently, in the discussion of previous studies, we will refer only to *mayors* and *council-manager* governments.
3.  Sparrow's study of San Diego is updated and expanded in Chapter Nine of this book.
4.  Incompatible goals and blocking behaviors are the essential

53

53

features of conflict; see H. Zeigler, E. Kehoe, and J. Reisman, *City Manager and School Superintendents* (New York: Praeger, 1985). Cooperation is characterized by compatible goals, coordinated and supportive efforts, and sharing of rewards; see Svara (1990).

5. See S. Elkin, *City and Regime in the American Republic* (Chicago: University of Chicago Press, 1987), and C. N. Stone, *Regime Politics: Governing Atlanta, 1946–1988* (Lawrence: University of Kansas Press, 1989). Elkin and Stone argue that networks of economic and political influence (including elected officials) represent a regime that originates action and secures support for certain kinds of activities, usually related to economic development.

6. These observations are drawn from a paper presented by Larry Keller of Cleveland State University at the 1991 conference in Raleigh, N.C.

7. Mayors and chairpersons will exert greater or lesser influence over the choice of a new manager as a member of the council. Pete Wilson was unique in his efforts to move managers out of the office until he found one who would accept a limited position.

8. A veto also separates the mayor from council members in their policy-making activities, but this is a minor expression of separation of powers, one that does not alter the character of the government. Shifting the responsibility of appointing the manager from the council to the mayor, however, would produce substantial change.

9. By comparison, over 70 percent of the council members in council-manager cities consider the city manager to be a very important contributor to the policy process, and 38–46 percent of the council members (depending on city size) consider the manager and staff to be the most important policy initiator.

10. The proportion rated *highly effective* is as follows:

|  | *Mayors* | *Chairpersons* |
|---|---|---|
| Goal setter | 37.4% | 25.4% |
| Organizer | 43.6 | 28.5 |
| Policy advocate | 40.5 | 23.2 |

The assessments were made by 131 city and 59 county managers in North Carolina.

11.  See G. J. Protasel, "Abandonments of the Council-Manager Plan: A New Institutionalist Perspective," in *Public Administration Review*, 1988, *48*, 807–812. Protasel argues that directly elected mayors strengthen the leadership capacity of the council-manager form and increase satisfaction with the form, as evidenced by the fact that cities with directly elected mayors are less likely to abandon the form than are those that select the mayor from within the council.

12.  As I have argued elsewhere (Svara, 1989, 1990), the high level of managerial involvement in policy decisions does not necessarily undermine the council's policy authority or the manager's accountability to the council. When the council sets the mission of city government, the manager is able to develop recommendations within a framework set by elected officials. Indeed, the manager is able to help the council accomplish its intended purposes.

## References

Bellman, G. M. *Getting Things Done When You Are Not in Charge.* San Francisco: Berrett-Koehler, 1992.

Bennis, W. *Leaders: Strategies of Taking Charge.* New York: HarperCollins, 1985.

Bennis, W. *Why Leaders Can't Lead.* Reading, Mass.: Addison-Wesley, 1989.

Boynton, R. P., and Wright, D. S. "Mayor-Manager Relationships in Large Council-Manager Cities: A Reinterpretation." *Public Administration Review*, 1971, *31*, 28–36.

Bryson, J. M., and Crosby, B. C. *Leadership for the Common Good.* San Francisco: Jossey-Bass, 1992.

Covey, S. R. *The Seven Habits of Effective People.* New York: Simon & Schuster, 1989.

Cunningham, J. V. *Urban Leadership in the Sixties.* Cambridge, Mass.: Schenkman, 1970.

Dahl, R. A. *Who Governs?* New Haven, Conn.: Yale University Press, 1961.

Eberts, P. R., and Kelly, J. M. "How Mayors Get Things Done: Community Politics and Mayors' Initiatives." *Research in Urban Policy*, 1985, *1*, 39–70.

Feiock, R. C., and Clingermayer, J. "Municipal Representation, Executive Power, and Economic Development Policy Activity." *Policy Studies Journal*, 1986, *15*, 211–229.

George, A. L. "Political Leadership in American Cities." *Daedalus*, 1968, *97*, 1194–1217.

Gilmore, T. N. *Making a Leadership Change*. San Francisco: Jossey-Bass, 1988.

Greenleaf, R. K. *Servant Leadership*. New York: Paulist Press, 1977.

Kammerer, G. M. "Role Diversity of City Managers." *Administrative Science Quarterly*, 1964, *8*, 421–442.

Kiechel, W. III. "The Servant as Leader." *Fortune*, May 4, 1992, pp. 121–122.

Kotter, J. P., and Lawrence, P. R. *Mayors in Action*. New York: Wiley, 1974.

Kouzes, J. M., and Posner, B. Z. *The Leadership Challenge*. San Francisco: Jossey-Bass, 1988.

Lineberry, R. L., and Sharkansky, I. *Urban Politics and Public Policy*. (3rd ed.) New York: HarperCollins, 1978.

Pressman, J. L. "Preconditions of Mayoral Leadership." *American Political Science Review*, 1972, *66*, 511–524.

Rees, F. *How to Lead Work Teams: Facilitative Skills*. Amsterdam: Pfeiffer & Company, 1991.

Sparrow, G. "The Emerging Chief Executive: The San Diego Experience." *Urban Resources*, 1984, *2*, 3–8.

Svara, J. H. "Dichotomy and Duality: Reconceptualizing the Relationship Between Policy and Administration in Council-Manager Cities." *Public Administration Review*, 1985, *45*, 221–232.

Svara, J. H. "Mayoral Leadership in Council-Manager Cities: Preconditions Versus Preconceptions." *Journal of Politics*, 1987, *49*, 207–227.

Svara, J. H. "The Complementary Roles of Officials in Council-Manager Government." In *Municipal Year Book 1988*. Washington, D.C.: International City Management Association, 1988.

Svara, J. H. "Policy and Administration: Managers as Comprehensive Professional Leaders." In H. G. Frederickson (ed.), *Ideal and*

*Practice in City Management.* Washington, D.C.: International City Management Association, 1989.

Svara, J. H. *Official Leadership in the City: Patterns of Conflict and Cooperation.* New York: Oxford University Press, 1990.

Svara, J. H. *Continuity and Change in American City Councils, 1979–1989.* Washington, D.C.: National League of Cities, 1991.

Wikstrom, N. "The Mayor as a Policy Leader in the Council-Manager Form of Government: A View from the Field." *Public Administration Review,* 1979, *39,* 270–276.

# Part One

## *Models of Comprehensive Leadership*

# 2

*Dan W. Durning*

# Active Leadership in a Small Council-Manager City: Mayor Michael Mears of Decatur, Georgia

In late summer of 1993, the commissioners of Cobb County, a metropolitan county near Atlanta, attracted national attention by passing a resolution condemning the gay life-style as incompatible with community standards. In the midst of furious debate on the resolution, Michael Mears, the mayor of nearby Decatur, publicly welcomed lesbians and gays to move to his city. He told a reporter, "I am absolutely committed to the idea that no one's lifestyle should be an impediment to the full enjoyment of participation in the community" (Fitch, 1993, p. 10).

Mears's action was consistent with his operating style as mayor of this small city, from January 1985 until his resignation, in October 1993.[1] Mayor Mears resolutely pursued favored policies, despite the feeble formal powers of the office, and he espoused very liberal political views that may have disturbed the average Decaturite. Nevertheless, Mears never lost an election and was selected nine times by fellow city commissioners to be Decatur's mayor.

Given the incongruity of Mears's activist inclinations and the limited powers of the mayor's office, as well as the differences between Mears's political philosophy and the political views of most southerners, some interesting questions arise. Can a mayor with few formal powers and a nonmainstream political philosophy provide effective leadership in a small council-manager city in the deep South? If so, what is the nature of that leadership? To exercise it, what resources does the mayor call upon?

These questions are investigated in this chapter. I examine how Mears's leadership fits into the types of leadership identified in Chapter One. Then I discuss whether Mears met the definition of a facilitative leader, and, if so, what type of facilitative leader he was.

To carry out these tasks, I first describe the setting of Mears's mayoralty, outlining the social and governmental context of policy making in Decatur. Then I explain how a change of city regimes established a framework of values within which Mears and the city commission operated.

After that discussion, I examine how Mears was elected mayor, what major policy decisions were made while he was in office, and how he operated as mayor. Then I identify the leadership roles that Mears performed, his style of leadership, and the resources he used to enhance his effectiveness. The chapter ends with a summary of my findings.

### The Decatur Setting

Decatur is a compact, historic city about six miles from downtown Atlanta. The city is shaped roughly like a rectangle sitting on its smaller side, and it is divided by a railroad track into two areas of nearly equal population. The area north of the railroad tracks, the part bordering on elegant Druid Hills and Emory University, is inhabited largely by white residents. The area south of the tracks is home to most of the city's black residents, who comprise about 39 percent of the city's 17,400 citizens.

#### Decatur City Government

Decatur has had a manager-council form of government since 1921 (in Decatur, the council is called the *commission*). The city's charter divides responsibilities among the city commission, the city manager, and the mayor.

## The City Commission

The policy-making power of the city government lies with the five-person commission. Each year, at its first meeting, the commission elects a member to serve as its chair. This chairperson has the title of mayor.

The Decatur council-manager system changed little from its adoption in 1921 through 1984. It was a pure reform system: an elected commission, with no directly elected mayor; two-year terms; nonpartisan elections, held separately from federal and state elections; and commissioners elected citywide, rather than from districts. Since 1984, however, the system has been altered. Commissioners now serve four-year terms. Commission elections are held in November of odd-numbered years, instead of every December, and four of the five commissioners are elected from districts. Two commissioners represent the northern district (all of Decatur north of the railroad tracks), and two represent the southern district.

## The City Manager

The commission appoints a chief administrative officer who is responsible, according to the city charter, for the proper and efficient administration of the city government. The city manager serves an indefinite term and may be removed by the commission at any time. The position was held for about two decades by Curtis Branscome, who stepped down as city manager in February 1993. While he was Decatur's city manager, in 1988, Branscome gained national visibility by his election as president of the International City Management Association. After Branscome resigned as city manager, he was replaced by Peggy Merriss. Decatur has long followed accepted practice in reformed council-manager cities: the city manager administers city functions and hires, fires, and directs employees; the mayor and other commissioners have no immediate management functions, and they do not personally direct the work of city employees.

## Decatur's Mayor

Decatur's mayor is appointed to a one-year term; thus the mayor can be replaced every year if three of the commissioners are displeased with his or her performance or if new commission members want a different mayor. Typically, however (but not always), the commission reappoints the person serving as mayor until he or she wants to give up the office.

The mayor is the city's chief executive officer, enforcing and executing the city's laws, ordinances, resolutions, and rules and holding all officers, employees, and agents of the city accountable for their performance. In addition, according to the city charter, the mayor may be given power by the commission to carry out other tasks.

Although the mayor has substantial responsibility, he or she has few formal powers. The formal powers include presiding at all commission meetings and calling extraordinary commission sessions. The mayor has no veto power, cannot hire or fire city employees, does not alone appoint board and authority members, and has no staff assistance. Furthermore, the mayor serves part-time.

### The Context of Mears's Mayoralty

In 1979, Decatur's regime found that it could no longer govern. That discovery came when it proposed a massive downtown redevelopment that was hooted down by opponents. From that episode came a consensus about the future development of Decatur, as well as a reconstituted regime to implement it. This consensus helped create the conditions for Mears's selection as mayor and set the framework for his roles as mayor.

### Civic-Minded Business Leaders: The City Fathers

In southern cities like Decatur, businessmen have long been a major part of the regime, and the governing coalition has often been known collectively as the *city fathers*. I am using Stone's definition (1989) of *regime* as the "informal arrangements that surround and complement the formal workings of governmental authority" (p. 3).

The regime consists of the groups that together make and carry out governing decisions. According to Stone the core of the regime is the "governing coalition," the "body of insiders" who "come together repeatedly in making important decisions" (p. 3).

In the 1960s and 1970s, Decatur's regime consisted largely of "good government" businessmen and the city's elected officials. These city fathers were several notches above the ordinary businessperson, however. Many had ties to the Coca-Cola empire, Georgia Power Company, prominent law firms, and the three financial institutions headquartered in the city. Many of them commuted the short distance from Decatur to offices in Atlanta skyscrapers. Viewing Decatur as a place of residence, rather than a place of work, these leaders often wanted to enhance the quality of family life in the city, and they resisted measures to promote rapid economic development there. Reflecting this priority, the city government invested heavily in residential areas and passed ordinances to discourage behavior seen as detrimental to "family values."

### The Regime Begins Unraveling

The city's business-and-government regime began unraveling in the late 1960s and early 1970s, largely as a result of the destabilizing "white flight." As white households left and black households moved in, Decatur changed in another way: its downtown was abandoned; the city lost most of its major retail stores to shopping centers.

Those regime members who did not flee tried to stabilize the city by enacting policies to revitalize the downtown. Toward that end (and to avoid superhighways through the city), the city leaders supported construction of fixed-rail transportation to link Decatur to the rest of the metropolitan area. In 1971, after the project was approved by DeKalb and Fulton County voters, the Metropolitan Atlanta Rapid Transit Authority (MARTA) began building its transit lines, placing three stations in Decatur, with one downtown (Stone, 1989).

As MARTA laid its tracks during the 1970s, Decatur changed again. Many younger and well-educated white professionals moved into the city, and, as in Atlanta and other major cities in the United

States, many of these newcomers were inclined toward neighborhood activism (see Stone, 1989; Clavel, 1986). Some of these activists were disturbed about how decisions were being made in Decatur. They charged that local leaders were trying to "create for Decatur, not with Decatur" (Deardorff, 1991).

### The 1979 Downtown Development Proposal

Old and new Decatur clashed in 1979 over a regime-backed proposal to remake downtown Decatur. The proposal was the fruit of city leaders' efforts to rebuild the downtown. After years of frustration, they had succeeded beyond their wildest dreams: Gerald D. Hines, a major developer from Houston, wanted to build in downtown Decatur. Together, Hines and the city proposed a $62 million development, with three office towers (one fourteen stories high and the others ten stories each). They would also build a 300-room hotel, a 22,000-square-foot conference center, two parking decks, and a new city hall.

When then-Mayor Ann Crichton announced the project, in late July 1979, to about 125 assembled business and community leaders, she did not anticipate the visceral opposition it would stir. The first public hearing on the project drew 300 people, and it was dominated by opponents who made emotional speeches and carried signs with slogans like "Don't Sell Decatur to Texas" (Fossett, 1979a, p. 1A).

With unrelentingly harsh attacks on the plan and its supporters, the neighborhood activists prevailed. At its meeting on August 20, the Decatur city commission postponed action on the Hines proposals "until there has been adequate time for discussions and considerations of alternatives" (Fossett, 1979b, p. 1A).

### New Consensus, New Regime

In February 1980, responding to the ruckus over the Hines proposal, the city commission created the seventeen-member Decatur Downtown Redevelopment Task Force. To chair it, they appointed Lyn Deardorff, former head of the Decatur Neighborhood Alliance and an opponent of the Hines proposal. The members of the committee represented major groups in the community, including business-people, property owners, and neighborhood activists. As the task force prepared its report, it solicited extensive citizen participation.

The report, issued in 1982, proposed a slightly different Decatur than would have existed if Hines had built as planned. More important, preparing the revised plan brought people with different interests and perspectives together to agree on the shape of the city's future. The plan stated a new consensus about the city's future. Decatur would retain its small-town character. To do so, it would protect the integrity of its neighborhoods by containing commercial development within the existing boundaries, and the downtown development would be designed on a scale to ensure the city would keep its small-town feel. Another aspect of the consensus was the understanding that decision making in Decatur was to be an open process.

An outgrowth of the new consensus was that neighborhoods, through their advocates, joined the regime. Representatives of neighborhood groups began fully participating in the city's important policy decisions. Deardorff, one of the most visible of the neighborhood activists, was elected in 1986 to the fill the at-large seat on the commission.

## Michael Mears Becomes Mayor

The new consensus had been forged and the new regime was in place when Mears was elected to the Decatur city commission in 1983. Efforts to implement the plan were being made by the Decatur Downtown Development Authority (DDDA), the city commission, and others.

In January 1985, the Decatur city commission elected Michael Mears mayor by a vote of 3-2. At the time of his election, Mears was beginning the second year of his first term on the commission.

In retrospect, the Mears selection seems an improbable event. He has described himself as a "flaming liberal" (Cowles, 1985, p. 58A), and three commissioners at the time were conservatives. Mears had an ally in Elizabeth Wilson, however, the first African American to be elected to the commission, and he got his third vote from Candler Broom, described as an old-family conservative southern Democrat. Broom explained that he had supported Mears because of a "need for a change of leadership at the helm of the Decatur Commission" (Vardeman, 1985, p. 4XA). (Mears defeated Ted O'Callaghan, who had served briefly as mayor.)

When he was elected mayor, Mears had lived in Decatur for over fifteen years. He had moved to Decatur to teach Russian language and black history at Decatur High School. Mears had received his B.S. degree from Mississippi State University and had worked there on his Ph.D. During his college years, Mears had turned to radical politics, organizing for Students for a Democratic Society (Mears, 1990). He was active in the antiwar and civil rights movements and attended the 1968 national Democratic convention as a member of Mississippi's "alternative delegation" (Cowles, 1985, p. 58A). Mears decided to become an attorney and received his law degree in 1977, after commuting for three years to the University of Georgia law school in Athens, about an hour away. He went to work for McCurdy and Candler, the largest law firm in DeKalb County and the most prominent one in Decatur.

By 1983, Mears the 1960s radical was identified with the city establishment by virtue of his working for the McCurdy and Candler law firm. When Mears ran for the city commission, in 1983, he was, according to some observers, anointed for the commission by the local behind-the-scenes powers in Decatur (Cochran, 1991). He won the election with 63 percent of the vote.

As befits an establishment leader, Mears's initial comments as mayor were not about redistributing wealth or power or radically changing Decatur; interviewed the day he was elected, he said that his goal as mayor was to avoid "taxing people out of the city" (Ordner, 1985, p. 2B). He told another reporter that his election was a "symbolic change" in Decatur leadership: "The solutions to problems probably will be the same, but my style will be a little different" (Vardeman, 1985, p. 4XA).

More improbable than Mears's initial election as mayor was his reelection for eight more terms as his political views and controversial legal work became more visible. His establishment veneer was already wearing thin by 1988, when he cochaired Jesse Jackson's successful presidential primary campaign in Georgia and cofounded the New South Coalition, to promote Jackson's political ideas (Wooten, 1988, p. 2E).[2]

Mears's lawyering also regularly made headlines. He represented accused murderers in highly publicized cases, having left McCurdy and Candler in the late 1980s to set up his own law firm. From 1985 to 1990, he handled forty-two murder cases.

Despite his controversial opinions and notorious clients, or maybe because of them, Mears was reelected to the city commission by wide margins each time he ran. After his first election, in 1983, when all the commissioners were elected citywide, Mears was elected to represent the southern district of the city, in which 70 percent of the population is African American. In 1989, he won a four-year term against two opponents, receiving 71 percent of the vote.

### Policy Making in the Mears Years

In the years after Mears was selected to be mayor of Decatur, the commission enacted several major policies, many of which have helped achieve the consensus goals established in the early 1980s. Major policies include the following:

- *Public safety department, created in 1985.* Mears initiated this action soon after he became mayor.
- *Zoning ordinance and land-use plan revision, 1987 and 1988.* Rewriting the zoning ordinance and land-use plan took several years. The thrust of the plan is to protect neighborhoods from unwanted development by downzoning much of the city.
- *Tree ordinance, enacted in 1989.* This ordinance facilitates protection or replacement of trees, as part of land development.
- *Historic preservation ordinance, enacted in 1990.* This ordinance created the permanent Historic Preservation Commission and promoted the revitalization of historical properties in the city's commercial and residential areas.

Among the city's greatest efforts was the financing of a conference center and a parking deck, in conjunction with the construction of a new downtown hotel. (This project will be discussed later.)

While Mears was mayor, the city commission regularly

settled disputes over such things as requests for rezoning, speed humps, and licenses to sell liquor. The rezoning issues tended to be the most fractious, but the commission often resolved them within the framework of the consensus goals. Thus it typically denied requests for new commercial development outside the downtown and looked hard at any rezoning that would impinge on neighborhoods.

Remarkably, most commission decisions during the Mears decade were made without dissenting votes. According to Branscome, former city manager, at least 90 percent of the votes were unanimous. The unanimity came despite the diversity of interests on the commission. Representing the north district were Candler Broom (the southern conservative Democrat who had helped Mears become mayor) and Andrew Harris, a moderate backed by an insurgent neighborhood group. The south district was represented by Elizabeth Wilson, a black woman who managed a community health center, and Mears. The at-large position, as mentioned, was filled by Deardorff.

According to Harris and Deardorff, the commissioners tried to make consensus decisions as often as possible. The commissioners "talked things out" and "deferred to each other" to get a consensus because such decisions were important for the city (Harris, 1991). They listened to other points of view and worked until they had forged a consensus (Deardorff, 1991). The functioning of the city commission and of Mayor Mears are best illustrated through their handling of the different policy issues that faced the city; four examples follow.

### Downtown Development:
### The Hotel and Convention Center

When Mears was elected mayor, the most important issue before the city was the redevelopment of the downtown, implementing the plan adopted in 1982. The Decatur Downtown Development Authority had moved forward with the plan by helping private developers acquire and demolish an old hotel on the square, to make way for a new office building. However, the commissioners and DDDA members believed that a high-quality hotel was needed downtown before other first-class office space would be built there.

To move the hotel project from concept to reality, the city took a leading role. According to Branscome, the city changed from cajoler to active participant in the project. Direct city involvement in hotel development was, Mears says, the boldest and riskiest action the city took while he was mayor.

The city's role in the project proceeded as follows: Potential developers found that a high-quality hotel would be possible only if built in conjunction with a conference center and a parking deck. The developers were willing to build the hotel if the city would build the other facilities. The overall project required a $20 million investment, $12 million for the hotel and $8 million for the center and parking deck.

To build the conference center and parking deck, the city had to borrow through the bond market. To finance construction of the conference center, DDDA, a city entity, issued revenue bonds. To pay for the parking deck, the city created a parking authority, which sold revenue bonds. In addition, to help the developers finance their hotel, the city applied for and received a $2.7 million Urban Development Action Grant (UDAG), which provided a subsidized loan to the hotel developers.

The mayor was a central actor, pulling together the elements needed to get the project completed. In addition, essential roles in the project were carried out by Broom, Branscome, and DDDA head Lyn Menne.

Mears estimates that he averaged twenty-five to thirty hours a week for nearly two years working on this project. Among the roles that he played in the project were the following:

1.  Mears helped build a consensus among major business leaders for the city's decision to build a conference center and parking deck. Before the project began, he invited the city's banking leaders to a conference and asked their advice on whether the city should build a conference center and parking deck. With their support for the idea, he met with other community movers and shakers, to hear their views and get their backing.
2.  Mears and Broom kept the city commission's support behind the project. According to project observers, some of the commissioners did not fully understand the project, and Mears and

Broom had to keep pushing, explaining, and reassuring them
to keep their support for it (Branscome, 1991).

3.  He and Broom were the "cheerleaders" for the project, promoting it both within and outside city government. The project
took over three years from beginning to end, and the two
spokesmen for the city worked to make sure that influential
people supported it. In this role, Mears was the city's official
optimist, and the city manager was the pessimist. The city manager checked all the numbers in the feasibility studies and pro
formas, and he pointed out what could go wrong with the
project. Mears explained why everything would go right and
how the city would benefit from the project (Branscome, 1991;
Menne, 1991).

4.  Mears, Branscome, and Broom personally negotiated the acquisition of key property needed for the project. To build this
project, the city had to acquire land on which several shops and
a cafeteria were located. However, the city did not want to use
eminent-domain condemnation of the land, a controversial element of the Hines proposal. Instead, officials chose to negotiate
with the landowners. To get the project under way, an elderly
property owner had to be convinced to sell the city his property.
If he had not sold it, his property could not have been con-
demned, given the unpopularity of such a move. Thus Mears
and Broom had to persuade the man that selling the property
was in his and the city's best interest. They succeeded.

5.  Mears and Branscome represented the city in negotiations with
the developers, underwriters, and bond counsel. According to
Menne (1991), "It was great having a mayor who could go toe
to toe with the bond counsel and underwriters."

6.  Mears and Branscome went to the bond rating agency, and
Mears presented the city's case for a good rating. They traveled
to Wall Street to present information used to rate the city's
bonds.

7.  Mears went to the Department of Housing and Urban Development to ask approval for the city's UDAG application. He
said, "I literally begged them for the UDAG grant" (Mears,
1990). Decatur got one of the last grants before the program
went out of existence.

In March 1989, Decatur dedicated a new 185-room Holiday Inn, with rooms built around a five-story atrium; a 24,000-square-foot conference center; and a 300-space parking deck. Across the street was a new office building. Also in 1989, plans were announced for the development of additional office buildings on the land next to the hotel and conference center.

### Decatur's Sister Cities

Soon after he became mayor, Mears, along with Gary Gunderson of the Oakhurst Baptist Church, traveled to Burkina Faso (formerly Upper Volta), an impoverished land of about 7.5 million people, to find sister cities for Decatur. While there, they worked out tentative agreements with Ouahigouya, a town of about 400,000, and Bousse, a village with about 10,000 residents. According to Mears, getting sister cities in Africa was related to the city's efforts to redevelop the downtown: the development project did not interest most black residents, and so he wanted a project that would make them feel part of the city. To show that Decatur was "one community," he made a "dramatic gesture," choosing Burkina Faso to be the site of the city's sister cities (Mears, 1990). Mears says that most blacks in Georgia can trace their ancestry back to the Gold Coast of Africa, where Burkina Faso is. Thus many of Decatur's African American residents have roots there, and by establishing a sister-city relationship with the two cities in Burkina Faso, Decatur could show that it recognized that it is a biracial community and could thereby encourage black residents to feel at home in Decatur.

### The Bickersons: Decatur and MARTA

In June 1988, Commissioner Broom tried to ban MARTA buses from the Decatur downtown. He thought that MARTA buses were clogging downtown streets and that MARTA property "looks like a slum" (Bell, 1988a, p. 1XA). Broom complained that the large number of passengers waiting for downtown buses was hurting nearby businesses.

All five commissioners supported Broom's proposal, but they postponed action on it for thirty days, to give MARTA time to do something about the problems. Mayor Mears said, "I sincerely hope somebody at MARTA is listening, because we are dead serious about this" (Bell, 1988a, p. 1XA).

MARTA leaders responded by charging that the commissioners were bothered less by the bus traffic than by the low socioeconomic status of the bus patrons, that the city's street improvements had not kept pace with the city's growth, and that its appetite for special attention from MARTA was insatiable. Soon after that response, an editorial in the *Atlanta Constitution* called Decatur and MARTA "the Bickersons" ("MARTA and Decatur . . . ," 1988, p. 16A).

As the controversy heated up, Mears and David Chesnut, chairman of MARTA and the attorney for DDDA, attended a DDDA meeting. According to an Atlanta newspaper, "After the DDDA meeting, Chesnut and Mears met in private for about 15 minutes. When they emerged from the meeting both men said a settlement [of the dispute] seems possible" (Bell, 1988a, p. 9XA).

Soon after that, Mears and Broom met with the chairman of the MARTA board, the head of the state department of transportation, and others. According to Mears, "It was significant because it was the first time that we were able to get all the players sitting around the same table. . . . Once we finished pointing fingers at each other, we got down to serious business and I think we made substantial progress" (Bell, 1988b, p. 1XA). He said that the outlines of a tentative agreement had been worked out: MARTA would reroute some of its buses, and the city, with the assistance of the department of transportation, would improve some of its streets. At its next meeting, the commission voted to table Broom's resolution indefinitely.

### Resolving Neighborhood Disputes

The city commission encouraged parties to neighborhood disputes to resolve their differences through negotiation. Mears described the process in a draft version of his 1991 "state of the city" address: "In the past the city commission has sat as judge and jury in deciding neighborhood zoning issues. We still have to make that final decision, but the process is different now. We tell the neighborhoods that they have to work in good faith with developers. We tell the developers that they need to bring us solutions, not problems. It is a shotgun marriage, a forced partnership, but it works." According to press reports of various neighborhood disputes, Mayor Mears played a leading role in encouraging contending groups to look for common ground, rather than fight their battles before the commission (Harvey, 1989).

### Policy Leadership

The preceding four examples illustrate the diverse roles that Mayor Mears played in Decatur city government and the style of his leadership. They show that Mears was not just a ceremonial leader who presided over commission meetings and cut ribbons. He also at various times initiated policy, helped gather support for city projects, informed and persuaded other commissioners, helped implement policies, helped contending groups in Decatur resolve disputes, and helped represent the city in its dealings with external actors.

A key to this description of Mears's activities is the word *helped*. Mears lacked the time and resources to do everything himself, and he was not the only commissioner with policy ideas and resources. Thus Mears was often part of a combined leadership effort, with the city manager, other commissioners, or important groups in the city. Mears often helped others get things accomplished for the city.

The information presented in Table 2.1 reinforces the observations derived from the four examples of policy making in Decatur. To explore the roles of Mayor Mears more systematically, I asked him, Branscome, and two other commissioners to complete a survey and identify Mears's importance in various roles. The list of roles is taken from Svara (1987) and divided into four dimensions: traditional roles, coordination and communication roles, policy and organizational roles, and external roles.

Each person completing the questionnaire was asked to assign a value from 0 to 5 for each of the eleven leadership roles that a mayor could play in city government. The value of 5 was to be assigned if the mayor was the leader in carrying out the role; 0 was

Table 2.1. Mayor Mears's Leadership Roles in City Government.

| | | Ratings | |
| --- | --- | --- | --- |
| Category | Mayor | City Manager | Commissioners (average) |
| Traditional Roles | | | |
| Presiding officer: Presides at meetings of the commission; facilitates discussion and resolution of business at commission meetings | 5 | 5 | 5 |
| Spokesperson: Announces and explains positions taken by the commission; acts as spokesperson for the commission | 5 | 5 | 4.5 |
| Ceremonial tasks: Fulfills ceremonial duties, such as giving speeches, greetings, and awards | 5 | 5 | 5 |
| Coordination and Communication Roles | | | |
| Educator: Provides information to the commission, manager, and the public (beyond announcing positions taken by the commission) | 3 | 3 | 4 |
| Liaison with city manager: Provides liaison with the manager for the commission; increases communication and understanding between the commission and the manager | 3 | 4 | 3 |
| Team builder: Lines up a majority of commission members behind a proposal; helps build consensus in the commission | 4 | 4 | 4.5 |
| Policy and Organization Roles | | | |
| Goal setter: Sets goals and objectives; identifies problems; sets a tone for the commission | 4 | 5 | 3.5 |
| Delegator/organizer: Helps the commissioners and manager maintain their roles; helps commission members recognize their responsibilities; defines and adjusts the relationship with the manager | 3 | 3 | 3 |
| Policy advocate: advocates programs; helps develop proposals for action; lines up support for proposals | 4 | 4 | 3.5 |

Table 2.1. Mayor Mears's Leadership Roles in City Government, Cont'd.

| | Ratings | | |
| --- | --- | --- | --- |
| Category | Mayor | City Manager | Commissioners (average) |
| *External Roles* | | | |
| Promotes city: helps create a positive image; works to attract development to the city | 5 | 5 | 3.5 |
| Intergovernmental relations: serves as liaison with local, state, and federal agencies; promotes intergovernmental cooperation | 5 | 4 | 4.5 |

to be assigned if the mayor did not participate in the role. Values between 5 and 0 would indicate any other extent of the mayor's participation in a role.

The survey responses indicate that Mayor Mears provided many different types of leadership. To some extent, he carried out each of the eleven roles identified by Svara. He was clearly a key leader in the traditional and external roles. Although he was a less important leader (but still involved) in the coordination and communication and policy and organizational dimensions, he played major roles as a team builder, goal setter, and policy advocate.

Examination of Mears's leadership roles shows that he was neither an executive mayor, as found in mayor-council cities, nor a figurehead, like some mayors of council-manager cities. He was not an executive mayor, because he did not manage city employees and did not lead by command and control; such leadership would not have been tolerated long by the other commissioners, the city manager, or members of the regime. Mears was not a figurehead, because he played a broad range of leadership roles; a mayor who performed only ceremonial leadership roles would not have been acceptable in Decatur.

One way to describe Mears's leadership style is to use Svara's (1987, 1988, 1990) classification system. Given the array of leadership roles played by Mears, he can best be classified as a director (see Chapter One).

Instead of calling himself a director, Mears probably would

have called himself the head deacon of Decatur. He maintained that
Decatur city commissioners are like church deacons: they collect
and spend money, and they hire and fire the pastor. If this simile
is apt, then Mears was a head deacon who helped other deacons
make good decisions and helped the pastor manage the flock. Both
Svara's "director" and Mears's "head deacon" provide leadership
that guides, pushes, and prods, but they do not order things to be
done. In practice, Mears's leadership was characterized by the following elements.

1.  *He promoted compromise and consensus decisions.* As the ex-
    amples of Mears's roles in decision making show, he favored
    negotiated rather than dictated decisions. When disputes arose
    with MARTA or other external organizations, Mears tried to
    work out compromises (McKinney, 1991). When developers
    fought with neighborhood groups, Mears urged them to find
    compromise solutions. A reporter for a Decatur newspaper
    talks about "Mike-style" dispute settlement (Ordner, 1991). Ac-
    cording to her, this type of dispute settlement involved direct
    negotiation among the groups concerned with a decision, and
    the typical result was an acceptable compromise. Mears's style
    was to encourage, even force, contending parties to talk to each
    other. In addition, as the responses to the survey show, Mears
    was a team builder who helped the city commission make con-
    sensus decisions. He helped fashion compromises that united
    the commissioners behind policy alternatives.
2.  *He showed up, and he responded.* To lead, a leader must show
    up when decisions are to be made, and he or she keeps in-
    formed. Mears usually did both. He was a hands-on mayor.
    When someone complained about barking dogs, he was likely
    to go to the neighborhood to find out how bad the problem
    was. If someone complained about slow police-response times,
    the next night he was likely to go to the scene of a police call
    to check out the response time (Ordner, 1991). According to
    local business leaders, Mears not only showed up, he also re-
    sponded. They tell a story of calling Mears about a problem
    while he was out of the city trying a case. His secretary beeped
    him with the message, and he returned the call during the next

court recess (Lutz, 1991). These businessmen said they felt that they could call him—or, for that matter, any commissioner—late at night if they had city-related problems they needed to discuss (Dehler, 1991).

3. *He consulted.* When a decision was to be made, Mears was known to consult with many and varied people. He sought the views of the groups likely to have an interest in the decision. He was able to consult widely because of his extensive contacts with major groups in Decatur. As mayor, Mears attended many meetings of neighborhood associations and held monthly meetings with association presidents. He frequently went to meetings of the Decatur Business Association, and he often spoke at African American churches. Through such activities, Mears knew the leaders of important groups in the city very well.

4. *He exhorted.* Mears not only showed up, he also talked. Probably his most powerful leadership resource was his ability to persuade, inform, and urge. These tools were especially powerful because of Decatur's preference for consensus decisions and negotiated agreements. They also helped mobilize citizens' support for the city's policies.

### Constraints and Resources

To function as an effective leader, Mears had to operate within the constraints set by the regime, and he had to have resources to help convince others to act or follow. Because he had so few formal powers, his resources were primarily informal, based on his office and his personality.

#### Constraints on Mears's Leadership

Before Mears could lead effectively, he had to meet two conditions: he had to exercise power in a way acceptable to the regime, and he had to reflect the will of the majority of the city commissioners. He was able to lead because the regime and the commission permitted him to do so.

**The Regime's Policy Consensus.** The Decatur regime backed the consensus goals that came from preparing the revised development plan. Those consensus goals incorporated the regime members' agreements about the future of Decatur, and they provided the framework for the policy decisions made by the city government. To be mayor, Mears had to operate within that framework. If he had challenged the goals and values that were part of the consensus, he would have lost the support of regime members and would have had a difficult time staying in office.

*The Commission's Permission.* One result of annual election of the mayor by the commission is that the mayor must be sensitive to the views of the other four commissioners. To stay in office, the mayor must not do things that offend them or that are outside the bounds of the leadership they are willing for him or her to exercise. The mayor must also adopt a mode of decision making that is acceptable to at least two other commissioners. Mears succeeded in keeping the support of the other commissioners by working with them to find consensus solutions to policy questions. He helped the commission shape consensus decisions and assisted in implementing them. Like the other commissioners, Mears also valued participation and negotiation. As a result, his style of leadership was congruent with the style preferred by most other commissioners. If it had not been, his tenure as mayor might have been cut short.

### Resources for Leadership

Working within these constraints, Mears could bring to bear many resources that enabled him to be an effective, multidimensional leader. Most of these resources were informal, coming from either the position or himself. His resources included the legitimacy of the office, the expectation that Decatur's mayor would be a strong leader, the respect of regime members and other important social groups, his visibility as a defender of Decatur against external threats, and his personal characteristics.

*Legitimacy of the Office.* The city charter designates the mayor as the chief executive officer, even though it gives the mayor few formal powers to use in that role. As the chief executive officer, the mayor can function as an active leader without being questioned about the right to do so.

*The Mayor as a Strong Leader.* A mayor is often expected to be a leader because of the widespread impression that a mayor is analogous to a governor or a president and therefore should lead the city. In Decatur, that expectation has been nourished by a tradition of activist mayors. Thus regime members, commissioners, and the public were not surprised that Mears was a visible public figure.

*Respect.* Mears, more than any other commissioner, bridged the major groups in the city. As Svara (1987) says, leaders like Mears occupy a strategic location in the community. Mears was respected by businessmen because he owned and managed a small downtown business (his law office). He had connections with old-family Decaturites because he worked for the McCurdy-Candler law firm. He had the respect of many neighborhood groups because he attended their meetings and encouraged the groups' creation. He had connections with the black population through his teaching of black history in the city schools and his serving as Jesse Jackson's campaign manager. But Mears was not seen as the captive of any group. He was not a traditional good-old-boy Rotary Club businessman, nor was he (in practice) a neighborhood activist, and while he lived in the southern part of the city, his neighborhood was a white enclave. In short, he had ties to major groups in the city, but he was not really one of any of them. He kept his independence, which enabled him to be viewed as a city, not a group, advocate.

*Position as Defender of Decatur.* Decatur has seen itself as threatened and abused by many outsiders: developers, MARTA, criminals. When Mears stood up for Decatur against these outside villains, he gained stature as a city leader. As the city's protector against outside threats, Mears gained the respect and gratitude of many Decaturites. He used these positive feelings to enhance his ability to lead.

*Personal Characteristics.* Mears has several personal characteristics that enabled him to be an effective multidimensional leader. The list includes the obvious: intelligence and excellent communication skills. In addition to these, other characteristics were important, including a high energy level, love of the spotlight, and sincerity.

First, Mears devoted a tremendous amount of energy to the job. Helping build consensus, negotiating, showing up, responding, consulting, persuading, and exhorting require much more energy than performing ceremonial duties or ordering things to be done. An Atlanta reporter, writing about Decatur's city government, described Mears as a "47-year old with the eager energy of an adolescent" (Emerson, 1991, p. 4E).

Second, Mears clearly relished being on center stage in city government, and he had high visibility in the Atlanta area. People knew who Decatur's mayor was and what he was doing. This love of the spotlight inspired him to speak when invited, to carry out ceremonial duties, to represent the city in external disputes, and to be available whenever a story was written about the city.

Third, people who are asked about Mears often describe him as a person with sincere beliefs (Ordner, 1991; Dehler, 1991). His sincerity led people to support him even when they disagreed with his political views. For example, one local businessman said that Mears's political views might have been "wrong," but at least people knew where he stood on issues (Dehler, 1991).

## Conclusion

In 1979 and the early 1980s, power in Decatur shifted from a regime of business leaders and government officials to a new regime, which included neighborhood groups. At that time, the new Decatur regime reached a consensus on the goals that the city should try to achieve, including protection of neighborhoods and appropriate-scale commercial construction in the city's downtown. The new consensus included an agreement that governmental decision making in Decatur would be an open process.

The regime consensus has influenced the job of Decatur's mayor in two ways. First, the mayor and the city commission do not determine, from among competing values and goals, the ones appropriate for Decatur; instead, they enact policies and set up programs that help achieve the regime's consensus goals, adopted more than a decade ago. Second, the values of the new regime have made necessary a type of leadership that includes extensive citizen participation, openness, and consensus decisions.

Working within this context, Mears was an effective leader who, despite his notorious liberalism, was elected mayor nine times by his fellow commissioners. He accepted the consensus goals, and his leadership was devoted to helping Decatur achieve them. His open style of leadership fit well with the style expected by regime members, and he worked with other commission members to reach and implement consensus decisions. In short, Mears could be an effective leader in Decatur largely because his policy objectives and leadership style were congruent with the values set by the Decatur regime.

As a "head deacon" or director, Mears performed many leadership roles for the city. A combination of some of these roles and his leadership style made Mears resemble Svara's facilitative leader: he helped rather than controlled or supplanted other participants in the government process, and he was a guiding force in city government.

Mears's leadership style was characterized by his efforts to promote compromise and consensus, by a peripatetic presence and responsiveness, by his consultation of groups affected by decisions, and by his use of persuasion and exhortation. Despite weak formal powers, he functioned as a multidimensional leader because his office gave him the legitimacy to do so and because, in Decatur, the mayor is expected to be a strong leader. He could also lead because he had extensive contacts with and respect from major groups, both inside and outside the regime; he was not closely identified with any particular group, however. He also brought to bear impressive personal characteristics that enhanced his ability to lead.

This case provides a good example of how a mayor with minimal formal powers can use other resources to play a wide range of leadership roles within a given context. Mayor Mears clearly was a facilitative leader, as defined by Svara. His ability to lead was constrained, however, in ways that the facilitative leadership model does not discuss: namely, Mears's leadership was circumscribed by the decisions of a governing coalition that established consensus goals for the city. If Mears had tried to use his formidable leadership resources to function as an executive leader, or if he had tried to lead the city away from the consensus goals, he probably would have precipitated a fight with regime members, which would have resulted in his loss of the mayoralty or in the creation of a new regime reflecting Mears's values more closely.

Thus this case suggests that the study of facilitative mayors should be concerned with more than the roles they play and the resources they can bring to bear. The study of mayors should also pay attention to the context within which they operate—the leadership roles and styles permitted or expected by the city regime, and the regime-adopted values and goals that constrain the mayor as he or she provides leadership to the city.

## Notes

1.  Mears announced in early September 1993 that his resignation would be effective October 1. He said that he was resigning so that Mayor Pro Tem Elizabeth Wilson could serve out the remainder of his term and become the city's first female African American mayor. Mears also said that he would not seek reelection to the city commission because of the increased demands of his job as a public defender ("Decatur: Mayor to Step Down," 1993).

2.  In 1991, a reporter interviewed Mears about his possible candidacy for chairmanship of the Dekalb County Commission. He told the reporter, "I'd have a hard time being elected to anything . . . because my opponent is probably going to talk about me being a pinko, commie liberal. But why shouldn't pinko commie liberals be elected to office if they can act as responsible public servants?" (Emerson, 1991, p. 4E).

## References

Bell, C. "Bus Debate Travels a Bumpy Route." *Atlanta Constitution-DeKalb Extra,* June 16, 1988a, pp. 1XA, 9XA.

Bell, C. "Decatur Meets Two Transit Chiefs to Unsnarl Feud." *Atlanta Constitution-DeKalb Extra,* June 30, 1988b, pp. 1XA, 7XA.

Branscome, C. Interview by the author, Feb. 7 and Feb. 21, 1991.

Clavel, P. *The Progressive City.* New Brunswick, N.J.: Rutgers University Press, 1986.

Cochran, G. Interview by the author, Feb. 8, 1991.

Cowles, A. "Decatur Mayor 'Appeals to Community.'" *Atlanta Constitution,* Dec. 6, 1985, p. 58A.

Deardorff, L. Interview by the author, Feb. 28, 1991.

"Decatur Mayor to Step Down." *Atlanta Journal,* Sept. 8, 1993, p. C2.

"Decatur Taking Steps to Preserve its Past." *Decatur-DeKalb News/ Era,* May 24, 1990, p. 5C.

Dehler, M. Interview by the author, Feb. 7, 1991.

Emerson, B. "Mike Mears: How Did This Liberal Lawyer Get Elected Mayor of Decatur . . . Time and Time Again?" *Atlanta Journal,* Feb. 25, 1991, pp. 1E, 4E.

Fitch, J. "Come Out to Decatur." *Southern Voice,* 1993, *29*(6), 10.

Fossett, F. "Plans Draw Citizen Fire at Heated Public Hearing." *Decatur-DeKalb News/Era,* Aug. 9, 1979a, p. 1A.

Fossett, F. "Decatur Commission Postpones Redevelopment." *Decatur-DeKalb News/Era,* Aug. 23, 1979b, p. 1A.

Harris, A. Interview by the author, Feb. 21, 1991.

Harvey, D. "Citizens, Decatur Consider First Baptist Church Rezoning." *Decatur-DeKalb News/Era,* Dec. 21, 1989, p. 3D.

Lutz, G. Interview by the author, Feb. 7, 1991.

"MARTA and Decatur: The Bickersons (editorial)." *Atlanta Constitution,* June 23, 1988, p. 16A.

McKinney, C. Interview by the author, Feb. 15, 1991.

Mears, M. Interview by the author, Dec. 11, 1990.

Menne, L. Interview by the author, Feb. 15, 1991.

Stone, C. N. *Regime Politics: Governing Atlanta, 1946–1988.* Lawrence: University Press of Kansas, 1989.

Svara, J. "Mayoral Leadership in Council-Manager Cities: Preconditions Versus Preconceptions." *Journal of Politics,* 1987, *49,* 207–227.

Svara, J. "The Complementary Roles of Officials in Council-Manager Government." *Municipal Year Book 1988.* Washington, D.C.: International City Management Association, 1988.

Svara, J. *Official Leadership in the City: Patterns of Conflict and Cooperation.* New York: Oxford University Press, 1990.

Vardeman, J. "Decatur Has New Mayor, 1st Black Commissioner." *Atlanta Constitution-DeKalb Extra,* Jan. 10, 1985, p. 4XA.

Wooten, J. "Could the Good-Old-Boy Network Be in Trouble?" *Atlanta Constitution/Atlanta Journal,* Apr. 10, 1988, p. 2E.

3          *Mary Ellen Mazey*

# The County Commissioner as a Facilitative Leader: Paula MacIlwaine, President, Montgomery County Commission, Montgomery County, Ohio

In the 1990s, local governments will have fewer fiscal resources yet more functional responsibilities because of the diminishing role of the federal government in local governmental affairs. The local leader of this decade will be required to possess new leadership traits

*Note:* The author wishes to thank those who took their time to be personally interviewed about their observations of Paula MacIlwaine as a facilitative leader. Many are individuals she referred to as her "kitchen cabinet": Fred Bartenstein, director of the Dayton Foundation; Chuck Curran, Montgomery County commissioner; Tom Heine, president of the Dayton Area Chamber of Commerce; Mary Sue Kessler, president of Community Development Company, First National Bank of Dayton, and former administrative aide to MacIlwaine; Paige Mulhollan, president of Wright State University; David Ponitz, president of Sinclair Community College; Fred Smith, former CEO of the Huffy Corporation; Jim Van Vleck, former vice president of the Mead Corporation; Don Vermillion, administrator, Montgomery County; and Jim Walker, professor at Wright State University. Special thanks go also to Amy Wiedeman of the Office of Management and Budget in Montgomery County. Amy, a former student of the author, assisted in numerous ways with the documentation used for this chapter.

in meeting the demands placed on his or her unit of government. Such is the case in Montgomery County, Ohio.

Montgomery County has a population of 573,809 (1990), which makes it the fourth-largest county in Ohio and the eighty-third largest county in the United States (U.S. Bureau of the Census, 1992). The county is centered in the middle of a triangle encompassing Columbus, Cincinnati, and Indianapolis as its three points and is situated in the southwest portion of the state of Ohio. The central city of the region (known as the Miami Valley) and the county seat of Montgomery County is the city of Dayton, well known for its aviation heritage. The entire region has a long tradition of innovation and free enterprise and has been recognized as a center of manufacturing production because it contains the second-largest concentration of General Motors employees in the United States. However, it is currently moving to the forefront with high-technology industries, which have strong links to Wright-Patterson Air Force Base. The base is the major research operation of the U.S. Air Force and, as a center of logistics, employs a total of over 27,000 civilian and military personnel.

Like most other Ohio counties, Montgomery County does not operate under a charter form of government. It receives its powers from the State of Ohio through the state constitution and the revised code. The board of county commissioners serves as the legislative and executive body of the county. Therefore, the commissioners' governmental domain is delegated in specific areas, such as property-tax assessment and collection, land records, election administration, public welfare and social services, and certain legal and judicial services. In addition, the county provides discretionary services, such as parks and recreation, drainage systems, and economic development. Finally, the county contracts to provide most of its municipalities with solid-waste disposal and provides such services as police protection and subdivision regulations to unincorporated areas.

The Montgomery County Commission consists of three members. The president is elected by the other commissioners for a one-year term. The commissioners oversee a staff of approximately 1,500 employees. Since 1967, the county commissioners have operated with a county administrator. The commissioners share administrative responsibilities with eight separately elected county officials. In addition, there are nineteen municipalities, twelve townships, sixteen school districts, and five countywide special districts. Each of these jurisdictions has a policy-setting board and staff.

This chapter focuses on the role of one commissioner, Paula MacIlwaine, and the leadership skills she demonstrated in fourteen years of service to county government (1976–1991). She served as president for eight years during this period. A special emphasis will be placed on her facilitative leadership skills and her ability to take limited governmental powers and use them to enhance Montgomery County's role as a major innovator of public policy, not only in the Miami Valley region of southwest Ohio but also in the state of Ohio and the nation as a whole. The major thesis of the chapter is that Paula MacIlwaine established herself as a leader with a facilitative style that empowered others. The facilitative leader "accomplishes objectives by enhancing the performance of others" (Chapter One, p. 6, this volume). An analysis of her style of leadership provides valuable information for future policy-agenda setters.

## Paula MacIlwaine's Early Political Involvement

In order to fully assess MacIlwaine's leadership style, it is important to discuss her early life as an impetus for a political career. Paula MacIlwaine graduated from high school in 1958, at a time when it was assumed that women, even if they furthered their education, would continue to have as their primary role to seek a mate, marry, have a family, and maintain the major responsibility for child rearing.

Her high school and college years were a time of high academic achievement and active involvement in school affairs but were not remarkable. At Ohio Wesleyan University, she majored in political science and developed a liberal political ideology that continues to this day. Her keen ability to master complex subjects was evident. Her support of team efforts, and her style of supporting others' accomplishments as part of her own, were fostered in such experiences as high school cheerleading. She had not yet shown herself to be a leader during these years, however.

Paula MacIlwaine's initial political involvement was also traditional. She was active as a concerned citizen associated with the League of Women Voters, an organization dedicated to advocating good government. The league's philosophy of studying and researching an issue before taking a stand has been a model for MacIlwaine throughout her political career. As president of the league, she argued for the accessibility of elected officials and for the assurance that all meetings would be open to the public. She tested openness by monitoring county commission meetings on a regular basis.

She moved beyond the role of concerned citizen and, in effect, began her political career when she expressed her views about substantive issues and reforms. She criticized welfare fraud in the county system, a county budget deficit, and the lack of professional staff, particularly to run the county's multimillion-dollar solid-waste program. Through MacIlwaine's intense study of government as league president, she began to deviate from her traditional role because of her disillusionment with how county government was operating. She became a vocal critic of the status quo.

Because of her involvement with county issues through the League of Women Voters, Paula MacIlwaine sought the Democratic nomination for county commissioner in 1976. She decided she could no longer study and critique government but needed to become actively involved. She ran for public office in order to become a change agent in county government.

She assumed the office as the first woman ever elected to the commission in January 1977, after a landslide victory. It was noted immediately after her victory that she was an enigma: "MacIlwaine has never before run for public office. Although she has been clear in her stands on problems . . . she remains one of the key political question marks . . . the question involves speculation over whether the 35-year-old mother of three and past president of the Dayton Area League of Women Voters will knuckle under the Democratic party line. 'She's not a member of the club' " ("Ohio Area Voters Were Choosey," 1976, p. 26).

Soon after taking her seat on the commission, MacIlwaine set forth with a number of initiatives that placed her in a key leadership position. Moreover, her two fellow commissioners left office because of political wrongdoing, which thrust her to the forefront of county leadership. Coincidentally, the Carter administration was taking office at the national level, and she was solicited by the new administration as a spokesperson for local government. She was elected at an opportune time and had an immediate opportunity to utilize the leadership skills she had been developing.

## MacIlwaine's Approach to Leadership

There are four attributes that characterize the philosophy and style of Paula MacIlwaine's leadership: the use of inclusion, as evidenced by her repeated efforts to build coalitions; the concern to foster good government; a commitment to expanding the opportunities for women and minorities in government; and a predilection for risk taking.

### Inclusion and Coalition Building

MacIlwaine was committed from the beginning of her political career to bringing citizens, governmental staff, and elected officials together around common concerns. During her fourteen years as county commissioner, Paula MacIlwaine served eight years as the commission's president. In that capacity, she worked diligently to increase communication and team building, not only with her fellow commissioners but also among all the other elected officials in the county, including the treasurer, the county engineer, the auditor, the county prosecutor, and the sheriff.

She used task forces, experts, and skilled facilitators to develop policy initiatives. By fostering a philosophy of participatory leadership, Paula MacIlwaine developed a policy-action agenda that was supported by a team of elected and appointed officials of both parties, by the public, and by the business community.

She increased the information flow to the public and private sectors and expanded the number of citizens involved in political decision making. This inclusion created ownership of the policies and actions that were to be implemented. She has stated, "I have worked hard to keep people informed. I believe that communication should be at the top of everyone's list" (MacIlwaine, 1990).

County staff members at all levels knew her on a first-name basis, and she knew them. Such close working relationships established an environment of mutual trust and support. As a liaison with the county administrator and staff, she constantly facilitated communication and understanding between elected and appointed officials. MacIlwaine encouraged the county administrator to provide in-service training for staff, in order for them to better understand their roles as appointed officials and elected officials' roles as policy setters. In addition, MacIlwaine worked with the county administrator to hold regular briefing sessions in which staff participated by presenting material to commissioners. Nevertheless, MacIlwaine and the two other commissioners always funneled decisions to staff through the county administrator.

Her ability to network in the community helped her achieve major policy changes in county government. She was constantly interacting with the business community and elected officials, at all levels of local government and from both the Democratic and Republican parties. She used her networking abilities to promote adoption of her policies, not only at the county level but also at the state and federal levels.

### Good Government

MacIlwaine brought her League of Women Voters perspective to county government and became an advocate of honest, good government. This position brought her general support from citizens and most other leaders, who widely concur that Paula MacIlwaine worked to put a professional form of county government in place. Reflecting on her years with county government, MacIlwaine says, "We fired people and brought in professional staff and set very high standards to work here. We eliminated patronage, which didn't make my party chairman very happy, but it was the way to build a professional staff. . . . Every department had to set new policies and put them into writing" (MacIlwaine, 1990). In implementing the concept of good government, she insisted that elected officials should establish policy, whereas professional staff should run day-to-day operations and implement the policies. This division of responsibility did not preclude constant efforts to critique and analyze the performance of staff, thereby holding them accountable and monitoring the implementation of an action agenda.

### Opportunities for Women and Minorities

MacIlwaine also became known for her strong support of females and minorities in government. Therefore, it is not surprising that Montgomery County has two female deputy administrators, one of whom is African American. MacIlwaine was instrumental in the hiring of women and minorities as professional staff and has also worked to ensure equal representation of women and minorities on appointed boards and committees: "We created the Commission on the Status of Women and Minorities to ensure that women and minorities were equally represented on all appointed county boards. We appoint forty-eight boards, and whenever an appointment is made by the county, I always make sure that women and minorities are represented on an equal basis. I do not know anyone else on the commission who pushes it as much as I do" (MacIlwaine, 1990). Research indicates that a female in a key elected leadership position can make a positive difference for women in municipal government employment (Saltzstein, 1986), and Paula MacIlwaine's leadership substantiates this finding.

### Risk Taking

A central feature of Paula MacIlWaine's leadership was risk taking, a behavior she engaged in and expected of others. As she put it, "I prod people to take chances. In government, everyone is afraid of what people are going to say. It's paranoia. Who is going to be against you, or what is the newspaper going to do? Any decision you make, you are going to upset 50 percent of the people, so you might as well go into it with that attitude and do what you think is right" (MacIlwaine, 1990). She was willing to take unpopular stands on issues in which she believed strongly and was not intimidated by others if they did not agree with her.

MacIlwaine's philosophy toward policy setting was centered on the belief that just because a policy has yet to be adopted does not mean it should not be undertaken; she would rather try it and fail

than not take the risk. She indicates that she has learned as much
from her failures as from her successes (MacIlwaine, 1990). In fact,
Paul Leonard, former lieutenant governor and former mayor of Dayton, feels that she has the key leadership ingredient, "the willingness
to lose"; and a current Dayton city commissioner calls that quality
in Paula MacIlwaine "the courage . . . to fight to the death to see it
through" ("MacIlwaine's Quitting . . . ," 1990, p. 1B).

## Type of Leadership

The type of leadership Paula MacIlwaine provides can best be described as that of the "director" because she made the governmental
process run smoothly and provided direction. MacIlwaine exemplified the communication and network building that promotes effective interaction among officials and with the public. From the
council and from the public she also maintained the strong support
necessary to being a successful director.

## Policy Initiatives and Accomplishments

MacIlwaine provided strong policy leadership, as her policy accomplishments indicate. She is a prime example of the elected
leader who initiates policy, secures support for it, oversees its implementation by delegating staff responsibilities and accountability, and finally mobilizes community groups to provide the
necessary grass-roots ownership of the policy initiatives. Her major
policy initiatives and accomplishments were a result of her strategic
planning efforts, the expansion and redirection of resources, and
welfare-reform initiatives.

### Strategic Planning

MacIlwaine initiated a number of strategic planning ventures at the
county level while she served as commissioner. The first such initiative was implemented immediately after she took office, in 1977,
at a time when strategic planning was virtually unknown in the
public sector. This early effort involved business leaders, labor leaders, and political figures with the county commissioners in setting

priorities and the county's policy agenda. Because of the broad range of citizens involved, public and private partnerships were formed to launch several new initiatives. One of these was the formation of the human service levy, which put social service funding under one funding mechanism. Another was the creation of county housing programs for the low-income population.

### Expansion and Redirection of Resources

During MacIlwaine's tenure as county commissioner, the county budget grew from approximately $250 million to over $400 million. Some of this increase was due to her ability to increase sales-tax revenues by facilitating "buy in" from the county's citizens. The sales-tax increase passed in the late 1980s was supported by the business community because the new revenues were targeted toward innovative programs. MacIlwaine was instrumental in linking the sales-tax increase to an economic development initiative that created a tax-sharing program and cooperation among local jurisdictions in Montgomery County. This program takes $5 million annually for the ten-year period 1991–2000 and allocates the funds to an economic development competition. Each year, the funds are disbursed not by the commission but by a group that has representatives from the public and private sectors. With a predetermined set of policy guidelines, the group recommends to the county commissioners which economic development projects will be funded. Then the new funds generated from the economic development projects are distributed through a government equity fund. Each participating township, village, and city in Montgomery County makes an annual contribution into the government equity fund, based on a single countywide growth–contribution formula, and receives an annual allotment determined by a distribution formula based on population. In general, the difference between the contribution and distribution formulas should result in net distributions for declining, stable, or slow-growth jurisdictions and new contributions for fast-growth jurisdictions. The tax-sharing program is a prime example of the county government's taking its limited governmental power and expanding its role into the realm of economic development while fostering cooperation among the city, village, and township governments within the county.

A second use of the increased sales-tax revenues was in offering incentives for a wide range of cultural and arts groups to coordinate their activities. These groups previously had been making separate requests for support. The county commission allocated $1 million annually of the sales-tax revenues and mandated that the groups work together to obtain county funding.

Both of these initiatives put county government in an innovative new role, as a coordinating body among other organizations. The county, rather than create its own new programs or seek to mandate activities for other organizations, initiated these incentives to foster voluntary cooperation. Getting these programs passed required facilitative leadership because the final agreements were based on consensus building and coalition development.

### Welfare Reform

MacIlwaine's work on welfare reform reflected her background and her approach to leadership. As a League of Women Voters activist, she had been concerned about welfare fraud, and early in her elected career (1979) she testified before Congress about welfare reform. Her ideas for welfare reform demonstrate strategic thinking and careful analysis of underlying problems. For example, she proposed the following:

- Instituting contracts between the government body and the client to outline the amount of welfare benefits the client will receive each month in exchange for the client's going to school, training for work, or entering a program designed to find employment
- Giving a pregnant teenager who is receiving welfare benefits a cash bonus for finishing high school
- Giving the client a check twice a month, to cover food and rent, instead of a check plus food stamps ("MacIlwaine Winner . . . ," 1987)

All three of these initiatives demonstrate her reliance on incentives to achieve change. She sought to permit people on welfare to help themselves, an approach similar to the general style of facilitative leadership, which is to empower others.

Having examined the underlying structure of the welfare program, MacIlwaine made specific recommendations on how the system could encourage independence and initiative, become family-oriented, create flexibility, decrease rigidity and paperwork, address special needs, change the Medicaid system, and expand the private sector's interest in improving the program (MacIlwaine, 1987). Her program for welfare reform was all-encompassing, with child-care provisions, health benefits, an innovative electronic fund-transfer card, training and education, and federal and state waivers for implementation. She worked with welfare recipients, the county welfare staff, the business community, and other elected officials to gain support for welfare reform in Montgomery County. In 1990, five hundred more welfare mothers were able to establish employment because of Montgomery County's innovative policies (Rice, 1991).

*Other Accomplishments*

MacIlwaine's other accomplishments include the public budget hearing for Montgomery County's annual appropriation, which allows elected county officials to present their budget priorities to commissioners; the merger of job-training programs between the city of Dayton and Montgomery County; and the merger of the city of Dayton's and Montgomery County's jails. The latter two efforts exemplify her progressive thinking, her commitment to improved efficiency in government, and her ability to bring individuals and organizations together. By forging innovative and creative partnerships, she was able to initiate change, both within the public sector and between the public and private sectors. In so doing, she moved the county and its region into the new way of working together for the 1990s.

### Expanding Public Recognition and Support

Paula MacIlwaine worked to see these reforms through in her own county, and she became known for welfare reform both within the state of Ohio's system and in the National Association of Counties (NACO). She was NACO's spokesperson for welfare reform, which was ultimately adopted by the federal government in 1989. Considered an expert on welfare reform, she worked with the National Governors' Association on this issue. She made appearances on national television and before national organizations—both rare for a locally elected official.

This record demonstrates her leadership abilities and her strength as a policy advocate at home. Furthermore, Paula MacIlwaine served on the platform committee at the 1988 Democratic national convention and remains the only person in the history of Montgomery County to address a national party's convention. (As president of the National Democratic County Officials and as co-chair of Michael Dukakis's Ohio delegation, she was one of five locally elected officials to address the delegates.) This kind of national recognition, visibility, and reputation helped MacIlwaine garner local support for her county-level policy initiatives. She knew how to work well with the media, and her visibility at the state and national levels helped her public image in Montgomery county.

## Assessment of MacIlwaine as a Leader

Paula MacIlwaine's record demonstrates substantial impact despite limited power. In fourteen years, she established a local, state, and national reputation as a social reformer, with high visibility in the area of welfare reform. She was a prime example of the innovative elected official who is willing to take risks and change traditional methods. Her approach to policy initiation was always to include a broad spectrum of elected officials and business leaders. Moreover, through networking and coalition building, she empowered a wide range of participants and facilitated the creation of a consensus for the changes she wanted to accomplish. Her purpose was never to establish a personal power base but rather to expand the capacity of county government to act on its own and foster cooperation. Personally observing Paula MacIlwaine in 1991, as she served as a member of the steering committee of a regional strategic planning process, I was particularly impressed with her ability to pinpoint

the major issues that needed to be addressed and to provide immediate and creative ideas for solutions.

## Conclusion

Paula MacIlwaine resigned from public office on January 6, 1991,
in order to pursue a career in the private sector. When she was
elected, in 1976, she was known as an independent thinker with a
stand on critical county issues. In 1991, she was recognized for her
innovative approaches to governmental reform, particularly in the
welfare arena but also in the expansion of county governmental
powers. She left office known as "the person who runs the county,"
and as she said, she departed "on a high"—unquestionably well
respected by the citizens of the county, elected officials from both
parties, and the power elite of the business community.

Few would question that Paula MacIlwaine is a role model
for all locally elected officials, but particularly for women. She came
to office as the first female commissioner, and she left office midway
through her term, but she remained vice chair of the Montgomery
County Democratic Party. Her replacement on the commission was
the first African American woman commissioner. Paula MacIlwaine's support for women is also demonstrated by the county's
record in hiring women for high-level positions.

Her key roles categorize her as a directorial type of leader. In
her years on the Montgomery County Commission, she worked to
provide a sense of direction for the county and excelled as a facilitative leader. She constantly promoted governmental professionalism and reform and empowered others with her ideas, through
networking, consensus building, and information sharing. Finally,
her style of leadership and accomplishments while in office indicate
that facilitative leadership is well suited to county government and
is not just a style for council-manager cities.

## References

MacIlwaine, P. "Suggestions for Welfare Reform." *Urban Fiscal
    Ledger*, 1987, *4*, 1-2.
MacIlwaine, P. Interview by the author, July 19, 1990.

"MacIlwaine Winner; Page in a Squeezer." *Journal Herald,* Jan. 19, 1987, p. 1, 8.

"MacIlwaine's Quitting Leaves Big Shoes to Fill." *Dayton Daily News,* Dec. 9, 1990, p. 1B, 4B.

"Ohio, Area Voters Were Choosey." *Dayton Daily News,* Nov. 3, 1976, p. 26.

Rice, S. Address delivered to Montgomery Council Commission, Dayton, Ohio, Jan. 6, 1991.

Saltzstein, G. "Female Mayors and Women in Municipal Jobs." *American Journal of Political Science,* 1986, *30,* 140–164.

U.S. Bureau of the Census. *Census of Population and Housing.* Washington, D.C.: U.S. Bureau of the Census, 1992.

# 4

*James H. Svara*

# Roles of the Facilitative Mayor: Mayor Jim Melvin of Greensboro, North Carolina

As an observer of urban affairs in Greensboro, North Carolina, in the 1970s, I was struck by the disparity between the dominant themes in the limited literature on council-manager mayors and the widespread recognition of the contributions made by the incumbent mayor. Although the nature of his leadership was clearly different from that associated with the executive mayor in mayor-council cities, he appeared to exercise leadership nevertheless. This chapter examines the leadership style and resources of that mayor—E.T. "Jim" Melvin—who served on the city council from 1969 to 1981 and occupied the mayor's office from 1971 to 1981. Research on Melvin in the middle 1970s was the basis for an initial reformulation of the mayor's office in council-manager cities.[1] In this chapter, it is possible to examine Jim Melvin's complete tenure as mayor and incorporate new information from extensive interviews with him and other leaders in Greensboro, conducted after he left office.[2]

## Background

Greensboro had a population of 144,076 in 1970.[3] The city had virtually doubled in size from its population of 74,000 in 1950, through in-migration and annexation, which increased the city's land area from 17.8 to 57.6 square miles. In 1970, the population was 71 percent white and 28 percent African American. The city's economic base was diverse, but textiles was the largest employer, accounting for 8,600 jobs (32 percent) in 1972. Reflecting trends in the state and the nation, textiles employment dropped to 7,500 in 1977 and to 4,600 in 1987. Other major employment sectors are chemicals and commercial printing, both of which expanded during the 1970s. Greensboro is also home to five colleges, including two state universities.

The city adopted the council-manager form of government in 1921 and, through the 1960s, used all the city governmental institutions associated with the traditional reform model. The council consisted of seven members elected at large on a nonpartisan ballot, with the mayor chosen by the council from among its members. In 1972, the charter was changed through referendum to permit direct election of the mayor. The council appointed the city manager, who had direct administrative control over all departments of city government.

The city had experience with strong managers, in particular James R. Townsend (1947–1961), a retired general who was highly respected within the city and in the city manager profession. A new manager, Thomas Z. Osborne—a longtime city employee and public works director—was appointed in 1973, and he served throughout Jim Melvin's tenure as mayor, resigning in 1984 to become president of the Chamber of Commerce.

Jim Melvin was born in Greensboro in 1933. He grew up in modest circumstances in a working-class neighborhood, which would later become predominantly poor and black, in the southeast section of the city. He spent many hours as a child, working around his father's filling station in the neighborhood.[4] He received his undergraduate degree in marketing in 1956 from the University of North Carolina, Chapel Hill, and a graduate degree in banking from Rutgers. In 1963, he served as general chairman of the Greater

Greensboro Open golf tournament, a major community event sponsored by the Jaycees, and he was president of the organization in 1965, when it received a national award for its accomplishments. As has been the case with other public officials in Greensboro, this experience was a stepping-stone to elected office. He was elected to the council in 1969. Two years later, he campaigned vigorously to be the top vote getter on the seven-person at-large council. By virtue of his first-place finish, the council named Melvin mayor. In 1973, he was chosen mayor in the first direct election for the mayor's office and was reelected to three more terms. In 1981, he chose not to run again.

At the time he was elected mayor, he was senior vice president of North Carolina National Bank. In 1978, he was named president of Home Federal Savings and Loan Association. He commented in interviews in 1986 that he had not realized until the end of his term the extent to which he was viewed as a representative of elite business interests. Although he continued to think of himself as the local boy who had done well in his bank job, he came to recognize that, to many people, he was "the lightning rod of the establishment." Since leaving office, he has been instrumental in mobilizing business leaders and making them a stronger force in local affairs, through the Greensboro Development Corporation and the Piedmont Triad Development Corporation.

## Roles and Types of Facilitative Leadership

The media and scholarly literature alike suggest that only by achieving de facto chief executive status does the elected leader in a council-manager government become a "real" mayor. As discussed in Chapter One, the model for classifying executive mayors is not appropriate to the council-manager form. The council-manager mayor can be seen as a facilitative leader. As mayor, Melvin was illustrative of a type of leadership that is comprehensive and consistent with the basic features of council-manager government and the cooperative pattern of interaction among officials. The preconditions for this kind of leadership are readily attainable within the council-manager form. The potential of the office was recognized by Jim Melvin, and he fulfilled it completely.

Central to effective performance in the job is an understanding of the possibilities and limitations of political leadership for the facilitative mayor. Mayors have been handicapped by their limited appreciation of what the office entails; Jim Melvin, however, had a grasp of the position that was partly intuitive and partly an application of approaches that he had used successfully in his work as a bank officer and in his voluntary activities, particularly with the Jaycees.

The traditional functions of presiding, performing ceremonial tasks, and acting as the spokesperson for city government are often viewed as the totality of the mayor's duties and not as particularly consequential functions. Jim Melvin handled the traditional functions of the office with adeptness and demonstrated that they are the foundation on which other aspects of the position are built. In times of crisis—such as the period after the shooting of self-proclaimed Communist demonstrators by members of the Ku Klux Klan, in November 1979—filling the traditional roles well can be crucial to the functioning of city government. Melvin also provided leadership in three other areas: coordination of officials to improve the effectiveness of their interaction, guidance (as opposed to control) in the formation and accomplishment of goals, and handling of promotion and "external relations" for the city.

Drawing from interviews with and about Melvin, we can see how he filled roles that involve the four components of the mayor's office. Changes in his attitudes and behavior over his twelve years in office suggest what the effects of an extended tenure as mayor can be.

Before examining his specific roles, however, it is important for us to understand how Jim Melvin viewed the office and his approach to leadership. Referring to his experience in the top position with the Jaycees, he said, "This is the greatest training ground. . . . If you can motivate folks when you're not paying them anything, think what you ought to be doing when you've got them on your payroll." As mayor, he worked with council members over whom he had no control and with the manager and staff, who were on the payroll. To Melvin, motivation and leadership mean "salesmanship, persuasiveness, getting the job done, [and] being right." He was inclusive but always sought to win others over to his point of view: "The way you had to make it work was through your ability to sell." He was also skilled at hearing both sides in a disagreement and seeking a middle ground, particularly in his early years in office.

By the end of his tenure, his effectiveness had been somewhat diminished by his growing impatience to get things done more rapidly than was possible through team building, persuasion, and negotiation. Toward the end, he observed, friends began to tell him, "You've gotten mean," and he acknowledged that there was some truth to the comment. In part, he feels that this was a necessary shift from trying too hard to be accommodating; given the number of decisions to be made in city government, "you just can't wait. You can't study them to death. At some point you've got to do it." In his final years, however, he moved from decisiveness to a real relishing of the battle and "really enjoying letting them [his opponents] have it." At that point, he did not seek to change the office to give the mayor more clout; he concluded that it was time for him to leave.

Observers of council-manager government typically note the mayor's responsibility for a variety of ceremonial tasks, which may involve appearing at various meetings, at dinners, and at other special occasions. The mayor, as spokesperson for the council, also enunciates positions, informs the public about upcoming business, and reacts to questions about the city's policies and intentions. In the two latter roles, Melvin built extensive contact with the public and the media, and this was a valuable resource in his performance of his other roles. Through his relationship with the public, he was able to develop the leadership resources that, as Boynton and Wright (1971) observe, are not available to any other officials. As representative of the city and spokesperson, the mayor also becomes an important channel for citizens' input. Melvin augmented and formalized this contact by instituting neighborhood meetings, which he attended along with one other council member, the city manager, and various city staff members. The city council also initiated the use of hearings on the budget in each quadrant of the city before the start of the budget-formulation process in city departments. In this way, projects designed to respond to citizens' requests could be incorporated into budget planning from the beginning. As presiding officer at council meetings, Melvin set the tone and exerted a mild influence over the timing and outcome of deliberations. He created an open atmosphere, which invited citizens to participate, but he did not refrain from asking pointed questions of those who spoke to the council. In council meetings and other public appearances, he signaled his positive attitudes toward staff members and promoted an understanding of the respective roles of elected officials and staff.

These traditional roles took on special significance in the aftermath of the 1979 shootings. Enormous strain was placed on the city government as it sought to cope with a media invasion, handle subsequent marches and demonstrations, conduct and be the subject of investigations, and provide security for the trial of the assailants and the possible aftermath of the jury's decision. Although routine services continued to be provided effectively, the city government virtually came to a standstill during the year after the shootings. Melvin filled a critical public-relations role, in cooperation with the city manager and staff, and helped the city meet and survive this challenge.

Melvin also contributed to higher levels of communication and facilitated action by officials. Beyond straightforward transmission of the council's views to the public, he was also an educator. In his relations with the council, the public, the media, and the city manager, and without promoting a favored position, the mayor identified issues and problems for consideration, promoted awareness of important concerns, and sought to promote understanding across the city by exchange of information. For example, to increase awareness that low-income housing was a problem in the city, he organized a bus tour through blighted areas and allowed council members to see for themselves that action was needed.

As liaison with the city manager, Melvin linked the two major components of the system—the legislative body and the administrative apparatus—and facilitated communication and understanding between elected and appointed officials. He increased the city manager's awareness of the council's preferences and could indicate how the council would react to administrative proposals. Not only did the mayor promote communication between the council and the city manager, he and the manager were also a complementary leadership team, sharing ideas about all aspects of city government. Each was viewed as the acknowledged leader in his respective sphere—the council-community sphere, and the organizational sphere (March, 1980). Tom Osborne's high standing as city manager was substantially attributable to his strong personality, his intimate knowledge of city government and the people who worked in it, and his ability to blend new managerial systems with his personal command of what was going on in government. His position was reinforced, however, by the clear support of the city council, reflected in and shaped by its close working relationship with the mayor.

Melvin was particularly involved in the role of team builder, working to unify the council and build consensus. Promoting coalescence is conceptually distinct from taking a group in a particular direction. The mayor, as team leader, seeks to promote full expression, helps the council work through its differences expeditiously, and encourages the council to face issues and resolve them decisively. Under Melvin, the council used a group psychologist as a consultant. This facilitator met with the council once a month for several hours, throughout Melvin's tenure, to assess and improve the council's group process, examine its goals and objectives, and explore such issues as leadership and followership. The sessions also examined roles and division of responsibility between the council and the manager and promoted more effective interaction. This was an innovative and unusual commitment to strengthening the process of the governing body, one that was not well understood elsewhere. "I've been asked to speak in other places in the country," Melvin said after leaving office, "and I'd tell folks that I honestly believed that this was one of the most significant things we did, and they thought I was crazy."

The roles we have considered so far have been concerned with communication and coordination. The next group involves influencing the conduct and direction of the city government's affairs and the content of policy. As goal setter, Melvin concentrated on bringing the council into active involvement with establishing goals and objectives for city government. He considered the setting of common goals to be the most important task a council should perform: "I think that [during] the first 90 days [after] a council is elected, [the members] should do almost nothing until they've caused themselves to be together enough to hammer out [their] goals and objectives. If they don't do it in the first 90—and, at the absolute outside, 180—days, they will never make it." Goal setting was an important part of the regular meetings with the group-process consultant. According to Melvin, instead of arguing about which street to pave, the council members "were really talking about . . . what we should be doing to cause this city to move forward." Melvin found it useful, on the basis of his experience in the private sector, to use goals and objectives in setting a framework for decisions by the city government.

He was also active as an organizer and stabilizer of key relationships within city government. He guided council members to a recognition of their roles and responsibilities in the council-manager form of government. The mayor, in this role, helps define the pattern of interaction between council and manager, monitors it, and makes adjustments to maintain the complex division of responsibilities between council and manager. Melvin was particularly intent on protecting the manager and his staff from interference by council members. Often, new council members or mavericks felt "ordained to go run the city." Maintaining the boundary between council and staff was of major importance to Melvin: "I guess the only combative position I ever took with any independent council member was on that issue." The mayor would intervene when other members of the council were out of bounds.

During this time, a procedure for evaluating the city manager's performance was instituted. The council assessed the manager's performance every ninety days. Meeting separately with the council, Melvin asked each council member what the manager is doing "that you like, and what is he doing that you don't like." He would then include one other council member in a meeting with the manager, to review the session.

Melvin and the council were concerned with promoting a high level of organizational and staff performance. They did away with annual cost-of-living salary increases and instructed staff to develop a merit pay plan. They stressed the use of management by objectives in city government, encouraged concern for productivity and economy, and discouraged the addition of new staff members. The council directed the city manager to create a system for tracking citizens' complaints and to add community representatives to his office, who would help citizens get their complaints resolved. The council also encouraged the manager to initiate sensitivity training for employees, to make them more customer-conscious. This was particularly important in the police department, where the relationship between officers and citizens had been adversely affected by the racial tensions of the late 1960s. In these activities, the mayor and the council were careful not to interfere with the city manager in the details of management.

Finally, Melvin was a policy advocate. As an active guide in policy making, the mayor developed proposals, lined up support for them, and crystallized the policy orientation of the council. In these activities, as in others that influenced the decisions made by the council, it is difficult to separate Melvin's own policy preferences from those of the council as a whole and those developed by the manager and staff. This is the mark of a facilitative leader. Melvin believed strongly in the need to establish a commitment to the goals toward which one is working: "You better know where it is you are trying to go, and I don't mean just you personally. I'm talking about the council and the group that is supposed to be going with you . . . . There are going to be a lot of folks out there to convince you otherwise. That is not to say that you get a mindset that you don't ever change. But you better feel pretty strongly about it, because if you don't, you are going to end up trying to please everybody, and you're going to please nobody. You are going to be just a mealy-mouth." He was recognized to be the agenda setter on the council and in the relationship with the manager. A newspaper assessment of the power holders in Greensboro in 1980 concluded, "If Osborne is credited with the efficiency of the city's operation, Melvin usually gets the credit as its idea-man" (March, 1980, p. A9).

Conceptually distinct from the preceding are Melvin's activities in promoting the city and representing it in a variety of external relations. The mayor may be involved in external relations and help secure agreement among parties to a project. In the promoter role, Melvin was an active initiator of contacts and helped develop possibilities for the city. As official representative, he had extensive dealings with officials in other governments and served as a key participant in formulating agreements with state and federal officials, developers, and others who sought joint ventures with city government. The mayor took the lead in projecting a favorable image of the city and sought to "sell" others on investment in it.

Melvin was effective at building relationships and networks. At the beginning of his tenure, there was a great deal of tension between city government and the Chamber of Commerce. He convened a monthly informal meeting of the "leaders' group," including the top officials in the city, the county, the Chamber of Commerce, United Way, the school board, and the airport authority. Working relationships were improved. For example, the city and the county developed a plan for the joint construction of a new city hall and county courthouse. He also convened regular meetings of top leaders in the business community, to get their ideas and share his proposals.

## Impacts

Many of the program accomplishments of the 1970s represented a commitment to carrying through on the general plans set by earlier councils, particularly with respect to completing the thoroughfare and capital-improvement plans. The city took the approach, innovative for North Carolina cities in the early 1970s, of passing local bonds to provide matching funds for state highway projects and then did the construction itself, rather than wait for the state. By moving up the completion of major projects, Melvin says, "we were able to control our own destiny." Throughout a decade of opposition, the city stood firm in its resolve to build a regional sewage-treatment plant, an enterprise that entailed repeated studies and steadily rising costs.

The mayor and the council, in harmony with the fiscal orientation of the manager, decided to use federal funds, especially general revenue sharing, for capital improvements. Nevertheless, the mayor and the council did oppose demands to expand the involvement of city government into social programs, given their doubts about the efficacy of such programs and the feeling that county government should remain the primary provider of social services. This position reflected Melvin's personal philosophy and the prevailing opinion in city government: "In government, it is just as important to say no as it is to say yes," and expanding the scope of city services was seen as "a sure slide to fiscal suicide."

He also said no to the use of district elections in selecting the members of the city council. In 1975 and again in 1980, he opposed a referendum that would have created a modified district-election process, with a majority of council members elected from districts and the remaining members and the mayor elected at large. He personally believed that council members should be concerned with the welfare of all citizens, and he feared that district elections would splinter the council and weaken support for projects and programs that were citywide in scope. He also insisted that the city council and the staff were committed to the equitable delivery of services to all parts of the city and that capital improvements in community development and recreational programs were concentrated in low-income and minority areas of the city. He feared that the use of districts would lead to pressure to provide the same facilities in all districts, including the higher-income areas of the city that the council had "discriminated against" in its commitment to target the areas of greatest need. During a decade in which the cities of Charlotte and Raleigh had adopted the use of districts, Greensboro voters, influenced in part by the mayor, held out.

Change came, however, the year after Melvin left office, and with his concurrence. Under pressure from the U.S. Justice Department, the city council approved a modified district plan—five district members, three at-large members, and the mayor elected at large—in order to secure clearance under the Voting Rights Act for a major annexation that the city wanted to complete. Melvin and other former opponents of the district plan also came to the conclusion that officials and citizens should put the continuing debate behind them and get on with the business of running the city.

Melvin and the city government took a cautious position on the city's involvement in downtown development. After some modest efforts at urban renewal in the early 1970s, officials decided that it was better to signal to private interests with downtown property that the city was not going to bail them out. According to Melvin, the prevailing view was that "if we ran an awful good city and gave folks high-quality services at very low cost, that would be our only role in economic growth." Although the city would provide infra-

structure[5] and assist with specific projects, such as using the powers
of urban renewal to assemble property for a new insurance
building, it was not going to be the major initiator of change. That
hands-off approach had been successful throughout the middle
1970s. Decisions on economic development would have to be made
by the private sector.[6] After leaving office, however, Melvin con-
ceded that the city should have been more proactive: "We never
primed the pump."

An exception was a proposal for a civic center connected to
a new hotel downtown. Melvin pushed hard for approval of this
project. He was successful at lining up support within city government and at securing backing and pledges of investment from the
business community, but a bond issue to finance the project was
rejected by voters in October 1979. The rejection resulted in part
from public confusion about whether a downtown facility was
needed or would be successful, when a private hotel and convention
center were being built on the edge of the city. Moreover, the bond
had been pushed forward quickly, before public support had been
developed. The careful attention to persuasion and coalition building of Melvin's early years in office had been missing.

## Type of Leadership

The kind of mayoral leadership provided by an incumbent depends
on which roles the mayor performs and how well he or she handles
them. Jim Melvin's record shows him to be a good example of the
directorial type of mayor, who not only contributes to the smooth
functioning of government but also provides a general sense of
direction. A primary responsibility of the council is to determine the
mission of the city government and its broad goals. A directorial
mayor contributes significantly to such consideration of the broad
questions about purpose. According to Melvin, "My toughest job
was keeping the council's attention on the horizon, rather than on
the potholes" (but he also said that the city's commitment to pre-
ventive maintenance had prevented potholes).

The mayor stood out as a leader in the eyes of the council,
the press, and the public, and he used that recognition as the basis
for offering guidance rather than imposing control. He enhanced

the influence of elected officials by unifying the council and guiding policy toward goals that met the needs of the community. Furthermore, he was involved in monitoring and adjusting relationships within city government, to maintain balance, cooperation, and high standards. He promoted the constructive interaction that is needed for effective performance. Melvin was careful not to supplant the manager's prerogatives or diminish the manager's leadership. In the organizer role, he worked to enhance the ability of the manager to function as the executive officer. At the same time, he strengthened the appraisal of the manager's performance. As a director, Melvin was the guiding force in city government.

In sum, Melvin is an example of the mayor in a council-manager city who fashions a unique type of leadership by the roles which he or she develops. Melvin maintained strong support from the council and the public through his effective performance in the traditional and coordinative roles. Mayoral leadership of the directorial type does not depend on a position of superior power if relationships are cooperative; rather, it utilizes the resources for coordination and communication that are inherent in the mayor's office. In fact, Melvin thought that attaching powers to the mayor's office would weaken it in a council-manager city. Providing a formal power like the veto would undermine the mayor's position by setting him apart from the council: "Once you give a mayor veto power, look out. He ain't ever going to ask those . . . councilmen . . . anything." Melvin looked askance at mayors from strong mayor-council cities who attended national meetings with large retinues of support staff. He thought the mayor's success should depend on his or her individual ability to "sell" ideas to others. Giving the mayor any executive powers over the staff would compromise the manager's position and, as a consequence, weaken the organization. Melvin had a clear conception of the job—its possibilities, interdependencies, and limitations—and an appreciation of the governmental process in which he operated.

### Resources

Melvin had a sense of purpose and his own ideas about what the city should do, but he was effective at working with others and accepted giving responsibility to them. Inclusiveness, sharing of information, facilitation of the expression of divergent views, and ability to resolve differences were important traits in his dealings with the council. In his relationship with the manager, he demonstrated tact, respect, ability to share authority, and trust in the manager's commitment to advance the goals of the city and to achieve the highest performance from government as a whole.

He was Greensboro's first directly elected mayor, after a change in the city charter, although initially he had been selected from within the council. He used his campaigns for reelection as a way to develop public support. He believed that direct election does enhance the mayor's position.

His interpersonal skills were highly developed. In the early years, he devoted considerable time to finding common ground between opposing positions. By his fourth term, he acknowledges, he had lost some of the patience that this approach requires: "The mayor becomes a lightning rod" for every decision that is made; "if you stay in office long enough, you've made everyone mad at you at least twice." In his view, this is the time to get out and let someone fresh take on the tasks of facilitative leadership.

This observation points to a final resource—a sense of enthusiasm and commitment. Melvin felt that this quality was crucial to success and that it cannot be sustained indefinitely: "Ten to twelve years is probably the absolute limit that someone could keep the enthusiasm up for the city job that we did and not have a tendency to burn out." In his view, the person who becomes mayor needs to "really give it a good shot and do all that you can. Just tear it up for a while, but then feel good about it and turn it over to somebody else."

## Conclusion

Melvin's example clearly demonstrates that council-manager mayors can contribute substantially to the performance of their governments and to the betterment of their communities. The position is not a pale imitation of the executive mayor's office in a mayor-council city; rather, it is a unique leadership position that requires distinctive qualities. This kind of mayor must utilize the opportunities for coordination and policy guidance that are present in the form, and he or she must display personal resourcefulness and drive, self-restraint, commitment to enhance the position of other participants in the governmental process, and flexibility. For council-manager mayors, effective leadership is built on strengthening the other participants in the governing process, rather than on controlling or supplanting them. The council-manager mayor can be the guiding force, coordinating the contributions of the council and the manager and providing a sense of direction and purpose to city government. The facilitative mayor increases the involvement of all officials and adds to the leadership capacity of the system as a whole.

Jim Melvin was an effective and successful leader before becoming mayor, and he has continued to be a major figure in community affairs since leaving office. In a newspaper analysis of the distribution of power in Greensboro in 1988, Melvin was still rated as the most influential person in the city (Williams, 1988). His tenure as mayor demonstrates how energy, creativity, good ideas, persuasiveness, a commitment to action, enthusiasm, and a strong desire to "be right" can be channeled through the mayor's office to energize a council-manager government. He was assisted greatly by a highly capable city manager, but it seems virtually certain that Jim Melvin and the council over which he presided would have secured the services of another talented manager if Tom Osborne had not been available; they would have elicited and reinforced a high level of performance from whoever was selected as manager.

Jim Melvin was also fortunate to have had able persons serving on the city council with him. The at-large election system through which they were selected was criticized for producing councils that were dominated by white businesspersons and professionals, overwhelmingly from the most affluent quadrant of the city. As individuals, however, they were dedicated and concerned with addressing the needs of the city as a whole. Even though they were largely homogeneous in background and/or attitude, the mayor enhanced their performance by providing a sense of purpose and by causing them to monitor and improve their interpersonal relations as a small group of decision makers. One can only speculate about whether he would also have been able to forge a council elected from districts into an effective working group, if district elections had been adopted in the 1970s. Given his talents as a leader, one suspects that he could have.

Effective leaders in council-manager government can stand out as individuals, but they also make the people around them look good by helping them identify and accomplish collective goals and perform at a higher level than they would have without the guidance of a facilitative leader. Jim Melvin epitomized this model of leadership.

### Notes

1.  These findings were first reported in James H. Svara and James W. Bohmbach, "The Mayoralty and Leadership in Council-Manager Cities," *Popular Government*, 1976, *41*, 1–6.
2.  The interviews with Melvin and other officials were conducted in 1986.
3.  The population in 1980 and 1990 was 155,642 and 183,521, respectively. The city added 3.1 square miles in land area during the 1970s through annexation. An additional 12.5 square miles were added during the 1980s. The minority population increased to 33 percent in 1980 and remained at this level throughout the decade.
4.  Melvin's father, who continued to operate his service station after most white-owned businesses had closed, was killed in a robbery at his business in 1973.
5.  The city's development effort was harmed, according to Melvin, by a sewer moratorium in the late 1970s, brought about by the delay in the construction of the new regional sewage-treatment plant.
6.  Since leaving public office, Melvin has been active in mobilizing the private sector for action and pushing government to support business development activities. He has helped inspire an energy and initiative in the private sector that he felt should have been displayed when he was in office.

## References

Boynton, R. P., and Wright, D. S. "Mayor-Manager Relationships in Large Council-Manager Cities: A Reinterpretation." *Public Administration Review*, 1971, *31*, 28–36.

March, W. "A New Way to Run City Hall." *Greensboro Daily News*, Nov. 25, 1980, pp. A1, A9.

Williams, E. "Power Is Fair Game for Master Player." *Greensboro News and Record*, Dec. 19, 1988, pp. A1, A6, A7.

# Part Two

## *Effective Coordinating Leaders*

# 5

*Timothy D. Mead*

# Leadership That Exceeds Expectations: Carla DuPuy, Chairperson, Board of Commissioners, Mecklenburg County, North Carolina

"Carla," I said, "I need to tell you something. When you were first elected to the board of commissioners and became chair of the board at your first meeting, I was skeptical that you would do well. But you have exceeded my expectations in every regard."

Carla DuPuy, chair of the Mecklenburg County Board of Commissioners from January 1984 to December 1990, had announced only a few days earlier that she would not seek reelection.

*Note:* The sources for this chapter include some interviews with people who have asked to remain anonymous. (Carla DuPuy is not currently holding any office, but rumors abound that she will seek high office in the future. In the event that she does, a few people will not want to have had their positions compromised by an interview for an academic volume.) As a member of the Charlotte–Mecklenburg Planning Commission, I had frequent opportunities to observe DuPuy performing her duties and so I too serve as a source. This chapter benefited from a careful reading and rigorous but friendly critique from Hugh L. LeBlanc, retired from the Department of Political Science at George Washington University.

This assessment of DuPuy's tenure as chair of the board of commissioners is widely shared among close observers of Mecklenburg County. Joe Bradshaw, former assistant county manager, captured the perspective well. He said that DuPuy "evolved" as chair of the board (Bradshaw, 1991). What follows is a case study that focuses on Carla DuPuy as a facilitative leader.

## The Context

Mecklenburg County is the most populous county in North Carolina. The 1990 census indicates that a little over half a million persons live in the county. Charlotte, a city of nearly 400,000, is the county seat. The metropolitan area, a portion of which is in South Carolina, has a population of well over a million (Jones, 1991).

Charlotte-Mecklenburg, as it is known locally, is the hub of the Carolina textiles and apparel industry. Traditionally, the textile industry has surrounded Mecklenburg County (Goldfield, 1982), yet Mecklenburg remained the vital service center of the industry.

While textiles has diminished in importance, other industries have taken its place. Three of the top five manufacturing employers are in nontraditional sectors: computers, food, and man-made cellulose fibers. Some have located in Mecklenburg County, but many of the new or growing industries have selected sites in outlying counties. Nevertheless, the extensive development of industrial parks in northern and western Mecklenburg County indicates confidence among investors that the market will continue to support industrial growth in the county (Urban Land Institute, 1990).

Further, Mecklenburg County is headquarters to major banking and finance activities. With expansion of several Charlotte banks into other regions of the country, Charlotte now ranks sixth nationally in the value of banking assets controlled from the city. Mecklenburg County also is the center of a regionally important trucking industry, with over 150 firms located nearby (Urban Land Institute, 1990).

Combined, these vigorous activities suggest to many local observers that Charlotte-Mecklenburg is emerging from the regional shadow of Atlanta—that Charlotte-Mecklenburg is "big league." The success of the Charlotte Hornets basketball franchise is symbolic of this progress; since early in the first year of the Hornets' existence, every home game has been a sellout.

Civic pride in the city and the region sets the context for political life. For nearly one hundred years, from 1868 to 1986, Mecklenburg County was governed by a five-member board of commissioners, all elected at large. After the Voting Rights Act of 1965, complaints developed that the at-large system effectively excluded some segments of Mecklenburg County's citizens from representation. At one point in the early 1980s, all five members of the board of commissioners attended the same center-city church.

A mixed system of district and at-large representation was voted in by the citizens in 1984 and went into effect in 1986. The board of commissioners now has seven members, three elected at large. In addition to the improved fortunes of black voters resulting from the use of districts, another "minority" also has been given an advantage—Republicans (Ingalls, 1988).

The chair of the board of commissioners in Mecklenburg County is elected by the board from among its members. Traditionally, the chair of the board has been the person with the greatest total votes received in the general election. No practice had emerged to deal with the contingency that someone might be the top vote recipient and not be in the majority party. Until very recently, only Democrats contested for seats on the board of commissioners. In November 1984, the candidate with the largest number of votes was Democratic incumbent chair T. L. "Fountain" Odom, who had served on the board since 1980 and had been chair since 1982.

Republican growth, however, was not solely a function of district electoral systems, and in the election before the mixed electoral system took effect, Republicans gained a majority on the board. DuPuy ran second in the general election and was the top Republican vote getter (Ingalls, 1988).

In 1962, the county manager system was instituted. In Mecklenburg County, this system functions in the classic fashion, with the manager serving at the pleasure of the board. The manager hires and fires the department heads, prepares an executive budget, and serves as principal adviser to the board of commissioners. As is required by the North Carolina constitution, however, some key county functions are under the jurisdiction of independently elected officials—in particular the sheriff, the district attorney, and the registrars of wills and deeds.

With few exceptions, prior to the appointment of Gerald Fox, in 1980, Mecklenburg County managers had been appointed from within. Typically, the level of professionalism was low. The appointment of Fox signaled an end to the previous pattern and a commitment to professional public management.

### DuPuy Becomes Chair

In 1984, only two Democrats were elected to the five-member board of commissioners. Commissioner Odom received the most votes, and traditionally he would have been selected chair for a third term. To the surprise of most observers, Republicans gained a majority on the board. Republicans wanted to claim the fruits of victory and select the chair of the board from among their number. Since only the Democrats had ever had a majority on the board of commissioners, there was no precedent for a party split in selection of the chair. None of the Republicans, however, had had any previous service on the board.

Among the Republicans, Commissioner-elect DuPuy led the ticket. Her fondest hope as a candidate had been that she would come in no worse than fifth, thus garnering a seat on the commission (DuPuy, 1991). Among political insiders, DuPuy had a reputation as a promising but untried rookie. Her previous governmental experience had been limited to service on the Mecklenburg County Library Board, and she had been chair of that group.

Perceptions of DuPuy were also influenced by her social standing. She was (and is) the wife of a prominent physician. Her campaign organization was dominated by friends made during her long service in the Charlotte Junior League. DuPuy is a petite woman, well dressed, with good interpersonal skills.

Fairly or not, these elements of DuPuy's origins and appearance led people to infer that she was a lightweight. She was inexperienced in the kinds of activities that many candidates for local office have engaged in, but she was not a lightweight.

Editorial writers for *The Charlotte Observer* made public

what many people were saying behind the scenes; even though the Republicans had gained a majority on the board and could claim the chair, experience should outweigh partisan advantage: "We'd like to offer a suggestion on that point. Mr. Odom now serves as chairman, and the three Republican newcomers would do well to keep him in that position for the first year of this two-year term. Then, having gained some experience and gotten to know each other, they can choose one of themselves to replace him" ("Good Choices for County Board," 1984).

In part, this suggestion reflected support for Odom; in part, it reflected reservations about DuPuy's possibly becoming chair. The speculation was that an articulate and vigorous accountant Rod Autrey, also a freshman commissioner, would make the most successful Republican chair. Political observers hoped that a year learning the ropes would make Autrey's prospects better, even though he had been only the second-highest Republican vote getter and only third-highest overall. DuPuy (1991) says that she did not feel at the time that there was a preference for Autrey, and she felt that if any of the newcomers to the board was to become chair, she had received the most votes and deserved the spot: "Why should I yield to someone else who had never been there either?"

In addition, support for DuPuy's assuming the chair was strong among women. After DuPuy announced that she would accept election as chair of the board of commissioners, she gained an endorsement from an unexpected source. Susan Green, former member of the board of commissioners and a prominent Democrat, spoke at a meeting of the Women's Political Caucus. Green urged women to come together behind DuPuy. Too frequently, Green asserted, women let other women in politics be ill treated. DuPuy was pleased but surprised by Green's support (DuPuy, 1991).

DuPuy decided to accept being chair of the board after Republican leaders told her that if she did not want the job, it would go to Autrey, and if he did not want it, then Jerry Blackmon, the third Republican newcomer, would be given the post. If none of the Republicans wanted to be chair, the leaders told DuPuy, then there would be consideration of a possible arrangement with Odom (Du-Puy, 1991).

Privately, the Democrats were divided. Some hoped that

Odom would be retained as chair. Some recognized that the Republicans had a majority and would select the chair, but they hoped that, as newcomers, the Republicans would flounder. A final perspective was that Republicans would choose the chair, and that the Democratic veterans would do as much as possible to make a success of the two years during which the Republicans held the chair.

From the perspective of observers of Mecklenburg County politics, DuPuy's tenure as chair of the board of commissioners started under a cloud of doubt. She had led the ticket of the majority party, but many saw her as the third most desirable choice for chair, behind Odom and Autrey. DuPuy recognized that she was in Odom's shadow, and she set out through her conduct to prove doubters wrong (DuPuy, 1991).

### Style and Substance

Formally, the chair of the Mecklenburg County Board of Commissioners has little power. As an elected member of the board, the chair votes on all issues. The only power that belongs to the chair alone is that of presiding officer at all meetings. Such leadership has been called "nonexecutive" (see the Preface); despite high public expectations for what such an elected official can accomplish, the power to generate outcomes autonomously is very slight. How, then, does such a leader lead? As Svara says in Chapter One, he or she does so by facilitating the efforts of others. In this sense, DuPuy was a facilitative leader.

### Facilitative Leadership of the Board

According to most of the people interviewed for this chapter, DuPuy's style of leadership was open, and she sought to be informed. She presided in an informal and relaxed manner yet kept close control over the progress of meetings. When tensions would build, DuPuy could use self-deprecating humor to defuse antagonists (White, 1991; Autrey, 1991). DuPuy recognizes that she utilized her sense of humor as a facilitative tool: "I tried to take the issue seriously, but not take myself too seriously" (DuPuy, 1991).

Her goal seemed to be to have people who had business before the board of commissioners (whether staff, developers, citizens urging the board to take a particular action, or individuals seeking redress for some wrong) leave meetings with the feeling that they had been fully heard. At rezoning hearings, for example, she would often give individual landowners, particularly those without legal or other professional assistance, a few extra moments to make their points, or she would ask questions that she thought would lead to the most rigorous explanation of a landowner's viewpoint, whether or not it was one she shared.

"I wanted to put minds together, get lots of participation, rely heavily on appointed bodies like the Human Services Council" (DuPuy, 1991). I recall having heard DuPuy ask in many meetings, "What do we have to do to make this work?" It did not matter to her whether the answer, or part of it, came from a staff member, another member of the commission, a member of an appointed advisory body, or a citizen; all ideas were grist for DuPuy's mill. Gradually, a plan would develop that most participants could claim at least some element of as their own.

As a leadership tool, DuPuy relied heavily on "being on top of every issue." She prided herself on reading all of the considerable amount of material generated by the county staff and by private interest groups: "Just doing the homework when others did not gave me a significant advantage. Over time, I proved that I wasn't a ditz brain" (DuPuy, 1991). She notes that almost immediately upon leaving office, she was appointed to the Chamber of Commerce's executive committee, one of the most influential private groups in the community.

A key element of DuPuy's knowledge of Mecklenburg County came from her constant presence. DuPuy made being chair of the commission a virtually full-time job. Announcing that she would not be a candidate for reelection, DuPuy said, "In the last five years, I have given this job 150% every day and for the year remaining in my current term I pledge to do no less" (Morrill, 1990, p. 3B).

Her daily presence had several consequences. First, it gave her a place and a time for reading background materials without distraction. Second, it put her in regular contact with the top-level administrative staff. She began to spend her morning break in the employees' break room, and shortly afterward she became friends with many staff members. She could be "both human and in charge" (Bradshaw, 1991). In the course of seeing her, people told her things that they would not have had a chance to tell her had she not been so available: "This was a unique part of her style. For six years we had a full-time, day-to-day chairman" (Autrey, 1991). Third, her knowledge became a major source of her influence. She could not be led astray by the strongly expressed assurances of staff, other commissioners, or the public. Gradually, others came to recognize that DuPuy really "knew." She surprised many with her knowledge. People quickly learned not to challenge her on her understanding of issues. She also soon learned to use her superior knowledge as a source of influence (Bradshaw, 1991). Fourth, her interaction with staff built confidence between the professionals and DuPuy and, through her, with the board of commissioners: "I could remember how important the library picnic was to everybody, and how disappointed they were when none of the commissioners showed up. So when I became a commissioner, I went to all those things. I was lucky that I did not have another career. Being commissioner was my career" (DuPuy, 1991).

### Personality and Facilitative Leadership

A distinctive element of DuPuy's leadership style was a function of her size and appearance. DuPuy is a diminutive and attractive woman; several people interviewed for this chapter noted her size and attractiveness, which no doubt had been factors in the original assessment of DuPuy as an unlikely leader.

DuPuy (1991) notes that throughout her life she has always been "the smallest, so I always had to try harder." Yet the result, in DuPuy's case, was not the classic expression of a Napoleon complex: a small tyrant. Rather, she learned a leadership style that was not threatening, and her physical presence added to her relaxed and gentle style. Consequently, those she worked with did not need to be defensive. Over time, the guard of other players was lowered (Bradshaw, 1991). Accommodation or policy resolution could be reached in an atmosphere of mutual respect.

Bradshaw perceives DuPuy's leadership as partly "family instincts. She wanted to create a family atmosphere—'We're all in this together.' She was more into nurturing than team building." He feels that DuPuy wanted to talk people through issues and smooth ruffled feathers. In particular, Bradshaw asserts, this was helpful at the county management level "because the staff all liked her, and she could go behind others and calm things down"; she was a "wound-healer" (Bradshaw, 1991).

The roles of facilitative leaders are also affected by the character of or the absence of formal power. The only formal power granted to the chair of the Mecklenburg County Board of Commissioners is the power to preside over meetings of the board, yet the chair is often able to use that power to enhance other, informal kinds of power. DuPuy took her multiple roles seriously as chair of the board of commissioners.

As presiding officer, DuPuy selected issues on which she would provide direction to the board. Autrey (1991) thinks that DuPuy consciously chose the issues on which she would spend the scarce resources of policy leadership: "She might have been saving a scarce resource. But she also was respecting that the chair carries weight and should be used appropriately. . . . On some developing issues that were a higher priority for her, she would try to facilitate the process, and you knew where she stood. . . . She would make her view known in the course of the discussion of the issues. . . . She did this wisely, because I don't have a feeling of issues of major significance that were not addressed." Examples of issues that Autrey sees as having attracted DuPuy's facilitative attention include the establishment of a recycling program, the siting of a landfill, and the provision of resources for emergency assistance in the Department of Social Services.

Autrey believes that, ordinarily, DuPuy would not "lobby" for her position in advance of board meetings. More typically, members of the board would not know how DuPuy was going to vote until she actually voted (Autrey, 1991). Another commissioner, however (Walton,1991), thinks that DuPuy's leadership role was that of a consensus builder. On controversial issues, she called the players to talk and to get the lay of the political landscape (Fox, 1991). Of course, both perceptions may be correct. DuPuy may have called Walton to lobby him more often than she called Autrey, or the two commissioners may have different perspectives on what constitutes a crucial issue, one on which they expect to get some signal from the chair of the board.

## Ceremony and Facilitative Leadership

DuPuy's leadership role was not limited to presiding over meetings or making phone calls to other commissioners to round up support. The core of DuPuy's role as chair was made up of ceremonial activities. Commissioner Walton notes, "She enjoyed her role as chair of the board. When she was invited, she went. She had the time, and she did it" (Walton, 1991).

DuPuy made the most of these opportunities. She was good at linking ceremonial activities with substantive concerns. She could take "pseudo-events" (Boorstin, 1961), the staged activities designed to generate publicity, and make them relevant to the policy directions that she wished to emphasize. Joe Bradshaw, responsible for solid waste and recycling while assistant county manager, recalls that "when we wanted to make a point about recycling, she climbed into a garbage can and let people take pictures of her peering out." She used ceremonies as occasions to be an "ambassador" for policy positions (Bradshaw, 1991).

Her role as ambassador was particularly noticeable as she led battles for various projects, often represented by successful bond referenda. During DuPuy's service as chair of the board of commissioners, no bond referendum was defeated by the voters. For example, when Gerald Fox arrived as county manager, capital planning was in disarray. Fox convinced DuPuy and the other commissioners of the need for more sophisticated capital-needs planning. DuPuy, Fox asserts, could articulate the need for human services and capital needs so that "the community would accept the need for higher taxes. She could carry the day on bond issues." These were "grubby duties," but she did them gladly, and her good "political sense" made for success (Fox, 1991).

DuPuy sees her role as having been one of "raising community attention." Examples that seem particularly appropriate to her include working on the management of the criminal justice system and paying attention to the apparent decline in the quality of education in the Charlotte–Mecklenburg schools: "It wasn't too hard to generate community interest when the DA's office could not handle all the incoming cases and the SAT scores fell" (DuPuy, 1991). When leaders of industry who were considering relocating to Mecklenburg County called to question her about rumors that the public schools did not provide good education, she called local business leaders and urged them to take a leadership role in generating public support for better education.

## Issue Selection

DuPuy did not seek out issues to espouse, nor did she have a preestablished agenda: "I processed incoming stuff, and issues came to me. Further, some of the issues that I pushed were things that no other commissioner wanted to be identified with. As chair, I could not pick and choose. So, I got the landfill, for example, because no one else wanted it" (DuPuy, 1991). According to Bradshaw (1991), she had the capacity to understand the crises represented by issues and to articulate them to the community (for example, the crisis of solid waste disposal). On such issues, she could be a risk taker in promoting her preferred solution.

To the extent that any policy thrust is likely to be associated with DuPuy's tenure as chair of the board of commissioners, it will be regionalism. In February 1986, DuPuy and council chair Murray White of York County, South Carolina, invited the chairs of Cabarrus, Gaston, Iredell, Lincoln, and Union Counties in North Carolina and Lancaster County, South Carolina, to join in a discussion of common problems. From this meeting the Carolinas Coalition was born (Pullen, 1988b).

There is fear in the adjacent counties of the impact of Mecklenburg and suspicion that it may exercise its political and economic influence to the disadvantage of its neighbors. Although she is not solely responsible for the apparent success of the Carolinas Coalition, DuPuy has played a key role in assuaging the fears of the adjacent counties. William McCoy, director of the Urban Institute at the University of North Carolina, Charlotte, has had a key position from which to observe the Carolinas Coalition. The Urban Institute has served the coalition as a secretariat. DuPuy's open style played a key role in facilitating the work of the Carolinas Coalition (McCoy, 1991).

DuPuy thought officials in adjacent counties realized that she was "a nonthreatening person. I never had any real power over them. I just wanted to share what we had here. I just tried to make them feel equal" (DuPuy, 1991). Even when she was unable or unwilling to accede to the wishes of nearby jurisdictions, DuPuy's openness kept lines of communication clear. The Carolinas Coalition met in places outside Charlotte, thus ensuring that Mecklenburg was not "summoning" other members to the vital center (McCoy, 1991), and DuPuy was ever alert to invitations from other jurisdictions to hear their points of view. They were not always happy with what they heard (Stowe, 1988), but they knew that someone from Mecklenburg had listened. *The Charlotte Observer,* shortly after she announced that she would not seek reelection, noted, "It's already predictable that Ms. DuPuy's most important legacy will be her leadership in initiating the framework for regional cooperation" ("Ms. DuPuy Talks About 1990," 1990). DuPuy left office with the cause of regional political cooperation well advanced and on a firm footing.

## Facilitative Leadership and Professional Managers

A key element of successful facilitative leadership is the relationship between elected officials and career managers. The traditional model advanced by political scientists has been predicated on conflict between political and career leaders, with a presumed loss of political responsiveness in council-manager systems (see Chapter One), yet success in such systems often depends on cooperative interaction between political and professional officials. Further, such cooperation, despite the model, is at least as common as conflict (Anderson, 1983; Mead, 1981).

DuPuy had a very positive relationship with the professional staff of Mecklenburg County. Joe Bradshaw, as assistant county manager, had a good vantage point from which to observe the relationship between DuPuy and Gerald Fox, the county manager. The responsibility of the manager is to make the chair and the board of commissioners happy, according to Bradshaw (1991):

"Early on, Carla learned to respect Fox and his opinion. She had confidence in him." Her skills and political sensitivity complemented Fox's managerial and technical skills. DuPuy, according to Bradshaw, quickly learned how to exploit and balance Fox's strengths and weaknesses with her own, and the two became a formidable team.

Fox (1991) also credits DuPuy with strengthening the manager system in Mecklenburg County: "The system is stronger now than when she came in. She never interfered in the gray area between management and policy. And she supported the staff in public every chance she got. So the staff had confidence in her and was eager to respond to her requests expeditiously. She depended on the staff to process, to give her information."

Most close observers of Mecklenburg County government would agree that the manager system is stronger now than it was a decade ago. DuPuy no doubt had a hand in enhancing the manager system, and so did Fox. Part of their mutual success was due to the willingness of each to give credit to the other.

DuPuy, Fox says, was a "quick study" who readily grasped issues, understood the positions of various players, and realized when she needed help: "She was smart enough to know when to lean on me and the rest of the staff" (Fox, 1991). Commissioner Walton thinks that a portion of DuPuy's prompt acclimation to county government was motivated by a desire to prove critics wrong. According to Walton, she rapidly acquired a greater "awareness of the relative roles of the staff and of elected officials" than most commissioners; "she did a crash course on county government" (Walton, 1991).

In turn, DuPuy thinks that Fox was a "wonderful administrator. He tried not to let his opinion influence the material he gave us. I generally knew how he felt. Sometimes, though not often, he came to me and said, 'This is what you really need to know about this.' He trusted the commissioners to do what needed to be done. Of course, I was down there so much, he didn't need to explain much to me" (DuPuy, 1991).

Commissioner Autrey believes that DuPuy was too close to Fox and the professional staff. As a result of the extended time she spent at the Charlotte–Mecklenburg Government Center, he says, she became too identified with the staff and lost her objectivity when issues of relationships between professional and elected officials developed (Autrey, 1991).

In any event, the "courthouse crowd" rapidly learned that DuPuy had been underestimated. She quickly proved that those who had expected her to be of little political consequence or to provide shallow leadership were wrong.

## Facilitative Leadership and Influential People

Gradually, DuPuy's influence spread to influential people in the community. Some argue that Charlotte–Mecklenburg, very much in the mold of Floyd Hunter's Atlanta, is run by powerful business-men (Mellnik, 1988). Neither DuPuy nor her husband were "players in the uptown community" when she became chair of the board. In early contacts with leaders of the business community, DuPuy could sense their perception that she was not up to the task, but they knew they needed to try to get along with her (DuPuy, 1991).

A key factor in her developing influence with the business community was that she kept plugging. White (1991) believes she knew that her success was partly dependent on support from busi-ness leaders, and so she simply kept in touch with them.

For untold years, the mayor of Charlotte and the chair of the board of commissioners have met with business leaders under the sponsorship of the Chamber of Commerce. During 1989 and 1990, this practice came under widespread attack from neighborhood groups and *The Charlotte Observer* (Chandler and Rhee, 1990). (Since then, these meetings have been determined to be covered by the North Carolina public meetings law, and they now continue without apparent controversy.) During these meetings, DuPuy simply convinced the business leaders of her ability. Autrey (1991) believes DuPuy convinced them that she was "predictable, thought-ful, accessible. She was astute enough to keep in touch with people who come together to make things happen." Fox (1991) perceives her as a valuable link to the "power structure," the bankers, and the Chamber of Commerce. Despite DuPuy's disclaimer, Fox thinks that her previous experiences on the Library Board and in the Junior League put her in contact with many of the people she needed to work with as chair of the board of commissioners.

Over time, no doubt, the business leaders also recognized that DuPuy was no fluke as chair of the board. She was successful in the coin of the political realm: she got votes. Three times she led the Republican ticket, and twice she was the top vote getter. In the last of those efforts, she rebuffed a determined effort by Commissioner Autrey to unseat her as chair of the board of commissioners (Pullen, 1988a). Walton (1991) thinks the business community had to take DuPuy seriously because she demonstrated over time that she had support in the larger public.

## Assessing Facilitative Leadership in Mecklenburg County

"She smelled like a rose because she was a rose" (Walton, 1991). Summing up DuPuy's success as chair of the board of commissioners with those words, Commissioner Walton captures what happened during her tenure. According to Autrey (1991), "She always had it. It was not something that she developed. She was absolutely dedicated to proving it, and she never backed down. She was never a lightweight. She might have been a flyweight, but she was world champion." Walton and Autrey, for different reasons, were the commissioners serving with DuPuy who were most likely to be critical of her performance. Those people, including myself, who had doubted DuPuy's prospects were wrong. She was more than we expected.

What factors contributed to DuPuy's remarkable success as chair of the Mecklenburg County Board of Commissioners? Any textbook can provide the lineaments of the reform movement and its assumptions concerning the mechanisms for leadership in municipal government. The reform movement was so successful in establishing its assumptions as operating principles that a recent study simply asserts, "Chief executives in the 'most reformed' cities are city managers" and overlooks the potential for facilitative elected leadership (Abney and Lauth, 1986, p. 139). Further, the professional literature directed toward city and county managers does not distinguish between council or commission members, on the one hand, and mayors or chairs of the board, on the other; all are simply "elected officials" with whom managers must deal (Anderson, 1983). Yet newspaper and television accounts of local politics and administration in reformed cities and counties are replete with assertions of responsibility and accountability directed toward chief elected officials. The textbook model may hold that elected leaders have been banished as a force in reformed local government, but practitioners think otherwise.

In the case of Carla DuPuy, there were a number of factors that contributed to her success. One factor, at least at the outset, was that she was seriously underestimated by those who needed to deal with her. As we have seen, her commitment to demonstrating that Mecklenburg County voters had not erred in electing her was something that energized her. The contrast between expectations and her actual performance brought reconsideration and led to early respect.

Another factor was her personality, which in turn affected her leadership style. It has long been recognized that personal qualities contribute to the performance of elected municipal leaders (Kotter and Lawrence, 1974; Pressman, 1972). DuPuy's open, friendly, nonconfrontational style led people to have confidence in her. Staff and citizens believed that they could tell her things without encountering prejudice from her. People brought her information, which she used to build agreement toward the goals she wished to reach. Officials from nearby counties, normally suspicious, were willing to accept her leadership on regional issues.

Still another factor was her reputation for a problem-solving approach—the "what do we have to do to make this work" perspective. A story, perhaps apocryphal, suggests this approach. Whether or not it is true in some sense is beside the point; people who followed the work of the Mecklenburg County Commission repeat this tale to one another: During DuPuy's tenure, a plan developed to privatize the provision of mental health services by transferring them to the Carolinas Medical Center, headed by Dr. Harry Nurkin, a vigorous advocate of the center and a tough bargainer. In negotiating the necessary contracts, Nurkin and County Manager Fox were unable to come to an agreement. Finally, the contracts were worked out personally by Nurkin and Fox. DuPuy got them together and did not interfere, but she would not let them leave until the work was done. While they ironed out their differences, DuPuy sat in the corner and knitted.

This kind of commitment, as a hallmark of DuPuy's leadership, was summed up by a *Charlotte Observer* editorial: "The statement read at the end of Tuesday's board meeting was typical of Ms. DuPuy: brief and to the point, not flashy or charismatic, but reflecting on the real and sometimes gritty business of local government. And it was, in her unassuming way, visionary" ("Ms. DuPuy Talks About 1990," 1990.)

DuPuy's confidence in the manager enhanced staff performance, which in turn reflected well on her. Productive relations between elected and professional leadership is perhaps the most important characteristic of local governments with high levels of management capacity (Mead, 1981).

It has come to be a given that elected leaders and professional staff must work together. Yet it is not a given of the manager-council system, as it is applied to counties, that such cooperation will exist. Hillsborough County, Florida, offers a contemporary example of the difficulties with policy and management that may result when harmony is absent (Gurwitt, 1989). An additional factor in DuPuy's success as a facilitative leader was her role as an intermediary among the various loci of power and influence. DuPuy controlled no resources that she could distribute or withhold to make brokering possible in the sense that Yates (1977) means. Yet DuPuy met regularly with officials of the Chamber of Commerce and other business groups, the mayor of Charlotte, Charlotte City Council members, representatives of the six smaller incorporated jurisdictions in Mecklenburg County, the Carolinas Coalition, and anyone else who wanted to meet. For two years, DuPuy and I served together on the Charlotte–Mecklenburg Planning Liaison Committee. A number of other elected officials served on this committee as well. None was as regular in attendance as she was. DuPuy came to these and other gatherings as part of her effort to serve as the node of as many policy networks as she could. Perhaps this is not brokering, but contact with a large number of people in a variety of positions contributed to DuPuy's success as a facilitative leader.

Her success was also a function of the fact that she understood politics. She knew who supported her and who did not, but—

as her ultimate political reconciliation with Commissioner Walton illustrates—she did not burn bridges. She was eager to work with anyone who wanted Mecklenburg County to work. (Her postservice appointment to the Chamber of Commerce's board of directors suggests the extent of her success in this regard.) DuPuy may not have possessed collaborative skill when she was elected to the board of commissioners; if not, she soon learned it. She learned to recognize the strengths of those around her and to exploit them.

Of all the insights into facilitative elected leadership gathered during my research for this case study, perhaps the most profound one comes from my interview with Gerald Fox. We had essentially finished our conversation. I put my notepad aside, and for a few moments we talked about personal matters. Suddenly Fox came back to the subject of facilitative leadership and offered a generalization about his relationship with DuPuy and his experience during a thirty-year career in local public management: "I don't think the council-manager system can work unless people like one another. Carla and I got along because we liked one another. That's why she was successful. People liked her, and she liked them." Does this comment suggest that friendship is the most important factor in facilitative leadership? I do not know.

At DuPuy's final meeting as chair, Fox characterized her tenure as "The Years of Carla" (Chandler, 1990). Six years earlier, very few of us would have imagined that. *Mea culpa.*

### References

Abney, G., and Lauth, T. P. *The Politics of State and City Administration.* Albany: The State University of New York Press, 1986.

Anderson, W. F. *The Effective Local Government Manager.* Washington, D.C.: International City Management Association, 1983.

Autrey, R. Personal interview by the author, Feb. 6, 1991.

Boorstin, D. J. *The Image: A Guide to Pseudo-Events in America.* New York: HarperCollins, 1961.

Bradshaw, J. Personal interview by the author, Jan. 29, 1991.

Chandler, L. "DuPuy Offers Farewell; 'Years of Carla' for County Close." *The Charlotte Observer,* Dec. 4, 1990, p. 1D.

Chandler, L., and Rhee, F. "Public Affairs Often Proceed Without Public." *The Charlotte Observer*, Feb. 19, 1990, p. 1A.

DuPuy, C. Personal interview by the author, Feb. 6, 1991.

Fox, G. Personal interview by the author, Jan. 30, 1991.

Goldfield, D. *Cottonfields and Skyscrapers: Southern City and Region, 1607–1980*. Baton Rouge: Louisiana State University Press, 1982.

"Good Choices for County Board." *The Charlotte Observer*, Nov. 11, 1984, Editorial page.

Gurwitt, R. "Cultures Clash as Old-Time Politics Confronts Button-Down Management." *Governing*, 1989, *4*, 42–48.

Ingalls, G. L. (ed.). *Elections, Parties and Politics in Mecklenburg County*. Charlotte: Charlotte/Mecklenburg Board of Elections, Department of Geography and Earth Sciences, and Urban Institute at the University of North Carolina, Charlotte, 1988.

Jones, R. "Census Recount Pays Off for Carolinas." *The Charlotte Observer*, Jan. 26, 1991, p. 1A.

Kotter, J. P., and Lawrence, P. R. *Mayors in Action*. New York: Wiley, 1974.

McCoy, W. J. Personal interview with the author, Feb. 4, 1991.

Mead, T. D. "Identifying Management Capacity Among Local Governments." *Urban Affairs Papers*, 1981, *3*, 1–12.

Mellnik, T. "Informal Influence of 'The Group' Helps Shape Charlotte's Future." *The Charlotte Observer*, Aug. 28, 1988, p. 1A.

Morrill, J. "Mecklenburg Board Chief Won't Run for 4th Term." *The Charlotte Observer*, Jan. 3, 1990, p. 3B.

"Ms. DuPuy Talks About 1990." *The Charlotte Observer*, Jan. 3, 1990, Editorial page.

Pressman, J. L. "Preconditions of Mayoral Leadership." *American Political Science Review*, 1972, *66*, 511–524.

Pullen, L. "DuPuy, Autrey Seemingly Battle for Chairmanship." *The Charlotte Observer*, Nov. 5, 1988a, p. 1A.

Pullen, L. "Regional Cooperation Aim of Counties Coalition." *The Charlotte Observer*, Mar. 8, 1988b, p. 1A.

Stowe, G. "2 Union County Mayors Take Carla DuPuy on Tour." *The Charlotte Observer*, Feb. 27, 1988, p. 14A.

Urban Land Institute. *The Charlotte, North Carolina, Region: An Evaluation of Development and Marketing Strategies for the Car-*

*olinas Partnership, Inc.* Washington, D.C.: Urban Land Institute, 1990.

Walton, B. Personal interview by the author, Jan. 31, 1991.

White, W. Personal interview by the author, Feb. 1, 1991.

Yates, D. *The Ungovernable City.* Cambridge, Mass.: MIT Press, 1977.

# 6

*Linda C. Winner*

# Leadership and Integrity: Mayor Noel C. Taylor of Roanoke, Virginia

If a list were compiled of top contemporary local government leaders in Virginia, the name of Noel C. Taylor, former mayor of Roanoke, would surely be found. Elected to the Roanoke City Council in 1970, Mayor Taylor became vice mayor in 1974 and mayor in 1975. Although a Republican in a community that is 60 percent Democratic, and a black in a community that is only 25 percent minority, he was consistently reelected until 1992, when he chose not to run, because of health concerns. His leadership was effective with four local government managers who had very different styles, and he saw numerous council members come and go. All the while, Roanoke developed a reputation as a progressive city, in keeping with the mayor's vision of what the community could be, his strong

*Note:* Thank you to Noel C. Taylor, who generously gave his time for lengthy interviews, as well as to numerous past and current Roanoke elected and appointed officials, who participated in the interview process on which this case study is based.

belief in the council-manager form of government, the promotion of citizen involvement, and partnerships between the private and nonprofit sectors and the city.

Perhaps the most interesting thing about Mayor Taylor is not just what occurred during his watch but how he led these efforts. His style is unconventionally low-key, highly inspirational, and based on bringing people together rather than on confrontational, back-room politics. A close look at Taylor in action reveals a mayor who used the traditional roles of mayor in a council-manager setting to provide facilitative leadership to his community. Mayor Taylor commented during his tenure, "As mayor, I'm on my way somewhere, and I want to take Roanoke with me." He did, and it is a remarkable story.

### The Setting

Roanoke, Virginia, is located midway between New York City and Atlanta on Interstate 81, 168 miles west of the state capital, Richmond. Settled in the middle of the eighteenth century and incorporated as Big Lick in 1874, Roanoke, at 100,000 citizens, is Virginia's southwestern hub of transportation, industry, finance, health care, and culture. Roanoke boasts a diversified economy, with over 92 percent of all census-defined industries located within its boundaries, and with high-tech companies becoming increasingly important players in the local business community. Since 1985, employment has increased by over 10,500 jobs, retail sales have grown by more than 40 percent, and effective buying income has increased by 21 percent. Roanoke also has managed to maintain a low unemployment rate (currently 3.9 percent) and stable property taxes while enjoying moderate growth.

The city provides the full range of services normally associated with a municipality: general administration, courts, public safety, public improvements, health and welfare, parks, recreation, and cultural and community development. In addition, the city provides water and sewage treatment for adjoining localities and, with Roanoke County, jointly owns and operates the regional airport. The city also owns and operates a mass-transit bus company.

Unlike many other Virginia cities, whose Main Streets fell on hard times and never recovered after retail businesses moved to outlying malls and suburbs, Roanoke focused on maintaining a vibrant downtown, which is now alive and well. Adjacent to the historic Farmers' Market, with its boutiques, galleries, and restaurants, is Roanoke's cultural heart, the Center in the Square. It is home to the Arts Council of the Roanoke Valley, the Roanoke Museum of Fine Arts, the Mill Mountain Theater, the Roanoke Valley Historical Society and Museum, and the Science Museum of Western Virginia. The scenic beauty of the Roanoke Valley, located between the Blue Ridge and Virginia Allegheny Highlands, also adds to the quality of life in the city.

In spite of its successes, Roanoke faces serious future challenges as the population and infrastructure age, the services provided by the city attract increasing numbers of people in need of such services, and the state's severe budget problems result in reduced aid to the city. The need for additional revenue will be especially challenging because annexation is not an option, and since a recent city-county consolidated government referendum was defeated by county voters (although strongly supported in the city).

## The Government

According to the Roanoke city charter, members of the seven-person council are elected for staggered four-year terms. Three members of the council stand for at-large election every other year, in May. The council member elected by the largest number of votes becomes the vice mayor for the succeeding two years. Since 1976, the mayor has been popularly elected at large every four years. Virginia is a Dillon's Rule state; consequently, the council's authority is derived from its charter, granted by the Virginia General Assembly and general laws of the commonwealth. The charter provisions regarding the appointment and authority of the city manager are standard ones. In addition to appointing the city manager, the council also directly appoints the director of finance, the municipal auditor, the city clerk, the city attorney, and the director of real-estate valuation. The council approves the appointment of the assistant city manager and the directors of utilities and operations, administration and public safety, human resources, and public works. The city clerk

keeps the council's records, and the city attorney prepares ordinances, provides legal advice to city officials, and defends the city
in court. The city council also appoints members to a number of
independent boards and commissions, such as the school board, the
library board, the Roanoke Redevelopment and Housing Authority,
the board of zoning appeals, the Industrial Development Authority,
and the planning commission. As provided by Virginia's state constitution, certain local officers in Roanoke are directly elected: the
city sheriff, the commonwealth's attorney, the commissioner of revenue, the city treasurer, and the circuit court clerk.

According to the charter, the mayor of Roanoke presides at
meetings of the council, votes but has no veto power, and serves as
the head of the city for ceremonial purposes, civil court processes,
and any military purposes. The mayor may also execute required
contracts and, in time of public danger or emergency, may take
command of the police with the consent of council.

## Background

Who is Noel Taylor? He delights in starting a conversation with
these words: "I have a saying that I'm the barefoot boy from Bedford
County, and I am. I was born in the adjacent county, twenty miles
from here. When people hear me say that, I don't know what they
think. I'm not bragging when I say it. I'm acknowledging my
identity—that I know who I am and from whence I have come."

He was born in rural, segregated Virginia, into a strong nu-
clear family where he developed a sense of pride, a willingness to
take risks, belief in the importance of education, the expectation of
success, compassion for people, and a strong belief that God uses
individuals to achieve His purposes.

Mayor Taylor's belief in the value of education is evident in
his own life. He graduated cum laude from Bluefield State College
in 1949 with a B.S. degree and from Virginia Seminary and College
in 1955 with a degree of Bachelor of Divinity. He later earned a M.A.
degree in religious education at the New York University Graduate
School, in 1963. In 1969, Virginia Seminary and College conferred
the degree of Doctor of Divinity on him, and Bluefield State College
awarded him an honorary doctorate of law in 1983. Mayor Taylor

is also the Reverend Taylor. He entered the ministry after a career as a public school teacher and principal, and he moved to Roanoke's High Street Baptist Church from a pulpit in Norfolk, Virginia, in 1961.

The 1960s, a time of racial unrest, found Noel Taylor assuming a leadership role. The first time he entered the city's Municipal Building, it was to petition the city leaders to repeal a law requiring blacks to sit in the back of buses. He became secretary of the Roanoke Valley Ministers Association and soon became the association's first black president, a position that increased his community exposure. As president of the Ministers Association, he was involved in many public and private business events and served ex officio on the Board of Roanoke Memorial Hospitals, demonstrating his ability to lead a previously conservative organization during a time of strife and unrest. His name became increasingly well known, and he had a forum in which his ability to bridge groups, persuade, and maintain principles became evident. This provided him an opening into public life. He also continued to move into the total community through his work on behalf of jobs for the underprivileged, the Board of Human Resources, the Library Board, the Arts Commission, and the Civic Center Building project.

### Getting Elected

As Roanoke's emphasis on brotherhood grew, the Reverend Taylor was becoming involved in a wider range of services. "This added to my yearning for a wider ministry," he says. "As exciting as the pastorate is, a pastor is localized to one group of people. When people ask what motivated me to run for council, I tell them that when I became a member of the council and then mayor, my parish became the entire city of Roanoke."

In 1970, efforts of the Black Caucus to secure a position on the Democratic Party's council slate were rebuffed. The black community is Democratic, and the black coalition was determined to have its own candidate. The Republicans were swift to enter the picture, approaching Taylor with the request that he become their black candidate. After much discussion, he agreed to be the candidate if the members of the Black Caucus would agree not to weaken the ticket with multiple candidates and to give his candidacy on the Republican slate their unanimous vote. He claims he never believed that there would be a unanimous vote for the Republican ticket, and since he did not want to run anyway, this would be his "out."

He was mistaken. People in the black community were learning that offering several candidates for the council was divisive, and that by putting their force behind one candidate, they could more effectively reach out to the total community.

Taylor says, "There was a sense that someone from the black community ought to come forward who could relate to the total community, who had some broad-based exposure, who would articulate the black experience and our need to become part of this total community." He led the ticket in 1970 on a broad base of votes. After this election, the council secured the change that allowed the council member receiving the highest number of votes to become the vice mayor. Taylor was elected vice mayor in 1974 under the new system.

In 1973, Taylor experienced his only political defeat, in a bid for the Virginia House of Delegates. Although this was obviously a painful experience, he looks back with acceptance and observes that if he had won he never would have become mayor, and that as mayor he had more opportunities to positively affect the life of Roanoke and its citizens. From this defeat, he learned lessons about timing and conducting campaigns, coping with disappointment, and not taking anything for granted: "I have to earn my support every day."

### Becoming Mayor

Taylor became mayor the first time not through a political campaign but by means of his selection to complete the term of Mayor Roy L. Webber, who died in 1975: "I admit to you I never dreamed, never thought about being the mayor. To my shock and surprise, the other five council members said they felt I should serve the unexpired term. It was only nine and a half months. I was sure one or more of the others would go after the full four-year term, so I decided to do it."

At that time, Roanoke was completing an annexation process. State law required that all seven council seats be up for election, in order to give the 16,000 new citizens representation, and provided for the first direct popular election of the mayor.

Behind the scenes, some powerful businessmen were concerned about the impact of possibly electing seven new people to the council. They wanted to preserve some continuity of experience. Late in 1975, one of these businessmen called Taylor, expressed the concerns of the group, and asked him to consider being the candidate for mayor and to help put together a ticket. Taylor was surprised, but he agreed. The candidates on the slate, including a candidate from the newly annexed area, a woman candidate, and a candidate from the Jewish community, ran as independents and were supported by the group of downtown businesspeople called Roanoke Forward. The Roanoke Forward ticket was elected. Mayor Taylor remembers that those who were in opposition made the statement that the city was being taken over by downtown businesspeople, but he never had a special request from any of the Roanoke Forward members.

Throughout his tenure as mayor, Taylor also maintained a strong commitment to his role as a minister, his primary calling. Mayor Taylor's desire to serve people, to go the second mile, and his firm belief that God uses people to accomplish His will motivate him in both the secular realm and the religious realm: "I know where I want to go, and I want to take the city of Roanoke with me. I want Roanoke to truly be the most exceptional place to live and work in the South."

## Making a Difference: Leadership Style and Roles

Mayor Taylor is credited by many with leading the economic revival of the city's downtown core. During his tenure, sixty new businesses opened downtown in existing buildings, eight major buildings were constructed downtown, $18.6 million in city bonds were sold to support neighborhood and economic development efforts, and downtown merchants asked the council to tax them above the established personal property rate so that they could form a service district to help plan activities for promoting downtown. Roanoke was honored three times during Taylor's terms with the National

League of Cities' All-American City Award for innovative projects that demonstrate a working partnership among citizens, businesses, and government. He was consistently selected as the most respected leader in the nation by the readers of Roanoke's newspapers, and although he did have critics (often blacks who wished he would be more militant), it seemed impossible to find an enemy.

There were three major themes in Taylor's approach to the mayoralty: cooperation between elected officials and professional staff, teamwork with the community as a whole, and creation of a positive atmosphere where good things could happen. Each of these themes is elaborated here, with comments from Mayor Taylor and other officials.

### Cooperation Between Elected Officials and Professional Staff

Mayor Taylor's view of the council-manager form of government and his role in it provided the framework for his leadership: "I think that fundamental to the effective government of any city is cooperation between the elected official and the administration. That leads to the kind of meeting of minds which permits a sharing of values, the development of a system of trust, open communication, the attainment of common objectives."

The council-management form of government in Roanoke permits separating "the operation of a city from the philosophy." Officials are not bogged down responding to "political necessity"; and, "most important, it has allowed one person to be responsible for efficiency."

The entire council is responsible for hiring the manager: "That's probably the most important decision we'll ever make." The nature of the relationship between the manager and the council is one of the mayor's primary responsibilities: "He has responsibility for the establishment of a relationship of trust between the manager and the council, the granting of authority, and the recognition of the values held by the manager, which he feels are of paramount importance. I think it's necessary that we have a commonality of goals. We may not always have a meeting of minds on certain issues, but I think it is important that we have some similarity in our value systems. That's something we have tried to accomplish."

Mayor Taylor worked with four managers, each of whom he describes as "uniquely different." It appears obvious that where common goals were established, success was more likely.

The manager who was in office when Taylor was first elected "tried to keep things on an even keel" during a difficult period of struggle over civil rights. He restrained the council when it was eager to act, "in order to keep the peace. He had a feeling for the things that could be controversial."

The next manager was a retired military man. Although he was a man of "great moral character," he did not respond adequately to the council's desire "to move this city progressively forward."

When this manager left, the council selected Bern Ewart. Before Ewart's selection, Taylor says, "we had a very forthright discussion about what we wanted to do, asked him if he thought he was ready to be involved in that kind of forward movement, and he assured us that he was. It was apparent from day one that Bern Ewart was a man on the move. We told him that was what we wanted. He had the spirit. He pulled off his coat and rolled up his sleeves." The council's role was "to encourage him." This was a relationship between a strong council and a strong manager: "One of the things I appreciated about him was that he believed in himself, in his ability, and he knew what he wanted to accomplish. He allowed us to give him our general direction, and he went to work to achieve that. He had a never-give-up spirit about him."

Taylor feels that the last manager he served with, Bob Herbert, and the council were "partners for progress": "The manager and council have developed the art of really talking to one another and listening. I think we've reached a point where the common concern and the importance of human development forms the touchstone of community improvement."

Mayor Taylor and the managers maintained open communication: "We [did] not have to agree with each other all the time, but we always agree[d] in our disagreements that we want[ed] the city to move forward, and we want[ed] to always look at the facts and do what [was] best for Roanoke." Honesty and shared responsibility were critical: "It's not a matter, as far as I'm concerned, of who is going to be the most powerful person or who is going to be the leader. I believe you can accomplish anything if you don't care who gets the credit."

City Manager Herbert appreciated the atmosphere of teamwork that the mayor established with the council. The mayor discouraged the council from making commitments before the manager had been able to formulate a recommendation. The council did not have to follow the manager's recommendations. Still, following the tone set by the mayor, the members of the council usually resisted taking any position on an issue before the manager and the staff could present a recommendation: "This help[ed] keep the city manager's position strong."

### Teamwork with the Community

Design '79, Roanoke's effort to change the direction of the inner city, was an example of how the council, the staff, community leaders, and citizens all became involved. It had three programs: Downtown Revitalization, the Neighborhood Partnership, and Roanoke Parks Today and Tomorrow. Mayor Taylor states that it is difficult now to determine exactly whose idea each one was, but providing for increased involvement of the people was his own contribution.

To develop Design '79, studies were made through the Chamber of Commerce and Downtown Roanoke, Inc., a consortium of downtown businesses. Citizens' opinions and ideas were solicited by means of prime-time TV call-in shows, a newspaper survey, on-the-street interviews, and a drop-in design room. The mayor constantly stressed his belief that enlightened and involved citizens could be trusted to act in the best interests of the city. He was correct. A 1979 bond issue funded $13.6 million in public improvements and resulted in a $132 million investment in downtown, of which 68 percent was private money.

During this time, the Neighborhood Partnership was formed. Mayor Taylor describes the effort: "We decided we would let the neighborhoods tell us what they wanted, what they needed, what was best for the neighborhood. We would not make all those decisions for them."

The third component, as mentioned, was Roanoke Parks Today and Tomorrow. Roanoke has parks in many diverse neighborhoods. Some neighborhoods are made up of mostly senior citizens; others are populated with very young couples. Once again, the city went to the people to develop the parks. The results, based on the ideas and needs of the neighborhoods, include different kinds of furnishings for the various parks.

Throughout the Design '79 process, with the mayor's leadership, the council took government to the people by holding meetings in churches, neighborhood buildings, and individual homes. Citizens came to believe that the council would listen to their voices.

### Creating a Positive Atmosphere

Taylor says, "You can accomplish almost anything if you can keep people talking." City Manager Bob Herbert describes the diversity in the community:

> We have a 25 percent minority population and about 25 percent elderly population. We have a mix of high and low income. . . . The mayor created a harmony in this community among the diverse groups that I think is unparalleled, at least in other Virginia communities I've seen. He sometimes took a real beating from the minority community—that he wasn't championing purely black causes. His response: "I've been elected by the citizens of Roanoke, and my job is to do what is best for Roanoke, not to do something that is just good for a certain group of black folks, nor to do something for a certain group of white folks."

The 1988 All-American City Award is credited to the same approach of creating an atmosphere in which good things can happen. Roanoke's entry centered on three projects: Project Self-Sufficiency, a program to help single mothers get off welfare and become economically self-sufficient; Roanoke Vision, the city's twenty-year comprehensive plan, developed through a series of citizens' workshops; and the Harrison Heritage and Cultural Center, the city's first black high school, in a building once abandoned but now renovated to house elderly and handicapped residents on the upper floors and a black cultural center on the first floor. It is a project that involved several community groups and aided in reinforcing community spirit and heritage. Bob Herbert thinks that the mayor's support for the strategic planning process was crucial to its success: "He did not dominate the process. He participated and was there throughout and allowed it to happen. This was him in the true role of facilitator."

Interviews with past and present managers and staff members provide further insights into Mayor Taylor's style and the leadership roles he played. He is described as being one who did not lead by developing specific policies; he believed he knew what was best for Roanoke and he wanted to be progressive, but he did not have a specific agenda. He wanted to be compassionate, fair, and accessible; the *how* and the *what* were less clear. One observer says, "He didn't lead by thinking through and creating a specific agenda or by making deals on the telephone." Another says, "He allowed ideas to bubble up in the public arena, and then he helped modify them. He's a terrific listener, and when you are open to ideas, people will bring them to you."

His effectiveness seems to have been solidly based on his credibility with the vast majority of the people and the council members. He was not suspected of having a hidden agenda. One colleague stated, "The mayor didn't think in terms of 'Oh, this is a contest. I have $x$ number of votes and they have $y$.' He thought in terms of right or wrong. If something was supposed to be confidential, it was confidential. People trusted him, and that helped give him credibility. And he's so personable. You like him. You didn't want to let him down. You always wanted to give your best."

Perhaps because he was not elected mayor by the council and therefore did not have a strong need to build internal political coalitions with council members on specific issues in order to win their support for the position, Taylor often did not get out in front on issues or make dramatic public statements. If someone had to do that, it was usually the manager, his staff, or someone in the community. Taylor seemed to want to stay above it all. Advocates of a particular issue on the council knew that he would not try to sabotage it. He might not vote their way, but he wouldn't embarrass them in public. His skill was to avoid confrontation and keep people talking. One council members observes, "When there was no consensus in executive sessions, and spirits were weary, and sharp feelings came out, he tried to reach out, help us to focus on why we were public servants, what we were trying to do for Roanoke."

Bob Herbert attributes this orientation to Taylor's background as a counselor and minister: "He did not dominate. He presided and let the others do most of the talking." He did not work to line up votes, even when others asked him to; that would have compromised his credibility. He was never perceived to be acting out of self-interest; he did what he thought was right. Says Herbert, "I've been here since 1979, and I never saw him cast a political vote."

Mayor Taylor is noted for having surrounded himself with generally positive, forward-thinking people and for having been willing to take advice in leadership. Herbert says, "It takes a very strong person to surround himself with people and be open to thinking. Sometimes I worried about being seen as a manipulator, but he listened to me. He's a very good listener. It takes a very smart person to admit he doesn't know all he needs to." In Herbert's view, staying quiet indicated not a lack of leadership but a natural desire to learn.

Mayor Taylor prides himself on being accessible. He wants to be with people: "I think it's important to be able to understand the thinking of others and to be mindful of their wishes and desires." As Mayor, he had an open-door policy. Every Friday, citizens came from 1:00 to 5:00, at thirty-minute intervals, as well as at other times.

Walking down a city street with Noel Taylor is a unique experience. He stops and talks with numerous people. He is greeted warmly by almost everyone. What would ordinarily be a ten-minute walk may take thirty minutes: "I call that being accessible to the people. It worked well for us. I think I'm here as a servant of the people. There is a lot of love in this city, and I hope I have made a contribution. My desire is to be among the people, and that is what I enjoy doing. I want to learn about their needs and their wishes. I think that is what it is all about—people helping other people to establish a better quality of life for all. This is what I have tried to do here." Taylor also served on the boards of banks and hospitals and had extensive contact with other community leaders.

Mayor Taylor communicated his vision for Roanoke in several ways. One was his annual "state of the city" address to the council at the first meeting in July, where he took a look at the immediate past, at the council's successes and failures, and set the challenge for the future. He would conclude with a series of recommendations, derived from the public and the professional staff, about what would "allow the city to move progressively ahead," and he would strike a note intended to inspire and challenge. The majority of these recommendations were sent to the manager for his study and recommendations and then back to the council for possible implementation.

Everyone gives Noel Taylor high marks as an ambassador for the city. He is praised for his relationships with state and federal officials and businesspeople, and "average" citizens received the same treatment from him. During his tenure, one city official observed:

> He treats people like the perfect mayor should. He is perfect representing the city out front. When a case for Roanoke needs to be made, you tell him what the point is, and he'll do it. They all walk away saying, "You've got a great mayor!" It's the same thing in council meetings. The public comes. He treats them like the perfect mayor. He handles them well when they get angry. They may not like what was voted on, but they go away believing they've been treated well and had a chance to speak. He makes the rest of the council's job easy.

He is also described as a deal closer. For example, in 1983 the city was dealing with Coca-Cola. The company wanted to move its facility from downtown and build a major new facility on thirty acres outside of the city. The city wanted the company to stay and redevelop the area. Roanoke planners and economic development staff put together what they believed to be a viable plan, but corporate real-estate experts were skeptical. A group of seven officials from the city, including the mayor, went to Coca-Cola headquarters. After presentations on technical aspects of the proposal, as one of the planners described the meeting, "the mayor got up and talked about what a difference it would make to the community. He's so sincere when he talks that you start shaking your head, saying, 'Yes, I believe that.' By the time we left, the chairman said, 'You have my commitment to put it in Roanoke.' He's a deal closer. He can make you feel like he's doing you a personal favor. He's so warm and sincere."

The family that owned the parent company had made a major commitment to downtown Miami, and the mayor touched that interest by talking about inner cities and making a commitment to hiring minorities. The project cleaned up thirty to forty acres and provided jobs. In the mayor's presentation, the key to success was effectively communicating the human consequences: "It wasn't just an economic development project. It was a community development project."

Instilling civic pride was another strong suit of the mayor's. Under his leadership, celebration became a strong force in the city. He established thank-you receptions for citizen volunteers, welcomed countless conventions and conferences, cut ribbons, and broke ground. He encouraged the development of sister-city relationships with Wonju (Korea) and Kisumu (Kenya) and served as host to their visiting delegations and as head of the Roanoke delegations visiting them. Special events, such as the Roanoke centennial, became means of holding inclusive public events. As one citizen observed, "He'd come to a ceremony and be the last one to leave because someone would have their children, who wanted to speak to the mayor. He'd get down on their level and speak to them."

In summary, there is little evidence that Mayor Taylor developed specific programs and lined up support or organized opposition to proposals. Instead, he had a significant impact on the direction of Roanoke by bringing his style of expressive, cosmopolitan, nonconfrontational, populist leadership strongly to bear on a variety of mayoral roles:

1.  He excelled at ceremonial tasks and was thus an important channel to the council and the city manager for citizens' attitudes and ideas.
2.  He was an exceptional presiding officer, facilitating the council members' open discussion without dominating, keeping members focused, and calming short tempers as necessary. He handled citizen participation at meetings with diplomacy and finesse.
3.  He performed in the educator role by identifying issues or problems for consideration, promoting awareness of important concerns, and seeking to promote understanding across the city through the exchange of information.
4.  As a liaison with the manager, Taylor played a crucial part in facilitating communication with the council and developing the timing for bringing issues forward. He was also a team builder, helping council members work through differences while promoting full expression.
5.  Taylor was a goal setter. His goals, usually broad in nature (especially as set forth in his "state of the city" address), served to point out directions and priorities.
6.  The mayor was an organizer and stabilizer of key relations within the city government. He effectively articulated the roles and responsibilities of the council and used standing-committee appointments to facilitate the council's work.
7.  Taylor was an outstanding promoter of the city of Roanoke. He is described with enthusiasm as a "grand salesman."

## Resources for Leadership

As mayor, Noel Taylor had all the usual resources of mayoral leadership in a council-manager setting: status and authority, demonstrated popular support, visibility, an office in the Municipal Building, staff support, a degree of control over council proceedings and committee assignments, and access to the media, the public, the city manager, and other professional staff. Yet his ability to hold on to the mayorship in a contradictory political and demographic setting and his effectiveness as a leader also stemmed from several other sources.

Mayor Taylor thinks that his being a popularly elected mayor, rather than one chosen by the council, provided a resource for leadership that worked to his advantage and to the advantage of the community. He believes that it enabled him to be a true representative of the people and allowed him to develop a relationship with council members that was not divisive or confrontational. His obvious popularity across racial, economic, and political lines increased his ability to garner respect for his ideas and gave him a position of influence that others found difficult to challenge.

Moreover, his understanding of the mayor's role with respect to the roles of others enabled him to strengthen not only his own leadership but also that of others. The fact that he was able to sustain a strong cooperative relationship with the city manager and the council lessened his need for power outside the formal system. He did not view leadership as a zero-sum game, and so he provided an atmosphere where elected and appointed officials enhanced one another's effectiveness.

Not to be overlooked are Noel Taylor's considerable personal resources. He brought to the office of mayor the willingness to devote a high level of energy and time to his duties; an unusual capacity to foster cooperation and teamwork, to articulate values, to communicate a vision, and to keep people talking; an aversion to confrontation and politics in the pejorative sense; and a high level of credibility. His strong morality, his Christian beliefs, his positive self-regard, and his firm conviction that he was chosen to be part of history were all resources that gave his leadership a power to inspire and bring out the best in others.

Asked what he took greatest pride in as mayor, Taylor cites the All-America City Awards and his ability to form effective partnerships. "And we gave the city back to the people," he adds.

Serious challenges remain for the city of Roanoke: regional economic development, a regional transportation system, a downtown residential area, a graying population, an increase in rental property, increasing stress for the city as the sole provider of services to the poor in the region, and the needs of public education. "There are no endings, just new beginnings. You never have the complete fulfillment of your dreams," Neil Taylor observes. In this city, where people followed because they believed in the leader, they came close.

## Conclusion

The notion that the council-manager form of government precludes strong mayoral leadership, unless the mayor takes on the attributes of the executive mayor, is belied by the Roanoke case. In his relationship with the city managers with whom he worked and the councils with which he served, Noel Taylor has shown that the form does not necessarily contain inherent conflict. A strong and effective city manager, an effective council, and a mayor can exhibit collective leadership without altering the basic character of the system. As Mayor Taylor explains, "This form of government allowed two areas of leadership to develop. It has served us well." This was true partly because Noel Taylor believed it to be true and did not treat leadership as a power struggle. In Roanoke, the importance of shared values among the mayor, the council members, and the manager was demonstrated. In this context, the opportunity for leadership by all was realized, and everyone was allowed to function fully, to the benefit of the city.

Mayor Taylor's vision of a city moving progressively forward has become a reality; in fact, Taylor is an example of a successful mayor who made a positive impact without executive powers. It is Mayor Taylor's conviction that his primary role as mayor was not to initiate specific policies, but rather to establish and maintain an environment that enabled all the participants to be as effective as possible. This, he believes, is what made him a successful facilitative leader.

On the basis of this case study, certain conditions and circumstances seem to be important for facilitative mayoral leadership to flourish:

1. The mayor should not attempt to control or supplant other participants.
2. The mayor should be willing to share leadership and form partnerships.

3.  The mayor should surround himself or herself with positive, forward-thinking people.

4.  The mayor should value and maintain mutual respect and trust.

5.  The mayor should develop ways to avoid unnecessary confrontation and manage conflict.

6.  The mayor and the manager should develop a successful working relationship and be encouraged to play an integral role in the policy-making process.

7.  The mayor should facilitate the creation of shared vision, values, and goals that shape policy direction.

8.  The manager should give the council members room to be responsive to the community and bring them in to share his vision.

9.  The council should not delve hastily into administrative matters or take positions on issues without hearing the manager's recommendations.

10. The council should communicate clear expectations and general directions to the manager.

11. Citizens' involvement should be prized.

12. Open communication and accessibility should exist among elected officials, professional staff, and citizens.

Clearly, such a vision of cooperation, partnership, and progress cannot be established by edict or by the use of power or coercion. A leader needs to step forward who can consistently act on this vision and personify it, someone who provides meaning and commitment. In the case of Roanoke, Virginia, Noel C. Taylor was that leader.

7

*Craig M. Wheeland*

# A Profile of a Facilitative Mayor: Mayor Betty Jo Rhea of Rock Hill, South Carolina

The facilitative leadership model offers council-manager mayors an approach appropriate for their form of government. Mayors can be important leaders who not only perform traditional symbolic roles but also provide policy and programmatic direction in their communities. This model is applied in this case study of Mayor Betty Jo Rhea of Rock Hill, South Carolina. Mayor Rhea is a lifelong resident of Rock Hill and has served in various positions in Rock Hill government for the past twenty-three years. She has been mayor since 1986 and in 1989 won a second term unopposed. Mayor Rhea excels at facilitative leadership. She is the type of mayor whom Svara (1990) has in mind when he writes, "Mayors need to be flexible and capable of shifting the emphasis they place on different roles. More than any other official in this form of government, the mayor is the stabilizer who acts in those areas in which contributions are needed at a given time. He or she will be more or less central, more or less public, more or less assertive as conditions warrant" (p. 117). Her case serves as an excellent example of how council-manager mayors are real leaders who make distinctive contributions.

## Research Design

The data were collected with interviews, questionnaires, and newspaper articles. Mayor Rhea completed a questionnaire consisting of seventy-two closed-ended questions, later participated in a three-hour interview, and provided a résumé. Forty-seven leaders from Rock Hill, York County, and the state of South Carolina were interviewed with a schedule consisting of twenty-one closed-ended questions and five open-ended questions. They also were asked to explain their responses to eight of the closed-ended questions. Thirty-eight other Rock Hill leaders were sent a questionnaire consisting of thirteen closed-ended questions and five open-ended questions. Twenty questionnaires were completed.

The participants were promised confidentiality, in the interest of obtaining an accurate assessment of Mayor Rhea's performance. A total of sixty-seven people participated in the study. Participants included members of the city council; the city manager; both assistant city managers; five other city staff members; two county council members; the county manager; five members of the state legislature; four political scientists from Winthrop College; seven business leaders; three journalists; two school board members; the school district superintendent; two Winthrop College administrators; a York Technical College administrator; eight civic leaders; fourteen chairs or vice chairs of the boards, committees, and commissions in Rock Hill; and representatives from the South Carolina Association of Counties, the South Carolina Municipal Association, and the South Carolina Advisory Commission on Intergovernmental Relations.

## Politics in Rock Hill and the Rise of Betty Jo Rhea

Rock Hill has a history of competitive, issue-oriented politics. Political parties have not been important in Rock Hill politics, although they may become important in the future, since the Republican party is becoming more active. Citizens do not register by party in South Carolina, and so data on the party affiliations of voters are not available. Election returns, however, do reveal the dominance of the Democratic party. To be successful in Rock Hill politics before 1990 meant running in the competitive Democrat primaries. The general elections, held in January, have not been competitive.

In the absence of party competition, community politics since the early 1970s have centered on the proposed solutions to several main problems: the decline of the textiles industry; the decline of downtown; the influx of many new residents, who have raised the city's population nearly 25 percent since 1980; the threat of Rock Hill's becoming just another suburb in the growing Charlotte metropolitan area; and the need to secure the participation of the African American community, which was one-third of Rock Hill's 1990 population of 44,000. Debates through the years have focused on issues arising out of these five problems, such as building Cherry Park, developing a downtown mall (and, later, removing the roof from the mall), preserving historic buildings, sponsoring public art, and changing the electoral system.

Over time, factions have formed around basic approaches to responding to these problems and issues. Betty Jo Rhea has been a member of a faction described by several community leaders as the *progressives*. They are opposed by the *conservatives*, who, according to one community leader, "want to refrain from using tax dollars to finance economic redevelopment, the arts, beautification, and recreation." The progressive faction has been able to control the majority on the council for most of the past two decades. This faction's dominance is evident in the consensual decision-making process on the council; close observers of the council's voting behavior estimate that less than 5 percent of all council votes have been split four to three.

The conservative faction has enjoyed more success in controlling the mayor's office. Between 1978 and 1986, a leader of the conservative faction held the mayor's office. He defeated a challenger from the progressive faction in a closely contested reelection bid in the 1981 Democratic primary (Parris, 1981). After serving two terms on the council, Betty Jo Rhea decided to run for mayor in

1985, in order to use this office to help promote the progressive agenda.

Betty Jo Rhea first became interested in community politics in the early 1970s:

> I first became involved in volunteer efforts. Then I was asked to be on the Parks Commission. We were getting government grants, and I decided I needed to get involved more if I was to make important decisions. So I decided to regularly attend council meetings. After a while, I'd go just to say to the council, "I'm here. I support you. You're doing great." Then, one night, I decided I could do this. So I ran for the at-large seat on the council in 1978 and won on the first ballot, even though there were many candidates.

Indeed, she received 1,813 votes in the eight-candidate primary, which was almost 800 votes more than any other candidate ("Rhea Nominated . . . ," 1977). In the 1981 primary, she again led the five-candidate field, collecting 1,979 votes (Parris, 1981). On the council for two terms (1978–1986), she pushed for city beautification and recreation programs. She was a leading supporter of the most controversial issue in the 1980s, building a city park in an area along Cherry Road that was a prime location for business development. With its walking track, soccer fields, and tournament-quality softball fields, Cherry Park is now one of the most popular places in Rock Hill.

The confidence she gained from serving on the council and speaking out on a tough issue led Betty Jo Rhea to run for mayor in 1985: "I felt qualified to run for mayor. I knew all phases of the council's work. I knew the city. I had a positive view of my role and ability. And I knew I could work with Joe [Lanford, the city manager]. I felt we'd make a good team."

She campaigned hard in the primary against a fellow council member, who was a leader of the conservative faction. She explained her strategy as "a door-to-door appeal to people who supported an effort to be progressive. I wanted to offer them a vision of how Rock Hill could grow right away." She believed that some of her opposition came from people who "thought a woman can serve on council, but as mayor—no way. Had I been a man with the same amount of experience, no one would've run against me." Betty Jo Rhea won the Democratic primary, receiving 2,296 votes (53.8 percent), and she won votes from every part of the city, especially among younger voters and the black community (Pettibon, 1985). Her campaign to push planning for the future, ensuring a quality-of-life approach to development, and attracting new industry had been successful. At the age of fifty-five, she was elected mayor of her city.

The style of leadership that Mayor Betty Jo Rhea used during her first term and continues to use during her second term is described in the rest of this chapter. Her record demonstrates how council-manager mayors can perform a facilitative role and make major contributions to their communities.

## Preconditions for Facilitative Leadership

What specific factors affect how a mayor performs? According to studies of mayoral performance (Svara, 1990; Ferman, 1985; Wikstrom, 1979; Boynton and Wright, 1971), there are at least three main preconditions for facilitative leadership: a formal structure of government, an information network for the mayor, and certain characteristics of the mayor's personality, skills, and perspective on the mayor's role. Did these preconditions exist in Rock Hill?

### The Formal Governmental Structure

When Rock Hill adopted the council-manager plan, in 1915, it became the second South Carolina city to do so. The formal structure of the government did not change again in a significant way until the late 1970s. The enforcement of the Voting Rights Act of 1965 resulted in the creation of an electoral system with the mayor and three council members elected at large and three from districts (Handal, 1989). Two black council members were elected in 1980, but only one remained on the council after 1982. No other minority candidates were successful, and there was pressure to increase the chances of black candidates.

In 1989, the present election system was established. Six council members are now elected from wards. The mayor remains the only elected official running at large. The change to ward elections in 1989 was accompanied by a move to nonpartisan elections. Council members, including the mayor, serve four-year terms. Three council seats are elected along with the mayor, and three council seats follow two years later. The council members and the mayor are paid salaries of $8,000 and $12,000, respectively.

The mayor has an office at City Hall (near the city manager's office), a full-time personal secretary, and use of the services of several other city staff in the public information office. The mayor is a regular voting member of the council, presides at council meetings, and is the ceremonial representative of the city. The office does not have any formal administrative powers, such as appointment and budgetary powers. Indeed, state law restricts council members and the mayor from interfering with the city manager's administrative powers (Easterwood, 1984, p. 17). The mayor's position is intended to be a part-time job, but there are no formal restrictions on a mayor who wishes to devote more time. Council members also are expected to work only part-time.

The council has the power to appoint the city manager on the basis of executive and administrative qualifications. The city manager may advise the council on appointments to committees, boards, and commissions. In addition, the city manager retains the powers to appoint and remove all city employees, prepare and submit an annual budget, prepare and submit an annual report, keep the council informed about the needs of the municipality, and recommend courses of action. The city manager serves at the pleasure of the council. If the council chooses to dismiss the city manager, written notice is required, and the city manager may request a public hearing.

This formal structure provides Mayor Rhea with the opportunity to exercise facilitative leadership. The main structural preconditions identified in the literature—voting status, salary, office, staff, length of term, method of election, and powers—are present. As already mentioned, she is elected at large to a four-year term.

*The Mayor's Information Network*

Mayor Rhea's information network is extensive. Her contacts include organizations at the local, state, and national levels. She has been a member of several community organizations, including the Chamber of Commerce, the United Way board, the Junior Welfare League, and the Fine Arts Association. She has served in leadership positions in associations of elected officials, including the U.S. Conference of Mayors, the National League of Cities, the South Carolina Municipal Association, and the South Carolina Advisory Commission on Intergovernmental Relations. She has been active in organizations promoting policies in which she has a strong interest, particularly the National Recreation and Parks Association, the South Carolina Parks and Recreation Society board, the "Come See Me" Festival board, the Rock Hill Sierra Club, and the South Carolina Museum board of trustees.

Mayor Rhea says that her extensive involvement helps her "learn a lot from other people." She gets "excited to hear what other cities do to promote their culture, beauty, and history—the quality-of-life things that help attract business." She wishes that "the other council members could attend conferences, so they could learn how important the arts, beautification, and historic preservation are to a community."

When Mayor Rhea wants to learn about the administration of programs and gain more information about policy matters that are before the council, she relies on five main sources, which she ranks as follows in importance: the council packet prepared by the city manager, reports from boards and commissions, public hearings, citizen complaints and comments, and experience on the council.[1] She explains, "I receive the packet on Thursday, and I always read it over the weekend." She also always reads the reports from boards and commissions. She listens to citizens' comments at public hearings during council meetings, and "while I'm grocery shopping, walking in Cherry Park, or walking down the street, people just come up and talk to me about a problem or something they like that the city is doing." Her fellow council members also provide useful ideas and information during council discussions: "Just going to meetings and listening is important."

Mayor Rhea supplements these main sources by privately discussing topics with various participants in the political process, especially the city manager, members of boards and commissions, and "rank-and-file citizens" (see Table 7.1). She admires City Manager Lanford, "a dreamer, a visionary." "Joe educates himself all the time," she explains. "It is a wonderful experience working with him." She talks by phone with the chairs of the boards and commissions, and she sometimes attends their meetings. Mayor Rhea also often consults the local news media, especially the two newspapers. Only the department heads are not part of her information network: citing state law, Mayor Rhea reports that she "talks with Joe rather than with department heads."

Clearly, Mayor Rhea has used her strategic position in the community to develop an extensive information network. She uses a mix of formal and informal sources and taps multiple sources of information, including the city manager, the council members, other public officials, and the public.

**Table 7.1. Frequency of Conversations Between Mayor Rhea and Other Participants.**

| Participants | Policy Matters Before Council | Administration of Programs |
|---|---|---|
| City manager | 1 | 1 |
| Members of boards and commissions | 1 | 2 |
| Rank-and-file citizens | 3 | 2 |
| Council members | 3 | 3 |
| Representatives of interest groups | 3 | 3 |
| Department heads | 4 | 4 |
| Mean Response | 2.5 | 2.5 |

*Note:* Mayor Rhea was asked a series of questions structured as follows: "How common is it for you to talk privately with _____ about the administration of programs?" and "How common is it for you to talk privately with _____ about policy matters before the council?" The responses are coded as follows: 1 = very common, 2 = common, 3 = somewhat common, and 4 = not common.

## The Mayor's Personality, Skills, and Perspective

In survey and interview responses, people recognized a number of strengths that Mayor Rhea brings to the job (see Table 7.2). Community leaders say that she is a warm, friendly person who, as one person put it, "doesn't know a stranger." She is totally dedicated to the job and undertakes her responsibilities enthusiastically. This commitment leads her to work seven days a week, over ten hours per day. Her dedication led one community leader to say, "Mayor Rhea has spoiled us. I don't know who could possibly run for mayor after her, she has set such a high standard for us."

Indeed, Mayor Rhea also worries about the effect that the demands of public service has on the willingness of younger com-

**Table 7.2. Mayor Rhea's Perceived "Strengths" and "Weaknesses."**

| Strengths | N (%) | Weaknesses | N (%) |
|---|---|---|---|
| Love of Rock Hill | 28 (41%) | Too sensitive | 11 (16%) |
| Attitude toward job | | Intergovernmental relations | |
|   Enthusiasm | 13 (19%) | at local level | 13 (19%) |
|   Dedication | 16 (24%) | | |
| | | Relies on city staff (for | |
| Personality traits | | policy ideas and details) | 12 (18%) |
|   Friendly/gracious | 22 (33%) | | |
|   Sincere/honest | 9 (13%) | Inflexible | 6 (9%) |
|   Positive/dreamer | 12 (18%) | | |
|   Courageous/decisive | 10 (15%) | Formal presentations | 5 (7%) |
| Positive image or reputation | 18 (27%) | | |
| Knowledge or intelligence | 11 (16%) | | |
| Public relations skills (informal, small group, one-to-one) | 30 (45%) | | |

*Note:* Participants ($N$ = 67) were asked the following questions: "What are Mayor Rhea's strengths?" and "How can Mayor Rhea's performance be improved?" The open-ended responses were coded by means of a two-stage process. First, key adjectives or topics mentioned by each respondent were simply counted. Second, general categories were created, in order to combine the comments into a more meaningful package. Two people coded responses to ensure accuracy.

munity leaders who have families to run for public office, especially for mayor: "Maybe mayors in council-manager cities need more pay, much more pay, so younger people can do all that I do as a full-time mayor."

Her total commitment stems from her strong love of Rock Hill and its people. Her eagerness to go to any event, wherever she is invited, has helped her develop a thorough knowledge of the Rock Hill community. Some community leaders suggest that she is too sensitive, and that her love of Rock Hill impedes her ability to work better with other local officials in York County. Mayor Rhea acknowledges this possibility but is reluctant to change: "When you spend as much time as I do, you can't help but care deeply. I think most women in government do this. We care for our communities. Its like a child that I'm responsible for. I just have to give it my all. If I backed away from it, maybe I wouldn't be as good a mayor. Would people not want me to care? Its true that I wear Rock Hill on my shoulder. Its like this: 'Say anything you want about me, but don't say anything about my husband, my children, or my city!'"

Community leaders also believe that Mayor Rhea likes to focus on the positive and enjoys dreaming about the future. One community leader said, "The mayor's favorite word is *positive*." Commenting on why she first decided to run for mayor, Rhea says, "I felt I had a vision of how Rock Hill could be in the near future. I wanted to focus on the positive things we could do to make our community better. I had the experience, and . . . I knew I could do a good job as mayor." The mayor does like to focus on the positive, and she does take criticism hard, but she also is willing to make decisions and defend them before critics. Even an observer who on more than one occasion has disagreed with Mayor Rhea admires "her determination and courage to take a stand on tough issues."

Mayor Rhea's skills in public relations aid her effort to build community support for policies and programs. Reading a speech in a formal setting is not her forte, but Mayor Rhea has the interpersonal skills to be effective in informal meetings with small groups and in one-to-one meetings with individuals. Community leaders describe how easily she meets people and makes them feel at ease; most would agree with this respondent's statement: "You always know she is present. She is a very stylish, flashy dresser and is known for her scarves. She is a real character with a good sense of humor. Betty Jo is a delightful hostess who can make people feel comfortable. She'll talk about family or children, and after an hour people think they're her best friends. And it isn't a put-on. She's sincere!"

She also is not shy about introducing herself to people in any setting, such as an association meeting, a public reception, or the state legislature. One observer of her efforts in the state legislature says that Rhea is "well known, well respected, and knows how to practice politics." Her network of contacts at the state, regional, and national levels often has amazed city staff. One staff member who attended a national meeting with the mayor says, "They rolled out the red carpet when we arrived, and everyone seemed to know Betty Jo Rhea."

### Type of Leadership

Mayor Rhea's personal qualities and skills suggest that she can act as a facilitative mayor. But what particular type of facilitative mayor does she want to be? a symbolic head? a coordinator? an activist or reformer? a director? Exhibit 7.1 and Table 7.3 indicate that Mayor Rhea wants to be a coordinator type of facilitative mayor (high on coordination, low on policy guidance). In Exhibit 7.1, Mayor Rhea agrees with the statements concerning her performance of the first three categories of mayoral roles. Her responses to the statements concerning the fourth category (organization and guidance) require closer examination. Mayor Rhea endorses some of these statements. For example, she agrees that a mayor should use her visible position in the community to mobilize people on behalf of her favorite programs, and she thinks that the mayor has more responsibility for ensuring that the manager and the staff perform their jobs well. But she does not endorse some of the other statements. In particular, she is neutral on the notions that the mayor should be a source of ideas for new policies and programs and that the mayor should build support in the community and on the council for being the key decision maker in city government.

Mayor Rhea likes to refer to the council–mayor–city manager relationship as a team effort. She acknowledges that she depends on the city staff for policy ideas and for the details of policies and

**Exhibit 7.1. Mayor Rhea's Responses to Statements
About the Mayor's Role in Council-Manager Government.**

---

*Statements (and responses)*

Ceremonial and Presiding Duties
An important part of the mayor's job is to attend events sponsored by various community groups. (Agree)
The mayor presides at council meetings and uses this position to maintain an orderly discussion. (Agree)
Meeting with community groups in order to promote city programs and policies is an important part of the mayor's job. (Agree)

Communication and Facilitation
When the council is divided on an issue, it is the mayor's job to arrange compromises. (Agree)
It is the mayor's job to make sure the council works together as a team. (Agree)
A mayor should promote an informal exchange of information among manager, council, and staff. (Agree)
The mayor should act as a liaison between the council and the manager. (Agree)
The agenda for council meetings is established by the mayor and the manager working together. (Agree)
Listening to citizens' complaints and informing the council, the manager, or staff about them is one of the mayor's main tasks. (Agree)

Promotion
A mayor can serve the city well by participating in associations of elected officials. (Agree)
The mayor's job includes representing and defending the city's interests before other municipalities, the state government, and the national government. (Agree)

Organization and Guidance
The mayor has a visible position in the community and should use it to mobilize people on behalf of his or her favorite policies and programs. (Agree)
The mayor, more so than the council as a whole, has the responsibility to ensure that the manager and staff perform their jobs well. (Agree)
A mayor should be a source of ideas for new policies and programs. (Neutral)
A successful mayor is one who will build a base of support in the community and on the council in order to be the key decision maker in the city government. (Neutral)
A mayor should not hesitate to give direct orders to the manager or city staff. (Disagree)

---

*Note:* When Mayor Rhea read these statements, they were not grouped under the four headings. She read a list of sixteen statements, randomly ordered.

Table 7.3. Mayor Rhea's Allocation of Her Time.

| Job Component | Percentage of Time |
|---|---|
| Ceremonial and Presiding Duties | 35 |
| Attending ceremonial events | 15 |
| Speaking to community groups | 10 |
| Presiding at council meetings | 5 |
| Meeting with the media | 5 |
| Communication and Facilitation | 30 |
| Meeting personally with the manager | 15 |
| Meeting with council in special work sessions or retreats | 15 |
| Promotion | 22 |
| Participating in associations for elected officials | 10 |
| Meeting with representatives of other municipalities, the state, and national governments | 7 |
| Traveling on behalf of the city | 5 |
| Organization and Guidance | 13 |
| Developing programs and policies | 8 |
| Directing the manager and staff | 5 |

*Note:* When Mayor Rhea read this list of activities, they were not grouped under the four headings. The coding of each statement was confirmed during the interview with Mayor Rhea. When Mayor Rhea speaks to community groups or meets with the media, she generally relies on city staff to provide detailed explanations and follow-up services. She acts mainly as a spokesperson. Mayor Rhea also sees her role as that of a team player who facilitates discussions, who provides ideas drawn from her associational activities, and who will work through and with other council members. In light of this approach to the manager and the council, meeting with the manager and with the council were coded as communication and facilitation activities.

programs. Mayor Rhea thinks that she "may be a catalyst providing the opportunity to pursue ideas, such as with efforts to promote city beautification, historic preservation, and the arts, but the details are developed by the staff." Her job "is to continue to build community support for decisions made by the council-manager team." She tries to create a supportive environment where certain kinds of policy ideas can emerge from the city staff and from the community.

The way she presides at council meetings reflects her desire to support participation by council members, staff, and citizens. She explains her approach as follows:

> I feel we try to work together as a group. We try to build support together. I run meetings according to Robert's Rules. The previous mayor let citizens and council members get personal and curse at each other. But I don't let anyone get personal. I try to keep the discussion open, cordial, friendly, polite, and businesslike. I want them to feel like they have a voice at the meetings, so I encourage participation constantly. Since I preside at meetings, I let my views be expressed and defended by a couple of other council members and Joe [Lanford]. I don't think of the council as being *my* group. It needs to be a lot of people's agenda. I try to get more people involved. You build on what many people want. Then it makes it everyone's idea. No one person needs to claim it.

Clearly, Mayor Rhea does not seek to draw power to herself personally but prefers to work with and through others. This is a chief attribute of a coordinator-type facilitative mayor.

Mayor Rhea disagreed with only one of the sixteen statements in Exhibit 7.1. She does not think the mayor should give direct orders to the manager or the city staff. Mayor Rhea qualified this response, however, by typing in the margin of the questionnaire, "The manager—yes; the city staff—no." In the follow-up interview, she explained that it is appropriate for her to give a direct order to the city manager, but it is the manager's job, not hers, to issue orders to the staff: "Under the law, I have to go through Joe. I may run things by Jack or Russell [the assistant city managers], but I generally respect Joe's authority. He does the hiring and firing."

This discussion of organization and guidance indicates that Mayor Rhea should be rated low on policy guidance. She does care about policies, but she does not try to develop them, nor does she seek to direct other public officials and community leaders to adopt them. Her policy leadership is therefore general in nature. Her intent is to serve as a coordinator-type facilitative mayor.

Mayor Rhea's allocation of time to the four components of her job reflects this approach as well. As Table 7.3 shows, Mayor

Rhea spends 65 percent of her time on ceremonial and coordinative activities and 22 percent on promotional activities. Her partnership with the manager permits her to focus on building relationships within Rock Hill, between Rock Hill and other governments, and in associations. Therefore, she spends less of her time on organization and guidance.

### Evaluating Mayor Rhea's Performance

How well does Mayor Rhea perform as a coordinator? How do community leaders and other observers rate her performance? What are Mayor Rhea's specific accomplishments? The data in Table 7.4 indicate that community leaders and other observers think Mayor Rhea's performance is distinguished. For her performance in general, she received an overall 1.68 average rating on a scale of 1 (excellent) to 5 (poor). Mayor Rhea earned her highest ratings (falling between 1 and 2) on ten of the eleven activities associated with three of the four core components in the facilitative leadership model: ceremonial and presiding duties, communication and facilitation, and promotion. She received her lowest rating, a 2.56, for developing programs and policies to address city problems. Yet even on that rating, the consensus was that her performance was above average.

During the interviews, respondents provided examples illustrating how Mayor Rhea performed these various activities and describing her major accomplishments. Some of the most colorful and revealing examples that were discussed are part of the first category of activities. All twenty-four respondents who were asked to comment on her approach to ceremonial duties strongly agree that she loves this part of the job.

Respondents offered numerous examples of Mayor Rhea's skill at ceremonial activities: participating in the dunking booth at the city employees' picnic, sponsoring the frog-jumping contest in the annual "Come See Me" Festival, and dressing up as the Statue of Liberty in a neighborhood Fourth of July parade—something she has been doing since before she became mayor.

A college professor describes Mayor Rhea's talk to students at Winthrop College as an example of how she uses her political

Table 7.4. Evaluation of Mayor Rhea's Performance.

| Job Component | Rating (N = 67) | |
|---|---|---|
| Ceremonial and Presiding Duties | 1.56 | |
| Representing the city at ceremonial events | 1.21 | (n = 62) |
| Inspiring community pride | 1.27 | (n = 63) |
| Speaking to community groups about city policies and programs | 1.51 | (n = 61) |
| Presiding at council meetings and insuring an orderly debate | 1.79 | (n = 44) |
| Discussing city policies and programs with the news media | 2.02 | (n = 54) |
| Communication and Facilitation | 1.71 | |
| Ability to work with the manager and city staff | 1.53 | (n = 49) |
| Knowledge of city programs and policies | 1.66 | (n = 62) |
| Building a working relationship with council members | 1.79 | (n = 47) |
| Responsiveness to citizen complaints about city services | 1.85 | (n = 47) |
| Promotion | 1.11 | |
| Representing the city in associations for elected officials | 1.09 | (n = 66) |
| Promoting the city's interest before other municipalities, the state, and the national government | 1.12 | (n = 66) |
| Organization and Guidance | 2.35 | |
| Ensuring that city staff deliver services effectively | 2.13 | (n = 48) |
| Developing programs and policies to address city problems | 2.56 | (n = 45) |

*Note:* These statements were not grouped under the four headings when they were presented to each respondent. The number of respondents varies because of "don't know" responses, which were excluded from the calculation of the means. The scale used by respondents is as follows: 1 = excellent, 2 = good, 3 = average, 4 = fair, 5 = poor.

career to encourage people, especially women, to be active in their communities: "Mayor Rhea talked about her motivations to make the community a better place. She told the students how she came to realize that she could be a council member and, later, mayor. The jobs were not beyond her abilities, so she said her success should be an example to them. She stressed how having a positive outlook and getting involved can make a difference."

Mayor Rhea offers an example of her own, revealing how much these events mean to her: "I enjoy visiting schools and meeting with children. I went to the Richmond Drive School one day, and the children gave me a scarf with their handprints painted on it and their names under each pair of prints. They told me the prints were pats on the back for a job well done. Now, that's the kind of experience that makes this job great! I like these personal-type events the best." When performing these ceremonial activities, Mayor Rhea combines her love of the city, her sense of humor, and her friendliness.

Mayor Rhea successfully uses her visible position in the community to promote a sense of community and build working relationships among council members, staff, and community leaders. Several people have described Mayor Rhea's extra efforts to respond to citizens' requests and complaints during the recovery from Hurricane Hugo. One community leader says, "Many times, she answered the phone at City Hall to handle complaints during the Hugo relief effort. She made sure the staff called back. Betty Jo was always available."

Mayor Rhea also helped encourage people to participate in Empowering the Vision (ETV), the city's strategic planning effort. One community leader says, "She really pushes the public-private efforts. She wants the whole community to work together. The looking-ahead part of Empowering the Vision came from Joe Lanford, but the getting-everyone-involved part was all Betty Jo."

Mayor Rhea's desire to inform citizens and raise their awareness of developments in Rock Hill led her to be the first mayor to make an annual "state of the city" speech. The speech is broadcast on local television and radio and is reported in the local newspapers. Mayor Rhea explains her interest in doing a "state of the city" speech: "I just thought, if the president gives a State of the Union speech, and the governor gives a State of the State speech, then why shouldn't the city of Rock Hill also have a 'state of the city' speech? I gave my first speech in 1987, and it turned out well. People need to be informed about our achievements in Rock Hill."

Numerous people have commented on Mayor Rhea's supportive approach to council members and the manager. They appreciate her approach to the presiding officer's role. She keeps discussions focused on the topic, and she does not permit any personal attacks by council members on one another. She often refrains from participating in debates while the council is in session, in order to gain the confidence of all council members. She wants them to feel they have a fair chance to offer their opinions. Mayor Rhea expresses her views before council meetings, at workshops, and before voting. During regular council meetings, however, she prefers to have her views expressed by other members of the council with whom she agrees.

In addition to using her presiding role to promote good working relationships, Mayor Rhea occasionally acts as a liaison between the council and the manager. Because all council members have complete access to the city manager, serving as a liaison is not a role that she needs to perform. Still, fourteen of twenty-four respondents said that she discusses ideas with the manager and, later, with some of the council members, in order to clarify their positions. Sixteen of twenty-four respondents also said that she tries to arrange compromises on the rare occasions when the council is divided. This effort usually does not involve pressure tactics or actual negotiations; rather, Mayor Rhea stresses the need for members to work together. As one council member explains, "She promotes harmony because she doesn't like divisiveness." Another council member says, "Her fairness helps lead us to compromise. She tries to show us both sides, and she tries to influence us. She wants us to compromise—especially to protect the whole city's interests." One city staff member summarizes the predominant view by saying that Rhea helps the council and the manager work well together because "her strongest attribute is that she is a team player. The team is the council, staff, and citizens. She knows her limitations, so she does what she likes to do and lets others do their jobs. She knows how to lead *without* leading."

One of the components of the job that she enjoys most and performs exceptionally well is promotion of the city. Mayor Rhea's extensive participation in associations for elected officials, especially her success serving as a leader in those associations, has helped raise Rock Hill's profile around the state, the region, and the nation. This publicity is important to Rock Hill as it attempts to attract new businesses and new residents and to create a renewed sense of community pride and optimism about the future. "The businesspeople like her high profile because it attracts attention," says one citizen active in economic development. "We outshine the other cities in the Charlotte area because of her. We've been treated as the stepchild in this state because we're close to Charlotte. She has helped change this image."

Many people have also cited examples of how these activities expose Mayor Rhea to new ideas that have proved useful in Rock Hill. She learns at meetings. She goes on tours of other cities. She participates in workshops. She talks to other officials about their approaches to problems. Mayor Rhea's advocacy of city beautification, historic preservation, public art, and recreation, as important quality-of-life policies that support economic development, is inspired by these activities. As one community leader says, "Mayor Rhea has grown—she has learned—as a result of her travels."

When she returns from a meeting or a workshop, she reports what she has learned to the staff, the council, and citizens. She promotes programs and policies she wants to see in Rock Hill by defending particular policies or programs once they have been developed and proposed and by providing a sense of direction to the policy-making process in general. One council member explains a typical example of such effort on the mayor's part. Rhea had just attended a meeting in Birmingham: "She knew I went to law school at Samford University in that city. So she called me after her trip and described all the things they were doing to redevelop the downtown in Birmingham. Her intent was to convince me to support the proposals in Empowering the Vision intended to redevelop our downtown."

While she does defend particular policies or programs, Mayor Rhea's basic approach is, as mentioned, to provide general direction. She encourages the city manager to use his own planning talents and his staff's talents to develop proposals, and Joe Lanford welcomes the chance to think creatively about the city's future. He and the mayor share many approaches and ideas. Both have been described as visionaries and dreamers.

Empowering the Vision is the best example of Rhea's leadership style and teamwork with Lanford. Many observers give Mayor Rhea much of the credit for making a citywide strategic planning effort possible in Rock Hill. They say that her progressive approach helped establish the supportive environment needed to get ETV started in 1987. One business leader says, "Betty Jo wants to have a downtown. She believes a community needs a focal point. We've suffered through a textiles syndrome. In the late 1960s, we started to see this play out. Now the economy has turned around. Betty Jo says we have to build a new city for our new era. She deserves credit for generating community interest and support. She is trying to keep us moving forward."

Mayor Rhea's friendship with Martha Kime Piper, president of Winthrop College, provided a forum for originally discussing the idea of a citywide strategic planning process. Mayor Rhea arranged a meeting with Piper, Lanford, and Michael Gallis, a planning consultant working for Winthrop College, to discuss the possibility of combining their planning efforts. Lanford, building on the ideas discussed at this meeting, and with the full support of the mayor, developed ETV. Rhea and Lanford worked together to gain sponsorship of ETV from the Chamber of Commerce, York County, Rock Hill School District #3, Winthrop College, York Technical College, the city of Rock Hill, and the Rock Hill Economic Development Corporation. After a two-year planning process involving over one-hundred citizens, Rock Hill produced its ten-year strategic plan, focusing on six major themes: culture, gardens, history, infrastructure, education, and business.

Mayor Rhea's progressive approach supported this planning process, and some of her specific programmatic concerns were also integral parts of ETV. For example, her desire to use a public art program, as a way of promoting the city's sense of identity and its attractiveness as a place to live and conduct business, helped make public art a major part of Rock Hill's strategic plan. The details of the public art program—especially its main product, the Gateway Project—were developed by the staff, consultants, and citizens who participated in ETV. The Gateway Project features two historic columns from the Masonic Temple in Charlotte, four sculptures by New York artist Audrey Flack, and landscaping. Mayor Rhea did not develop the details of the Gateway Project, but her advocacy of public art created the context for its development. Other parts of the strategic plan—such as the creation of historic districts, a fall arts festival, and expansion of the wildflower program—also are attributable to her support for a quality-of-life approach to city development.

Not only has Mayor Rhea's involvement in various associations helped promote Rock Hill, she has also had an impact on municipal finance reform in South Carolina. She realized one of her major intergovernmental achievements while serving as president of the South Carolina Municipal Association, in 1989. In South Carolina, voters must approve the sales tax in a referendum. She helped persuade the state legislature to pass a law permitting a local-option sales tax. The law is intended to allow local governments to use a 1 percent sales tax to lessen their dependence on property taxes. Most of the sales-tax revenue must be used to roll back property taxes, but eventually 29 percent of the revenue may be used as an alternative source of funding for county and municipal governments. Several observers of Mayor Rhea's efforts as president of the association have praised her performance; all would agree with the following comments by a state leader: "She is held in high regard by members of the state legislature. She is personable and approachable. She knows politics. She's savvy. She clearly understands the nature of coalition politics. She has been accepted because she's a pro. She represented all cities in South Carolina, not just Rock Hill, and spoke of their financial plight. All of her colleagues in the association trusted her to get the message across without being abrasive, too forceful, or too arrogant. She excelled during her tenure as president."

In summary, Mayor Rhea's performance is widely recognized as distinguished. She has performed all eleven roles in the facilitative leadership model with skill, and her efforts have been effective. Mayor Rhea has had an impact not only on Rock Hill but also across South Carolina. Her performance demonstrates that council-manager mayors can become important leaders, guiding the policy-making process in their communities, by enhancing the chances of council members, the city staff, and citizens to participate in that process.

## Conclusion

Case studies describing the performance of council-manager mayors can reveal the importance of this office in community politics. As

Svara says in Chapter One, the council-manager mayor is not a pale imitation of the mayor in a strong mayor-council government. Council-manager mayors can be facilitative leaders, promoting the participation of council members, staff, and citizens in the political process and guiding their communities toward policy and programmatic objectives. Mayor Rhea's performance clearly reveals how this can be accomplished. Svara's description (1990) of the facilitative mayor fits Mayor Rhea: "The mayor must be effective at working with others and willing to give certain responsibilities to them. Inclusiveness, sharing of information, facilitation of the expression of divergent views, and ability to resolve differences are important traits for the mayor to have in dealings with the council. The relationship with the manager requires tact, respect, ability to share authority, and trust in the manager's commitment to advance the goals of the city and to achieve the highest performance from government as a whole" (p. 117). Mayor Rhea's case supports Svara's general theory regarding mayoral leadership, but her case also leads to three specific observations.

First, Mayor Rhea's partnership with Joe Lanford, a manager who specializes in city planning, is a key factor explaining her success. They share an approach to city development and an appreciation of planning as a tool for affecting the future. They have established a division of labor that uses the talents and interests of each of them in a way that produces strong executive leadership in the policy-making process. It is doubtful that either one would be as effective without the participation of the other. Clearly, Mayor Rhea's case indicates that the mayor–city manager relationship can be a key factor in whether council-manager mayors can be facilitative mayors.

Second, Mayor Rhea's voting status appears to be a key structural feature that supports her efforts to promote a cooperative approach to policy making in Rock Hill. She presides at council meetings and votes as a regular council member, rather than holding veto power or being excluded from voting. Her fellow council members recognize her as more than a ceremonial representative of the city. She plays a central role in the business of the council. She is accepted as a member during all phases of the council's work, and her voting status legitimizes her efforts to influence the council at all stages of the decision-making process. Given Mayor Rhea's experience, as well as the evidence from other cases studies (Wheeland, 1990), it can be said that council-manager communities undertaking structural change should consider giving the mayor a vote on the council in order to provide a key structural precondition of facilitative leadership.

Third, Mayor Rhea's full-time commitment to her duties is another key factor in her success. The mayor's job in Rock Hill (and, typically, in any council-manager government) is intended to be a part-time job. Rhea is on the job every day, all day. She easily adjusts her schedule in order to travel on behalf of the city. Would she be as successful if she worked only part-time? Mayor Rhea believes that her success depends on her full-time commitment, and she suggests formally making the mayor's job a full-time position. Whether such a change is needed in the council-manager plan in order to have a mayor who acts as a facilitative leader is an important question that deserves further study. Mayor Rhea's case certainly supports the idea of a full-time mayor for a council-manager government.

## Notes

1.  Mayor Rhea examined a list of twenty-four sources of information often used by council members and mayors. She chose not to add any sources to the list. In turn, she identified the five sources she used when making policy choices and when learning about the administration of programs and ranked those five sources. Mayor Rhea indicated that she used the same five sources in the same order of importance for each type of effort. Sources that are not a *main* part of Mayor Rhea's information network are as follows: interest groups, local news media, conversations with council members from other communities, conversations with members of boards and commissions, associations for elected and appointed officials, performance evaluations of the manager, lobbying among council members, committee work, study sessions with the manager, budget sessions, staff lobbying, spouse, attendance at board and commission meetings, friends, manager-mayor conversations, council

member-mayor conversations, key community leaders, and city attorney/solicitor.

## References

Boynton, R. P., and Wright, D. S. "Mayor-Manager Relationships in Large Council-Manager Cities: A Reinterpretation." *Public Administration Review*, 1971, *31*, 28–36.

Easterwood, M. "The Municipality and South Carolina." In C. B. Tyer and C. B. Graham, Jr. (eds.), *Local Government in South Carolina*. Columbia: Bureau of Governmental Research and Service, University of South Carolina, 1984.

Ferman, B. *Governing the Ungovernable City: Political Skill, Leadership, and the Modern Mayor*. Philadelphia: Temple University Press, 1985.

Handal, C. "Single-Member Districts Approved." *The Herald*, Apr. 26, 1989, p. 1A.

Parris, L. "Jerome Stays In: Gill, Berry Out." *The Herald*, Oct. 21, 1981, p. 1A.

Pettibon, S. "Rhea Wins Mayoral Primary." *The Herald*, Oct. 16, 1985, p. 1A.

"Rhea Nominated, Gill, Poe in Runoff." *The Herald*, Oct. 19, 1977, p. 1A.

Svara, J. H. *Official Leadership in the City: Patterns of Conflict and Cooperation*. New York: Oxford University Press, 1990.

Wheeland, C. M. "The Mayor in Small Council-Manager Municipalities: Are Mayors to Be Seen and Not Heard?" *National Civic Review*, 1990, *79*, 337–349.

Wikstrom, N. "The Mayor as a Policy Leader in the Council-Manager Form of Government: A View from the Field." *Public Administration Review*, 1979, *39*, 270–276.

# Part Three

*Change
and the Viability of
Facilitative Leadership*

# 8

*Gary Halter*

# Mayoral Leadership
# in College Station, Texas:
# A Self-Analysis

This chapter is a self-analysis of my six-year term as mayor of College Station, Texas. It is an attempt to provide the unique perspective of someone who has both an academic background in public administration and city management and practical experience as a local elected official. Obviously, it may lack the objectivity of a study conducted by an independent observer. It provides a case study of mayoral leadership in a university-dominated community experiencing exceptionally high population-growth rates. The chapter's conclusion is that the collaborative or team model of mayoral leadership worked well with a council dominated by university faculty and staff, but the chapter also raises questions about the continued use of this model in a city with a council that is no longer dominated by university faculty.

## The Governmental and Community Context

College Station is a city of about 56,000 residents in central Texas, approximately ninety miles northwest of Houston. It is best known for being the home of Texas A&M University (TAMU). Bryan, Texas, a community of approximately the same population, adjoins College Station to the north. The metropolitan area has a combined total population of 140,000.

College Station operates under a home-rule, council-manager city charter. It has a seven-member city council elected at large by place for two-year overlapping terms. The mayor is elected at large by the voters. College Station has technically functioned as a council-manager city since it was chartered, in 1938.

During the time frame of this case study, College Station could best be described as a college town, with approximately 30,000 of the 41,000 students attending Texas A&M University living in the city. The city council traditionally had been dominated by university faculty members. To date, ten people have held the office of mayor, and all but one have been faculty members (the one exception was a retired director of the Texas A&M Association of Former Students). From 1939 to 1986, no more than two of the seven council positions on any one council were ever held by nonuniversity people. It was not until 1987 that the majority of the council seats were held by people not employed by Texas A&M University. The effective voting population in city elections is rather small, given the population; having 1 percent of the registered voters participate is not uncommon, and the highest vote total in any city election was a little over 3,000. Students take no part in city elections.

The city is a full-service, general-provider government. The city owns and operates an electrical distribution system, water and sewer service, the more traditional services of police, fire, parks, streets, and solid-waste collection. In 1986, the total budget for the city was about $58 million. The school system is operated by a separate unit of government, the College Station Independent School District.

### The Office of Mayor

The office of mayor is a nonpaying position, with few formal duties specified in the charter. The mayor presides over city council meetings, represents the city at official functions, signs documents, and may call special meetings of the city council. The rules and procedures adopted by the city council give the mayor authority to set the agenda for council meetings, but any member of the council can have an item placed on the agenda. The mayor, manager, and staff play a large role in setting the agenda. Thus, formally, the mayor's position has few powers and duties. The person occupying the position can choose to play many roles, from strictly ceremonial tasks to policy leadership. With few exceptions, the people occupying the office of mayor have played a strong leadership role. Ernest Langford, mayor from 1942 to 1966, established a pattern of strong leadership in the mayor's office. One can question whether the city, under Mayor Langford, actually did function as a council-manager city; perhaps *mayor-administrator* might be a more accurate description of the form of government under Langford.

Langford was followed by David A. Anderson, who assumed an active role in meeting the challenges brought about by a growing population. Mayor Anderson was an activist, succeeding with two bond elections and constructing a new city hall, a fire station, a police station, and a major park facility. In 1972, James B. Hervey became mayor. After two years, he chose not to run for reelection. Oris M. Holt was elected in 1974 and served two years as mayor. In many respects, Mayors Hervey and Holt were also activists. In 1976, Lorence Bravenec was elected mayor and assumed a more active leadership role. I was elected mayor in 1980 and served until 1986.

Many pressures faced the city during the late 1970s and early 1980s, most of them related to growth and development. The city could not simply stand still and was pushed along by outside forces. The population of College Station from 1970 to 1986 went from 17,000 to 53,000, primarily because of an increase in student enrollment and the oil boom. I had served on the city council for five years and had good insight into both the processes of government and the problems faced by the city. Given the growth of the city, my assuming a caretaker role would have shifted the leadership and policy-making functions to others, perhaps to the city manager. Thus my role was dictated as much by circumstances and tradition as by personal predisposition. With few exceptions, as I have said, the office of mayor in College Station traditionally has provided strong leadership for the council and city government.

*Mayor-Manager Relationships*

The office of city manager has been relatively stable, with only six people holding the position since 1939. Two managers dominated the office for most of the history of the city. Ran Boswell served as city manager from 1952 until 1974. Under Mayor Langford, Boswell's role was more that of an administrator under a "strong mayor." In 1974, North Bardell, a professor of civil engineering at TAMU, assumed the position and served until 1985. Bardell performed exceptionally well as city manager. He possessed an easy-going manner and interacted with people very well. During his tenure, the city staff became more professional, both in educational background and in experience. When Bardell resigned, the city was in an excellent position to attract well-qualified candidates. In 1986, William King Cole, MPA-trained with experience as assistant city manager in Denton and city manager of Bellair, was hired as College Station's manager. Cole died in 1988 and was replaced by his assistant, Ron Ragland. No manager has ever been fired by the College Station city council. Relationships between the mayors and the managers have been generally good and productive.

## Significant Changes in Political Patterns

For most of its history, College Station could be described as a quiet, sleepy college town. Its population size was to a large degree dictated by student enrollment. When the college grew, the city grew.

In 1975, when I first ran for city council, the politics in College Station could be characterized as village politics. Campaigns were casual affairs, politics conducted among friends and neighbors. Small informal networks, composed primarily of old-timers, controlled city politics. Being a "college person" and having the support of these informal networks ensured a candidate's election.

As growth accelerated and newcomers were added to the community, politics began to move toward a more open system, with media-campaign tactics. Newcomers successfully challenged the old-timers for control of the city council. Calling for "no growth," "limited growth," or "quality growth" was popular. Neighborhood

groups organized and brought a "NIMBYcratic" air to most campaigns.[1] Protecting neighborhoods from growth pressures became
the main issue and driving force in city politics. Conflicts surfaced
and captured the attention of the local media.

Growth pressures declined in the late 1980s. Most of the controversy has died down, but the network of informal coalitions of
old-timers no longer controls politics in the community. Campaigns are much more open and public, and the use of media is
commonplace.

### Bryan, Texas, and Local Politics

Into the political formula of College Station one would also have
to add an understanding of the relations with the twin city of Bryan,
Texas. Many college towns are described as having a town-gown
split, but that does not characterize College Station. There is, however, a town-gown split between the twin cities, with Bryan serving
the "town" function. The Bryan city council traditionally has been
dominated by nonuniversity people. In the last twenty years, only
one university employee has served as mayor, and only two have
served on the city council. The Bryan city council is dominated by
the business community, and the description "selected from the golf
team at the Rotary Club" (Novak, 1990, p. 16) would apply.

Relations between the cities of Bryan and College Station
could best be described as stormy. The disparity in the professional
and economic backgrounds of the councils in Bryan and College
Station complicates the task of governmental cooperation. The two
cities have decidedly different philosophies regarding significant
policies, especially in the areas of planning, zoning, and expendi-
tures for parks and recreation. College Station has always had some
form of zoning; Bryan adopted a zoning ordinance only in 1989.
College Station has been accused of being overzoned and overreg-
ulated; in Bryan, the individualistic political culture (Elazar, 1984),
which dominates Texas, prevails and results in limited governmental control over the private sector. The recent adoption of a zoning
ordinance represents less a change in philosophy than an attempt
to answer the charge that the lack of land-use controls was responsible for lower growth rates in Bryan.

### Texas A&M University and Local Politics

The largest single employer in the area is Texas A&M University. With the development of some industry and major retail establishments, the university's importance has lessened, although it still remains the dominant economic force in the community. The task of city governance is more difficult when one institution plays such a large role in community affairs. It is further complicated by the potential for council members employed at the university to be torn between loyalty to the city and loyalty to the university.

## Leadership Roles

Of the various roles that mayors play, three stand out in my experience: performing ceremonial duties, being a "complaint center," and being a policy advocate. The first two roles entail potential traps into which the mayor may fall, which then makes it more difficult to fill the third role.

### Ceremonial Role

The ceremonial role is perhaps the most obvious to the general public. The mayor is called upon to perform many ceremonial tasks by various groups in the community. The pressure to perform ceremonial functions became so great that I began to think a rule could be applied: "Wherever two or more are gathered together, there also is the mayor expected to be." Any group or organization feels that the mayor has an obligation to appear on demand and say kind words. In some cases, the people organizing an event view the appearance of the mayor as a triumph of their organizational skills and influence. Members of the group may view the appearance or nonappearance of the mayor as a sign to the group of how important it is.

As mayor, I felt some obligation to respond to invitations whenever possible, but I soon found out that the demand for such appearances took a large amount of time—so much, in fact, that I found myself neglecting my university work and other city matters that required my attention. This, of course, is the trap.

Falling into the ceremonial trap may not be obvious to the mayor. It is easy to attend to such activities. They are noncontroversial. You don't make anyone mad unless you fail to attend; you generally make people happy. People will say nice things about you and thank you for your efforts. The news media may even cover the event and afford you good press coverage. You make friends. Consequently, you can fall into the trap, and the deception of self-importance and your belief that you are "attending to duties" will only reinforce this behavior.

This is not to say that the mayor should not attend to ceremonial duties. Some such activities can be used to build support for important policy or program changes. The point is that a mayor should not become the captive of ceremony and neglect leadership in policy areas.

### The "Complaint Center" Trap

When I was first elected mayor, I received literally hundreds of phone calls from citizens with complaints and demands for special treatment or services. In some cases, the complaints were trivial (such as reporting a pothole) and could have been expedited with a call to the streets department. The volume of calls was considerably greater than anything I had ever received as a city council member. Many phone calls were from people who just wanted to complain and did not expect action. Part of your job, in the minds of some citizens, is to listen to complaints and be sympathetic. In a town the size of College Station, even a trip to the supermarket can result in citizens' complaints, often from total strangers who give you a piece of their mind.

I did not encourage such complaints from citizens, but some mayors do, making complaint handling their primary function. They become "complaint center" mayors. Every day, they produce a long list of complaints to give to the city manager for action. After a while, the job of the city manager also becomes solving citizens' complaints. The manager becomes a high-paid errand runner for the mayor and is not able to attend to the necessary management activities because he or she is solving the specific problems on the mayor's list. The mayor may follow up each complaint with a call to the citizen, to make sure that the problem has been solved. This puts additional pressure on the manager to respond, and it consumes still more of the mayor's time.

Becoming primarily a "complaint center" mayor has both rewards and problems. The rewards are primarily personal. The mayor will be viewed as responsive, caring, and concerned: "I called the mayor, and he solved my problem." In the next election, many citizens will remember the mayor for his or her responsiveness. The problems are twofold. First, the mayor may not have enough time left to deal with long-term problems of the city or provide any leadership or direction for the city or the council. The mayor becomes a link between the citizen and the staff for services, and leadership takes a back seat. Second, staff members neglect long-range problems and even daily administrative matters as they attempt to respond to the mayor's list of citizens' complaints.

Citizens have a right and even a need to complain to elected officials. Complaint handling, however, should not become the primary function of elected officials. For elected officials, the importance of complaints from citizens is that they may indicate problems in the city or pinpoint areas where the staff is failing. Citizens and officials alike are better served when it is easy for citizens to approach appropriate staff members directly with their complaints and get satisfactory responses without the interference of elected officials.

### The Role of Policy Advocate

Of all the roles played by mayors, that of policy advocate is the most difficult. Being a ceremonial or "complaint center" mayor seldom produces political enemies; for this reason, it is easy for a mayor to emphasize ceremony and complaints and avoid the policy role. A proposal that calls for a change in city policy will almost always result in conflict. New proposals often cost additional money dollars and may result in tax increases. Even when no new taxes are needed, existing groups may be denied services, and controversy ensues. Growth-related policy proposals, which seldom cause tax increases or decreases in city services, may still be controversial because they threaten existing life-styles and values. Any change in the

status quo may result in the creation of political enemies and potential rivals in the next election.

If the mayor is willing to deal with the potential controversy
surrounding an active agenda for change, he or she has a relatively
free hand to develop and pursue any new policy. The primary
group to win over is the city council, and the mayor must have the
support of the city manager. The manager has to be involved because of his or her control over information and resources, essential
elements in accomplishing change.

When the mayor develops a strategic plan of action and wins
the support of the council, the plan has a high likelihood of success.
Most city council members do not have agendas for action when they
are elected; if they do, their agendas tend to be limited to the specific
issues that motivated them to seek election. When a single issue (such
as a planning or zoning decision affecting their homes) has been
dealt with, such council members can often be led to embrace a larger
agenda if the mayor provides leadership and guidance.

### Areas of Positive Impact

I have chosen three areas to demonstrate the positive impact of
mayoral activity on city policies: planning and zoning decisions,
improvement in relations with the city of Bryan, and economic
development. These were chosen partly because they represent three
broad areas of policy: land-use controls affect both the life-style
values of residents and the business community; intergovernmental
relations involve the city in a broader sphere of activities; and economic development involves both government and the private sector. Furthermore, these areas are often in conflict with one another.
Formulation of strict planning and zoning policies can conflict
with economic development, and economic development efforts,
which competed with the city of Bryan, hampered intergovernmental relations. The interplay of competing and conflicting goals
complicates the process of leadership.

#### *Planning and Zoning Decisions*

One of the factors that encouraged me to seek election to the city
council was zoning decisions. Shortly after moving to College Sta-

tion, I attended a meeting of the city council at which a developer was asking for the rezoning of a large tract of land near my home. I attended out of concern about the impact on my home. During the meeting, the chair of the planning and zoning commission indicated that the commission favored the rezoning. The mayor then asked if anyone representing the landowner was present. The chair of the commission again addressed the council, this time representing the landowner, and spoke again in favor of the rezoning. The council voted to rezone the land. This dual representation by the chair was repeated on the next two items on the agenda. I finally objected to what was an obvious conflict of interest. The chair and I had an argument. He pointed out that being chair of the commission did not pay, and he had to make a living some way. I suggested that he choose one job—chair or developer. The local paper covered the event, and several people contacted me with similar concerns. We formed a group to watch the city council. In time, it became evident to me that there was no planning at all, and that rezoning was granted upon request.

This watchdog group recruited and sponsored candidates for the city council and, by 1977, had a majority on the city council. This was not a formal group with a name, but rather a loose network of people. We had gained the support of key individuals, and we won the election primarily through our personal contacts.

I felt that the city needed to revise its comprehensive plan and stop granting rezoning upon request. Planning and enforcement of the plan (zoning, subdivision controls) should be related. If zoning is changed from one category to another, there should be some compelling reason for change and that change should be compatible with the comprehensive plan. I had enough understanding of urban planning from my academic background to articulate these points. Between 1975 and 1980, partly as a result of my leadership on this issue, College Station adopted a comprehensive plan, a street plan, and a capital-improvement plan.

I came to realize the shortcomings of comprehensive planning when it is applied to a real-world political setting. I also came to realize the limits of mayoral leadership. Anyone who has observed politics in College Station for the last twenty years would note that city politics are characterized by frequent conflicts over issues directly related to land-development issues. A zoning ordinance provides a forum for public debate of these issues and thrusts the mayor and the city council into the position of being arbitrators of disputes. Easton (1953) has characterized politics as "the authoritative allocation of values for a society," and in the process of planning and zoning, many competing values are brought to the fore. The city council becomes the agency that authoritatively decides which of the competing values will prevail—or, more precisely, which values will be partially satisfied. These values have been described as the aesthetic value, a concern "for the visual and sensual properties of the built environment"; the functional value, which relates to the efficient movement of the people and things necessary for the city to function; the economic value, which states that land should be put to its highest and best economic use; the social value, which is related to the social needs of groups of citizens; neighborhood life-style values; and moral values, which have to do with the need for all citizens to be treated fairly and share in the benefits of the city (Johnson, 1989, pp. 24–34). Each of these values—aesthetic, functional, economic, social, and moral—has legitimacy; no one value is more legitimate than any other, and each has a valid claim on city resources.

During my time on the College Station city council, all of these values were constantly presented to the council for arbitration, and some citizens were partially satisfied. Conflict was frequent and public. As mayor, I had to provide leadership in this conflict-laden and often emotional atmosphere. I attempted to do this, but my leadership was often lacking. I did not suffer fools very gladly, and I now realize that this was a major shortcoming on my part. I felt that if the council had agreed on a plan of action that would have long-term effects on the city, it should stick with that plan and not bow to pressure from any group, including well-meaning concerned citizens acting as an angry mob at council meetings. Getting citizens to see the necessity of compromising their values (usually social) was next to impossible.

A good example of this shortcoming involved action on the street plan for the city. When I was first elected mayor, no such plan existed, and in several cases developers had been allowed to offset streets to accommodate land-ownership patterns and maximize profits for their developments. After the city developed a major street plan based on well-established planning principles that were designed to avoid these kinds of problems, developers were required to follow the plan when subdividing land. Several developers did attempt end runs around the plan, but the council was generally consistent in holding them to it. In these decisions, mayoral leadership was successful. With citizens, however, the plan was frequently altered. A neighborhood group would demand that a major street not be extended because it would bring in outsiders and unwanted traffic. Citizens would often make such comments as "When we bought our home, the real-estate agent told us that the street would never be extended, and now the city is going back on its word." Another person objected to a street extension and to the building of a church and parking lot in his neighborhood. He said, "In my home town, where I grew up, the city allowed a parking lot to be built across from my parents' home. Years later, when I returned for a visit, I found that my family home had turned into a Chinese restaurant. If the city allows this church and parking lot across from my present home, I certainly hope the neighbors are ready for Chinese food." In all these cases, the council abandoned the street plan and bowed to pressure from neighborhood groups; I was unable to convince the council to enforce its agreed-upon plan.

This is not to say that planning and zoning were unsuccessful. In many areas, they were. Our zoning ordinance is now much more discriminating. In addition, a strict sign ordinance has eliminated a source of the visual pollution so common to many cities, and a requirement for landscaping commercial areas has improved the appearance of the community. Subdivision ordinances have also eliminated substandard developments. In all these areas, a positive impact was made and will have long-term benefits. The lesson to be learned here is that if the council was quite willing to enforce the plan and city standards when it came to developers but was unwilling to enforce the city policy when neighborhood groups objected, it was partly because the council shared the values of the neighborhood groups. I was somewhat unsuccessful in convincing the council that all values have legitimacy. The council did not feel a sense of shared values with the developers and often viewed their motives with suspicion, (sometimes with good reason).

### Relations with the City of Bryan

As indicated, the relationship between the city of Bryan and the city of College Station was often strained by a town-gown type of conflict. The backgrounds of the two councils were often quite different, and communication and cooperation were difficult. Many longtime residents of both communities were very quick to point out past conflicts. Older residents of Bryan often referred to College Station simply as "the college": "You people out there at the college think you know everything, don't you?"

During my first term on the council, the controversy between the two cities was heightened by the fact that College Station purchased water and electricity from Bryan. The energy crisis of the early 1970s caused many rate increases, and both cities felt that they had lost out in the bargaining process. Between 1976 and 1980, College Station arranged to purchase its electrical power from another supplier and developed its own water system. Separation of the two city utility systems eliminated the primary source of controversy.

Thus, by 1980, when I became mayor, the field for cooperation was much more open. Even before the election (I had no opponent), I contacted the mayor of Bryan, Richard Smith, and suggested that we get together and discuss common problems. We both agreed that we should forget about past animosities and try to forge a new relationship. Mayor Smith had been reared in College Station and married into an old Bryan family; in some ways, he bridged the two communities.

We felt that there should be some joint project on which the two cities could cooperate, even if it was symbolic. We soon settled on the creation of a joint animal shelter. Neither city had adequate facilities for impounding animals, and both had experienced some rather bad publicity in the local paper over the treatment of animals. The local humane society was advocating a joint shelter, and Mayor Smith and I both felt that it was a visible project that could demonstrate cooperation and set the stage for improved relations.

But we underestimated both the ease of accomplishing the task and the problems that would have to be overcome.

The joint animal shelter opened for operation in 1983, but only after a number of problems had been overcome. There were controversies over its location, its functions, and its funding. Another major controversy involved the veterinary school at Texas A&M. A plan to utilize students to spay or neuter animals was scuttled when local veterinarians objected. Mayor Smith and I called a meeting of the local veterinarians' society and worked out a compromise: they agreed to a program whereby the shelter would issue a spay-or-neuter certificate when an animal was adopted, which could be used at local veterinary clinics; in exchange, the veterinarians agreed to provide, on a rotation basis, a veterinarian to examine all the animals taken into the shelter.

The Brazos County Animal Shelter has proved to be a great success. It is a visible example of cooperation between our two cities. Other projects followed. There is now a joint library program between the two cities. Bryan also contracts with College Station for a joint solid-waste landfill and recycling program and a joint emergency-dispatch agency.

### Economic Development

Not until the 1930s did a substantial off-campus population develop in College Station. Since Texas A&M University is tax-exempt, the city and the local school district have depended almost exclusively on residential property for property-tax support. Until the middle 1970s, the single largest source of sales-tax revenue for the city was the university-owned bookstore; most retail trade and all industry were in Bryan.

As the city of College Station began to experience very rapid residential growth, it became necessary for the school district to hold bond elections in order to gain voters' approval for new facilities. The school district lost two major bond elections because of a homeowners/taxpayers association revolt; the city was more successful with its bond elections since very few city operations are financed with property-tax money (most funding comes from utility revenues and charges such as license and service fees). Nevertheless, the city had received negative comments from both investment rating services because of its lack of reliance on property-tax revenues, which are generally viewed as stable.

Toward the end of Mayor Bravenec's term, he and I began the effort to promote a more diverse tax base in College Station, to help both the city and the school district. We attempted first to work with the Brazos County Industrial Development Foundation (BCIDF), which was part of the Bryan–College Station Chamber of Commerce. After a series of meetings, it soon became apparent that this group was not going to do much for College Station. We had put forward a number of proposals, all of which received negative comments. For the most part, our meetings with BCIDF consisted of the board telling us why it could not do anything for us.

After becoming mayor, I met with a local group of businessmen and proposed the idea of creating a similar body in College Station. I received very enthusiastic support. A few were suspicious because College Station had a reputation for being antigrowth, partly because of our planning and zoning processes. I had some difficulty convincing everyone that strict planning and zoning policies and a more diverse economic and tax base were not incompatible; good commercial and industry development looked to such regulations to protect investments. I felt that the city and the business community would profit from the recruitment of industries with these values.

From these meetings came the College Station Industrial Development Foundation. The city provided almost all the funding for this effort—some $50,000 the first year. A full-time director was hired, and office space and staff assistance were provided in the city's convention center. The foundation was a positive force in expanding and diversifying the tax base of the city and the school district. It can be difficult to judge the exact extent to which such a group actually has recruited development and the extent to which development might have occurred anyway, but there is no doubt that having a separate organization funded by College Station provided a positive voice for locating in College Station.

College Station's economic base greatly expanded from 1980 to 1986. Two major corporations, Westinghouse and Texas Instruments, located electronic plants in the city. The city also gained a major retail mall, containing 1.5 million square feet of retail space, and an additional 1 million square feet in other locations. Retail trade moved from Bryan to College Station, as evidenced by sales-tax revenues.[2] The city gained a hospital, two mental hospitals, and considerable office space for businesses and professions. In short, over a period of six years, College Station became the dominant business city in the metropolitan area.

Conflict among the goals can limit the mayor's impact on policy and make it difficult to stick with a consistent policy. For example, the defeat of the school bond elections in College Station was attributed to homeowner concern about the lack of diversity in the tax base, but an economic development policy that encouraged new development conflicted with the organized homeowners who saw increased growth as a threat to their life-style and social values. In turn, businesses wishing to relocate in the community at the urging of city government sought exemptions to city standards for signs, off-street parking, and landscaping of commercial areas. Recruiting retail trade, especially when businesses moved from Bryan to College Station, made improvement of relations between the two cities difficult.

As mayor, these conflicts were difficult to deal with. Do you compromise one policy to promote another? Do you abandon long-term plans to accommodate pressing demands? Do you slow down economic development activities that may be taking business away from Bryan to promote intergovernmental relations? These are difficult choices.

## Nature and Sources of Leadership

I feel that my leadership style is best described as "collaborative or team relationship" (Boynton and Wright, 1971), a term indicating a cooperative relationship among the mayor, the council, and city manager. A number of factors were involved. First, previous mayors and councils had enjoyed similar relationships with the city manager; conflicts between elected and appointed officials had been rare. Second, my own background and academic experience had provided me with an understanding of the council-manager form of government and the realization that appointed officials were not the enemy but were essential to accomplishing objectives. Third, the professionalism of the two city managers with whom I served contributed to a sense of mutual respect and support.

### Support of the City Council

An effective mayor must have the support of the council. This is especially true if a collaborative leadership style is to work. There are two basic ways, not mutually exclusive, for a mayor to secure the support of the council. First, the mayor can use persuasion, convincing other members of the council to accept or agree to a plan of action. Second, the mayor can work through the election process to ensure that the majority of those elected to the council have similar views. Both ways are difficult and time-consuming.

As I have said, many people elected to the College Station city council had very limited agendas (or, in a few cases, no evident agendas). This was true of the majority of the nineteen people I served with in eleven years on the council. In this vacuum, someone with a plan of action could gain support for an agenda. I certainly found this to be the case, especially during my first four years as mayor. Nevertheless, council members' lack of articulated agendas does not mean that the mayor can simply proceed to do whatever he or she wants; a consensus must be built.

I found goal-setting retreats very useful in helping the council reach a consensus or formulate a collective agenda. Our biannual retreats enabled the council to spend time discussing the mission of the city, identifying major goals, and developing a priority listing of the top ten goals to be accomplished during the year. In short, the council decided the major policy objectives of the city collectively. I found it important to have the first retreat in late May or early June, after council elections but far enough in advance of the budget cycle so that the staff would have the benefit of this information in drafting the budget. The second goal-setting retreat, usually in November or December, was to review progress toward achieving goals and to serve as a reminder of agreed-upon courses of action. As a process for establishing policy, council retreats are an effective tool of leadership for the mayor. The mayor can use a goal-setting retreat as a way of saying to the council, "Here is where we are, here is where we should go, and here is how we can get there. Do you agree?"

I usually began the process by asking council members to give their input. A council retreat can also be guided by an outside facilitator, although I never used one; I found that I could chair the session if ground rules to ensure participation were followed. I found that the most effective way to force all council members to participate was to ask each member, "What is the most pressing problem facing College Station?" I would ask one member to begin the process by stating one idea or problem, and then I would go to the next member and continue the process until all ideas or problems had been exhausted. This process ensured that everyone had an opportunity to state a view, and it forced members to think about problems. If a council member was newly elected, it allowed him or her to bring out any campaign promise or agenda he or she might have, even if it was a very limited one.

I also learned that silence does not mean consensus. Some council members sit quietly, say nothing before the vote, and then vote against a proposal. The round-robin statement of problems forced everyone to give input and, in many cases, members would bring up problems that everyone else felt were important. A person who brought up a problem often believed that it was his or her goal and became its chief spokesperson; the fact that others shared this person's idea did not matter, and consensus was achieved.

I found the goal-setting sessions to be the most effective way of getting programs accepted by the council and of achieving some consensus for action. The process became an effective leadership tool. (This is not to say that the council always stayed with the program; as indicated, the council would sometimes abandon a plan in the face of citizens' demands.)

During my terms as mayor, four council members resisted attending goal-setting sessions, especially if these were to be held out of town over the weekend; they were always too busy or could not miss church. I came to realize that some members did not want to attend, out of fear that their limited agendas would not be accepted by the council and that they would not be able to continue pressing for action.

Another option open to a mayor for gaining the council's

support is to work toward the election of council members with whom you share values. College Station elected three council members each year. I often encouraged people I knew to run for the council. I offered them my covert support and placed them in contact with people who could and would help them win. There was some risk in doing this if it became too public. There was some negative reaction to the slating of candidates; individuals were expected to run as independents. Of course, others also tried to get their candidates to run and be elected, and everyone denied that there was any slate making.

It was important to file early and hope to limit opponents, especially when there was no incumbent. Finding a candidate to oppose an incumbent was somewhat more risky, since I might have to work with the incumbent after the election. From 1980 to 1984, this process worked very well. After 1984, I had less success in finding candidates, partly because of the battles over zoning and street extensions, which led to the formation of the neighborhood groups. These groups were more successful in electing their candidates to office.

## Communication Networks

After I became mayor, I found that if I said something, it carried much more weight than if I had said the same thing as a council member. The word of the mayor simply has more weight with most people than the word of anyone else in city government. He or she can command more attention and press than anyone else can. By the same token, mayors must also be careful of what they say because of the credibility given to their words.

I have already noted the danger of falling into the ceremonial trap, but ceremonial tasks can be used as a forum for advocating the mayor's position or that of the council or city. This is the value of ceremonial appearances, and it is the reason why they should be chosen wisely.

Contact with community leaders is also important. A mayor receives many invitations to social events attended by community leaders; in many cases, it is not the mayor personally who is being invited, but the office. Such events often allowed me to communicate my position on an informal basis to others whose support was important, or simply to develop contacts for later meetings.

### *Relations with the City Staff*

Good working relations with the city manager and the staff are an essential resource for success. This does not mean that you must advocate policies supported by the manager, but rather that you and the manager must have mutual respect for one another's ideas and expertise.

In my experience, there were a few council members who viewed the staff both as the enemy and as fair game. They arrived at council meetings armed to play "stump the staff" in open public meetings. Such behavior may make a council member look good in the press, but it creates ill will with the staff and makes cooperation difficult in the future. The only effective way of handling such council members is to have the other members discipline them, but council members are reluctant to do this. Discipline cannot be public. I often tried talking to council members on an informal basis. You can also attempt to adopt a code of behavior that outlines rules. The College Station council now has a formal code of behavior, which was adopted after I left office. A code formalizes discipline and makes it less personal.

The city manager and I had a close working relationship and met frequently. Both city managers with whom I worked made a point, in a weekly memo to the council, of informing the members about our frequent discussions. This procedure protected the managers from the common complaint that council members are being kept in the dark by the manager and the mayor.

I also made a point of taking the political heat when controversial issues developed, and of protecting the manager from criticism. Some councils try to push the manager out in front to absorb criticism. I did not feel that this was appropriate. I was quite willing to take credit for things that went right and blame for things that went wrong. If the manager made a mistake, he received criticism from me and the council in a private forum.

The collaborative relationship that characterized my interactions with the council and the manager were an expression of the city's governmental tradition, the characteristics of the persons who held office, and my academic background. The structure of council-manager government enhanced this approach. Officials developed a sense of mutual trust. I respected the expertise and advice of the city manager and staff, as they respected mine. There was an openness in the exchange of ideas and information rather than the manipulation of information to support preconceived positions. In the last two years of my term as mayor—when the makeup of the council changed—this collaborative relationship began to break down.

### Change and the Viability of Facilitative Leadership

The homogeneous nature of College Station's population and the low involvement of students in politics resulted in a lack of major political controversies or divisions within the council. The fact that most ethnic minorities and most low-income citizens reside in Bryan means that any controversies over class and race are bifurcated between the two cities rather than occurring within the city of College Station. In addition, because most business leaders were residents of Bryan rather than College Station (during the time of this study), their ability to influence the election of the College Station City Council was limited. In short, a white, homogeneous community of professional educators with shared goals and values had made a tradition of facilitative leadership easier to achieve in College Station.

Toward the middle of my third term as mayor, in 1985, several factors began to erode the homogeneous nature of the city council. First, the neighborhood groups were successful in electing members of the council who had different values and attitudes, and who were unaccustomed to working in a collaborative, team-relationship setting. In most cases, their educational backgrounds were very limited. They viewed the mayor, other council members, and the staff with great suspicion but lacked any agendas for action beyond opposition to existing programs.

Second, the economic development policies of the city had been successful in attracting new businesses, diversifying the tax base, and increasing the number of business leaders who lived in the community. They also recruited and successfully elected members to the city council.

By 1987, only the mayor and two of the six council members were university employees. There were two businessmen, an attorney, and two neighborhood advocates. The makeup of the council has remained about the same from 1986 to the present, with no more than two or three university employees serving as members. This change in the makeup of the council has led to less cooperation and more diversity. Most of the public controversies of the pre-1986 era, which had revolved around planning and zoning issues, have disappeared with low growth rates, but there is far less agreement on common goals and objectives, and there is generally a lack of direction to the city staff from both the council and the mayor.

The 1990 bond election provides some evidence of this lack of agreement within the council and of the breakdown in collaborative leadership. In December 1990, after two years of study, the city council proposed a $15.6 million bond. The package contained eight propositions, but only two passed (street and sidewalk improvements, and some park improvements). The voters rejected $10.5 million for such projects as a library, park-land acquisition, public buildings, and an early-warning weather system; in five previous bond elections, from 1976 to 1985, the voters had rejected only two propositions out of some fifty proposed. Before the election, there had been great public disagreement among the council members, played up by the local newspaper, over portions of the bond package. For example, the location of the proposed library building was not specified because the council could not agree on a site. With this level of disagreement, it is perhaps not surprising that the voters so overwhelmingly defeated most of the propositions.

There are other signs of a breakdown in unanimity. The election of the current mayor, in 1986, was marked by some controversy when he defeated, with the support of the business community, a neighborhood advocate (who was later reelected to the city council in 1987). The presence of two to four council members representing the business community has broken the commonality of values on previous councils. Moreover, in the past two elections, three members of the city council have indicated their interest in running for mayor and their dissatisfaction with the current situation. There are also some indications of a more distant, less personal relationship among the current council, the mayor, and the city manager and staff. This relationship is very formal, both in public council meetings and at social affairs.

The city council in College Station recently adopted a code of conduct that defines appropriate or acceptable behavior during public meetings. The code deals both with interactions between members of the council and with interactions between the council and the city staff. It was adopted partly because of interpersonal problems. Such a code would probably be useful in any city council, but its recent adoption in College Station indicates the extent of the problems.

I did not seek reelection in 1986, in part because service on the council had ceased to be enjoyable. I found myself increasingly at odds with the elected representatives of the business community, who doubled as fiscal conservatives and spoke the Reagan rhetoric, and with the neighborhood advocate who opposed almost everything. My leadership style and abilities were not completely equal to the situation; someone with different abilities from mine was needed as mayor, to provide leadership to a more diverse council.

A personality and value system more in tune with the business world may be what is needed to lead this new council. The value system of the council has changed to such a degree that the person serving as mayor will have to possess the ability to work with people drawn from diverse backgrounds. The mayor may also have to seek new ways to work with the manager and the staff. One could argue that this situation calls out for an excellent facilitative leader.

### Conclusion

Facilitative leadership may be enhanced by a particular mix of value systems, background characteristics, and personalities. It is probably easier to achieve in a council made up of people from similar backgrounds. This mix may be affected by changes in the population or makeup of the city, as in College Station, or by a change from at-large to single-member district elections. Research into these factors will be extremely difficult and time-consuming, but it may help us understand successful leadership in council-manager government.

Is it more difficult for a mayor to be a successful facilitative leader with council members from very diverse backgrounds? If so, what changes in behavior are necessary for success? These questions deserve attention.

## Notes

1.  NIMBY, of course, is the acronym formed by the first letters of the phrase "not in my back yard."
2.  Texas cities have a local-option 1 percent sales tax, which is collected by the state and returned to the city government in which it was paid.

## References

Boynton, R. P., and Wright, D. S. "Mayor-Manager Relationships in Large Council-Manager Cities: A Reinterpretation." *Public Administration Review*, 1971, *31*, 28–36.

Easton, D. *The Political System.* New York: Knopf, 1953.

Elazar, D. *American Federalism: A View from the States.* (3rd ed.) New York: HarperCollins, 1984.

Johnson, W. C. *The Politics of Urban Planning.* Englewood Cliffs, N.J.: Prentice-Hall, 1989.

Novak, T. L. "Response." In H. G. Frederickson (ed.), *Ideal and Practice in Council-Manager Government.* Washington, D.C.: International City Management Association, 1990.

# 9

*Glen W. Sparrow*

# The Emerging Chief Executive 1971-1991: A San Diego Update

The role of mayor in the council-manager city has recently become the object of increased interest (Svara, 1990). An earlier look at the city of San Diego, California, and at Mayor Pete Wilson's tenure (Sparrow, 1984) posed the thesis that in a large and growing western council-manager city, size produces civic diversity, which in turn has a tendency to modify the roles of the manager and the mayor. This diversity produces cleavages within the population that require greater political leadership. Rapid growth leads to demand for services, which requires public choices over such issues as setting of priorities, service delivery and distribution, and questions of quality and quantity. Conflicts over land-use decisions and the rate of growth require further political decisions and leadership. As the need for political agenda setting, choice making, coalition building, and goal articulation increases in importance for the city's residents, there are greater opportunities and greater needs for the emergence of elected leadership.

From 1971 to 1982, Pete Wilson shaped and defined the role of mayor for San Diego. Upon his departure, the city experienced numerous changes, which produced upheaval and drift. This summary of the Wilson years and of the nine years following his departure will be instructive for those interested in the increasing executive role of the mayor in a large, western, council-manager city. It demonstrates the extent of the changes that Wilson made in the mayor's office and indicates the need for continued strong leadership. This chapter reviews the Wilson years in San Diego and discusses his impact on the evolution of the mayor's office. It goes on to examine the period following his departure and considers the utility of strong executive leadership in a large western city.

## Preconditions

Chief executives like Pete Wilson are able to do several things at once: articulate and place long-range goals on the city agenda; develop support for them from citizens, the city government, and the private sector; oversee at least the initial steps leading to their accomplishment; and ensure the effective delivery of municipal services. The experience in San Diego tells us that the conditions encouraging the evolution of a nonexecutive mayor to a chief executive in the council-manager system include the presence of the traditional reform model of municipal government, a population of at least 250,000, rapid post–World War II industrial growth, expanded boundaries, and an emphasis on land-use decisions as being among the most important public acts of government. This evolution also requires an individual who is ready and willing to exercise the combination of political, policy-making, and administrative skills that constitute leadership. The importance of the institutionalization of change in producing a smooth transition of leadership is clearly shown by the events that followed Wilson's departure. The absence of a successor who shared Wilson's vision of the office and Wilson's abilities suggests the need for formalization of the evolutionary process or for the election of an individual with the proper qualities. Clearly, however, subsequent experience in San Diego indicates that once change has been set in motion, it is difficult to retard the expectations that are produced.

## The San Diego Setting

By the late 1960s and early 1970s, San Diego was a fine example of
the modern reformed city. Experience in this city, as in many others
in the same category, indicates that while the reformers successfully
increased efficiency and decreased corruption, they did so at the
expense of conflict resolution. Underestimating the complexities of
city government, the reformers tended to see governance as "a problem in administration that could be solved through improved organizational techniques rather than a problem in politics that
involved the balancing of competing interests" (Harrigan, 1981,
p. 97). The flaw was not immediately apparent, however. Cities
with populations between 10,000 and 250,000 tend to exhibit a ho-
mogeneity that contributes to the stability of the council-manager
form, but further growth usually brings in its wake greater plural-
ism and more factions demanding to be heard. In the growing city,
the council-manager form continues to be effective at providing
goods and services, the first of what Banfield and Wilson (1963) have
described as government's two principal functions, but its rational
bureaucratic structure is less effective at fulfilling the second function, "managing conflict in matters of public importance" (p. 18).

In San Diego, as in other growing cities, the conflicts involved growth versus no growth, increased racial awareness, downtown versus the suburbs, new arrivals versus old-timers, and neighborhood versus neighborhood. All these demanded a form of conflict
management. The dilemma of the growing, reformed city is that it
is operating in a structural system that "demands an impersonal,
apolitical settlement of issues, rather than the settlement of conflict
in the arena of political battle" (Lineberry and Fowler, 1967, p. 710).
In effect, a council-manager city is not so adapted as to respond to
the conflicts that occur when the population increases beyond a certain size. Through brokering, however, the mayor is positioned to
provide the leadership required for the development of coalitions in
the pluralistic city.

Studies by Mollenkopf (1983) and Abbott (1981) seem to demonstrate that a progression of changing political relationships in
cities like San Diego had an impact on traditional power centers.
The roles of the city manager and the mayor were affected, not

because of formal restructuring or charter changes but because mayors were increasingly taking the initiative when faced with problems that demanded solutions. A long-term vision of what the city should be, a plan to achieve this vision, the informal and incremental pyramiding of power, an ability to take advantage of inherent weaknesses in the reformed political system, strength of personality, ability, and ambition—these were all hallmarks of this kind of emerging municipal chief executive. Pete Wilson was such a mayor.

Political observers in San Diego have little difficulty identifying the fault line that established the modern political era in the city. On November 2, 1971, Wilson, a thirty-seven-year-old state assemblyman, was elected mayor, and the city's political machinery began its evolution toward the new municipal chief executive model. During the eleven years of his tenure, the city government seemed to be based on his political strength and ability—elements not mentioned in the city charter.

As described by the charter, San Diego's government is a council-manager form. As is largely typical of reformed city governments, it is nonpartisan (as required by the state constitution for all local California governments). During the Wilson years, San Diego's electoral system deviated slightly from the reform model by providing for a mayor to be elected at large and for eight council members to be nominated by district and elected at large. When Wilson took office, in 1972, San Diego, with a population of 697,000, was the fourteenth-largest city in the nation and the third-largest city in the state. In the 1960s, the city had increased its population by 22 percent. Through a substantial effort at economic diversification, the city had changed its image from that of a sleepy Navy town, improved its attractiveness, and added tourism to its military and defense industries. When the recession of 1959–60 ended, the aerospace industry became the third major building block of the local economy.

In 1971, Wilson was a fresh face in local politics who had returned clean and untarnished from his stint as a state legislator in Sacramento. At that time, he had been perceived as a "pestiferous, but largely ineffectual, do-gooder" who articulated the concerns of "aesthetes, those worriers about the environment, land use, and pollution" (Keen, 1973, p. 77). Wilson did indeed find a home with these types and became the natural leader of this group. But he did so carefully, without alienating the downtown development and financial interests, which, like Wilson, were beginning to realize that the days of unrestricted growth were numbered. All the interests in this rather strange coalition found in the new mayor an intelligent, moderate Republican seeking to form a consensus that would support a reasonable program of controlled growth and economic progress. Wilson became the broker between the two factions and created policies that balanced their demands.

Relying on his expertise, energy, and ability to get diverse interests to work together, Wilson moved rapidly and made impressive strides in creating a growth-management plan, slowing suburban sprawl, and protecting the environment. As Wilson adroitly accumulated power, extensive changes were taking place: "The fiscal analyst reports to him; the transportation function has been transferred to planning, and the Mayor appoints the planning director; the Mayor is chairman of the legislative committee, so the city's lobbyists report to him; the Mayor is the City's representative in the Comprehensive Planning Organization [San Diego's Council of Government], so he participates in regional planning" (Keen, 1973, p. 77).

Wilson came to realize that while he had created a winning coalition, had gained support for his vision of a new era of progress in San Diego, and had expanded the role of the mayor, the city charter's council-manager form of government was a structural straitjacket. His ability to lead the city depended on his power of persuasion, not on the formal powers described in the charter, and so his leadership was severely limited: he had the responsibility to lead, but not the power. By 1973, the situation apparently had become intolerable, and Wilson proposed structural reorganization in the form of a charter amendment. The change would have given the mayor the power to create the budget, veto the council's acts, and hire and fire the city manager. The election was not even close; the measure was defeated by a vote of 102,000 to 62,000. In the minds of the voters, the reform ethic was stronger than Wilson's popularity, and he was forced to use other methods to consolidate the power he desired. During his five years in the California state assembly,

Wilson had observed firsthand, as party whip and close associate of Speaker Robert Monagan, the role of the speaker as leader of the assembly. Adapting this model to city government, Wilson devised a plan to increase administrative power by expanding his power as leader of the city council.

The popular (if simplistic) image of power in San Diego's government seemed to be that of a hydraulic system, whereby a decrease in the city manager's power would result in increased power for the mayor. Wilson's scheme—a city council committee system that would increase the role of the mayor and the council by reducing the city manager's role—played to this image. Less than two months after his proposed charter change was defeated, Wilson unveiled a proposal—adopted in 1974—that, by ordinance, created standing committees within the city council. Under the plan, the mayor would appoint the members and the chair of each of four standing committees, determine which legislation required committee review and which committee should review it, set the agenda of the city council and thereby decide the items to be listed for discussion and their order, and become chair of the Rules Committee, the most powerful of the committees. (The Rules Committee would consist of the mayor, the deputy mayor, and the chairs of the other three standing committees, thereby providing the mayor with almost total control over the committee—and the council.) Thus the mayor would hold the power of appointment and would control the flow of legislation, as well as the agenda. The appointment power would enable the mayor to place allies as chairs, to determine the membership of the committees, and to reward supporters. The mayor would also appoint the deputy mayor from among the members of the council.

To further diminish the manager's power, Wilson moved to lessen managerial control over the flow of information to the city council. He created several new positions, including an independent fiscal analyst within the mayor's office and consultants for each committee who were exempt from the city's civil service system and were therefore within his jurisdiction. The consultants, together with the new committee structure and a new Wilson-sponsored initiative (which the voters approved) to make the council a full-time legislative body, enabled the council to develop its own information independently of the city manager, draft ordinances, and undertake special studies. The budget, the primary determinant of city policy, was still created by the manager, according to the system that the voters had decided in 1973 to retain. But the fiscal analysts and the committee staff were now able to review and revise the budget to give the council an alternative proposal to consider. This significant expansion of policy control added greatly to the mayor's administrative power. Ray Blair, who served as city manager during a portion of Wilson's tenure, said of the full-time council members and their independent staffs, "That modification really changed the relationship between not just the mayor and the manager, but also the Council and the manager" (cited in Hill, 1990, p. 171). Another observer, retired State Appellate Court justice and charter commission chair Ed Butler, supports this view: "That was the spike in the heart of our city-manager form of government." Butler goes on to say, "No longer . . . did the council members act as 'the board of directors' of the city, but as independent department heads" (cited in Hill, 1990, p. 171). Of course, as would become apparent after Wilson's departure, increasing the power and autonomy of the council would be dangerous to the mayor if the mayor ever lost control of the council.

Wilson also moved to control appointments to city boards and commissions. Some of these bodies are limited in power and are merely advisory, but others have significant power. The ability to appoint over 150 allies to various boards and commissions shifted control over planning, spending, and administration of much of the city's future expansion into the mayor's office, in addition to providing Wilson with significant patronage power. Further increments of power came from changes in intergovernmental programs. Nixon's New Federalism, with its focus on decentralization, as exemplified by general revenue sharing and block grants, shifted greater control over federal programs to the offices of Wilson and other mayors throughout the nation. Money for federal programs, such as the Comprehensive Employment and Training Act, the Model Cities program, and general revenue sharing, flowed through the mayor's office, providing Wilson with a larger staff and greater control in critical areas.

In a 1976 reputational study of San Diego leaders, Pete Wil-

son appeared as the most influential person in the city—a big
change from the 1960s, when no local official had been listed (Erickson, 1977). The city was still listed by the International City Management Association as having a council-manager structure, and
the city's charter still adhered to the city manager form. But around
the City Administration Building, in the city's newspapers, at the
Chamber of Commerce, and wherever knowledgeable people discussed the issue, Wilson was recognized as the chief executive, the
person in charge. As Wilson's authority increased, a succession of
city managers found it difficult to operate under the mayor's evolving scheme. In 1978, after having outlasted three managers, Wilson
found one who was comfortable with his system. Indications of
popular support for Wilson's evolving chief executive form were his
reelections, by rather comfortable margins, in 1976 and 1980.

### The Emerging Chief Executive

Social, demographic, and economic conditions did pave the way for
alterations in the governmental structure of San Diego, but these
conditions did not guarantee Wilson's success or the evolution of
the office to that of a chief executive. The transformation required
Wilson to redefine the role of mayor in a council-manager government. Wilson's political leadership was assisted by a system that
called for a mayor elected at large and thereby gave him a constit-
uency that would support his efforts. His skills at getting elected
and reelected, raising money, forming a coalition of supporters in
this nonpartisan system, and assisting in the election of allies were
critical. As a young, attractive, articulate, well-organized, and well-
managed candidate who was not a part of the city's past political
system, Wilson was in a preferred position. The ability to appeal
to diverse interests in the city, to negotiate, to compromise, and to
form coalitions for managing conflict was also critical, given the
rapidly changing, heterogeneous population.

Wilson was the right person at the right time for San Diego.
His concept of leadership, which emphasized rational decisions
based on knowledge, matched the mood and expectations of his
generally well-educated public. Wilson appealed to the sense of
managed and controlled change, mixed with fiscal conservatism

and environmental preservation, that represented the view of the life-style liberal. He created his own political machine, based on his appeal and emerging power and on his ability to mediate conflict and build coalitions. He found and developed candidates, nurtured their progress, got them appointed or elected, raised money for them, and acted as their mentor. Wilson allowed his allies on the city council to operate independently on issues not important to him. On issues involving land use, downtown development, fiscal restraint, reduction of social services, appointments, or public employees, however, he expected and usually received support.

### "Après moi le déluge"

Pete Wilson left San Diego for the U.S. Senate in 1982, and the chaos that ensued and exists in the city to this day is testimony to the leadership, direction, and control he provided. After Wilson's departure, Roger Hedgecock defeated Maureen O'Connor in an acrimonious and expensive mayoral campaign filled with personal attacks by both candidates. Hedgecock eventually was forced to resign because of legal trouble over his campaign fundraising, and O'Connor was elected to replace him. Between the elections, during the mayor's court appearances, and at other times when there was either weak temporary leadership or no leadership from the mayor's office, the council moved to reduce some of the mayoral powers that Wilson had carefully accumulated. The council reduced or removed the mayor's appointment powers. It even overturned Hedgecock's appointments to council committees and inserted itself into the board and commission appointment process.

Before leaving office, Hedgecock had engineered the appointment of a new city manager. The new appointee arrived in San Diego and proceeded to operate as a strong city manager. He ran into trouble when he began to involve himself in community complaint functions and started to garner recognition in the media, both roles generally reserved for the mayor or the council or their personal staffs. He seemed not to recognize or care that the elected officials perceived that he was encroaching on activities from which they derived political power. In an ill-advised interview in the *Los Angeles Times,* he declared that he was going to be the most pow-

erful city manager he could be. Within eighteen months of his
arrival, he submitted his resignation to a city council that obviously
did not want a powerful city manager. Moving rapidly, the council
appointed from within an assistant city manager who had been
with the city for over twenty-five years. When that manager reached
retirement age and retired by his own choice, in 1991, the council
again turned to its own ranks to select the current city manager.

     After her election, Mayor O'Connor never exhibited the abil-
ity that Wilson (and even Hedgecock, before his legal difficulties)
had possessed to move the council in desired directions. Wilson had
sought out, nurtured, and helped elect council members; O'Connor
refused even to risk endorsements. Wilson had evoked a vision of the
city and moved through policy guidance to create it and through
administration to manage it; O'Connor seemed not to dream large
dreams and had problems articulating her vision, let alone creating
policies to guide and implement it. Wilson had controlled the council even in its deportment and public appearance; under O'Connor,
council meetings became chaotic and disruptive, and the members
seemed rude and/or bored. Wilson had maintained significant control over the budget; O'Connor allowed the city manager to dominate the budget process. Because of limited and sporadic direction
from the mayor, the council came to recognize its latent power,
which it had gained under Wilson (who had controlled it). But
without leadership from the mayor or from within the council itself, the council's power, like mayoral power in San Diego, drifted
toward entropy.

     The evolution begun by Wilson appears, given the expe-
rience of O'Connor in the same office, which retained most of the
powers created by Wilson, to have been based largely on his personal attributes. Without charter changes to preserve the alterations
made by Wilson, the evolution has become dependent on personality, rather than on formal powers and on the view of the office
held by the mayor. Permanence, predictability, and consistency
have become elusive, and each mayor redefines the office, consciously or unconsciously. The voters and the city staff are at the
mercy of the abilities and desires of the office holders, and the city
has no institutional integrity. One of the major lessons of San Diego's last two decades is that change must be institutionalized if it

is to resist the idiosyncrasies of personality. The confusion, drift, and lack of direction present in San Diego government are due in large part to the battle to fill the vacuum created by Wilson's departure. The council, the mayor, and the manager have attempted in turn to guide the city over the past nine years. For various reasons, all have failed. The lesson is that smooth transitions and continuity, without formal rules, are difficult to ensure.

## Quo Vadis?

As San Diego enters the last decade of the twentieth century, some twenty years after Pete Wilson's assumption of the mayor's office, how does it look, and what is its future? The 1990 census places San Diego as the sixth-largest city in the nation with a population of 1.1 million people, including a growing Latino and Asian population that, by early in the next century, will produce a city in which the Anglo population will be in the minority. The robust economy of the post-World War II era seems to be suffering from the worldwide recession and the reduction in defense spending. Nevertheless, the city's location on the Pacific Rim and its culturally diverse population should provide it with a sound economic future. The city, once dominated by a small group of economic notables, has given way over the last two decades to a politically, ethnically, economically, and geographically diverse community, which has become more pluralistic while retaining a political culture that favors a free-market economy (except for issues of land use), mainstream Republicanism, and fiscal frugality.

The political system continues to resemble a troika, with the council, the mayor, and the manager taking the lead at various times. Too often, however, the resemblance is to a team without reins. A 1988 charter amendment, which introduced district elections for council members, has had a profound effect on city governance. The first election after the amendment, in 1989, and the second, in 1991 (each one affecting four council members), removed three conservative Republican progrowth council members and one moderate Democrat, replacing them with four political neophytes who have slow-growth and populist views. Mayor O'Connor, who had seemed to benefit from the amendment by becoming the only member of the council elected citywide, continued to the end of her term, in 1992, to oppose the change. She was not successful in either forming or leading a coalition, even though there were more of her fellow Democrats on the council after the 1989 election than at any other time during her tenure.

A charter review commission projected its chair, Justice Butler, into the limelight and raised public discussion of the issue of strengthening the mayor's office. After the change to district elections, Butler said, "The momentum in city government is clear. With district elections you need a strong mayor" (cited in Hill, 1990, p. 168). The issue became conflictual, however, and the strategy for change became incremental. A potpourri of unrelated charter changes has been offered to the voters; none, however, directly addresses the issue of the mayor's role. This is unlike the experience in San Jose, where a charter commission presented a comprehensive plan for significant change in the council-manager plan, and voters agreed to the charter changes. San Diego moves more cautiously and incrementally. But, after twenty years of informal change, there does appear to be movement—if glacial—toward formal structural revision of the council-manager plan. Former city manager and strong council-manager proponent Ray Blair has publicly agreed to the need for comprehensive revision of the plan: "The mayor's office being strengthened is just one issue. The manager's role must be modified. The Council's role must be modified. The department heads' responsibilities, the budgeting process, the existence and role of the Civil Service Commission, the size of the staff of the councilmen, field offices, Council meetings, the continuation of the committee system—all of those are facets that must be looked at" (cited in Hill, 1990, p. 171). In the fall of 1993, an independent group of city leaders began drafting a charter amendment to produce a strong mayor–based form of city government to replace the council-manager plan. Initially, there appears to be widespread support.

### Conclusion

In San Diego, the council-manager system, viewed by many as being representative of progrowth forces and unable to provide for conflict resolution, continues to evolve toward stronger mayoral leadership.

The need for conflict resolution through political leadership has increased the visibility and the importance of the mayor. The eleven years of Wilson's transformations produced a new type of chief executive within the council-manager plan. Wilson expanded the mayor's role and the council's role but maintained control over the council. After his departure, there was a vacuum in the leadership ranks. City residents who had been comfortable with Wilson's view of the mayor's role have become uncomfortable with the lack of guidance currently provided by the mayor, the council, and the manager. Demands for leadership are growing, and it appears that changes to institutionalize the expanded role of the mayor, to move toward greater separation of executive and legislative powers, and to continue the move toward a chief executive are in San Diego's future.

## References

Abbott, C. *The New Urban America.* Chapel Hill: University of North Carolina Press, 1981.

Banfield, E., and Wilson, J. Q. *City Politics.* New York: Vintage Books, 1963.

Erickson, R. *Who's Running San Diego? A Sociological Investigation of Community Influence.* La Jolla, Calif.: Western Behavioral Science Institute, 1977.

Harrigan, J. *Political Change in the Metropolis.* (2nd ed.) Boston: Little, Brown, 1981.

Hill, M. "The Winds of Change." *San Diego Magazine,* Feb. 1990, pp. 100-105, 165-171.

Keen, H. "The Wilson Era: San Diego's New Power Structure." *San Diego Magazine,* May 1973, p. 77.

Lineberry, R., and Fowler, E. "Reformism and Public Policies in American Cities." *American Political Science Review,* 1967, *61,* 710.

Mollenkopf, J. *The Contested City.* Princeton, N.J.: Princeton University Press, 1983.

Sparrow, G. "The Emerging Chief Executive: The San Diego Experience." *Urban Resources,* 1984, *2,* 3-8.

Svara, J. *Official Leadership in the City: Patterns of Conflict and Cooperation.* New York: Oxford University Press, 1990.

*Edward Thompson III*
*David M. Brodsky*

10

# A Mayor in Commission and Mayor-Council Government: Mayor Gene Roberts in Chattanooga, Tennessee

The literature on the mayor has focused almost exclusively on executives in council-manager and mayor-council cities. More important, even though commission governments represent the initial effort at progressive structural reform, students of local government have failed to systematically examine mayoral leadership in commission cities. This chapter examines the effects of governmental form on political leadership, using data gathered from in-depth personal interviews conducted with government elites in a city that shifted from the commission form to the mayor-council form. Content analysis is used to answer two sets of questions. First, how do commission and mayor-council government elites perceive executive leadership? Do they hold differing perceptions of leadership exercised by the same executive? Second, how do commission mayors lead? Can they provide effective leadership?

## The Social and Political Context

Although a mixture of concerns motivated Chattanooga's 1911 shift to the commission form of government, race and partisan politics were the overarching factors. A small group of white Republicans formed a ruling coalition with African Americans, who were 40 percent of the population. Although whites dominated leadership positions, the ruling coalition was maintained by the appointment of a significant number of African Americans to government positions. The largely Democratic Hamilton County delegation to the Tennessee general assembly eventually succeeded in getting the legislature to amend Chattanooga's charter. The amended charter provided for the commission form of government, a system of at-large nonpartisan elections, and a reduction in the number of elected municipal officials from twenty-seven to five. In addition, the legislature eliminated "ward workers," who aided black voting, and made it illegal to pay another person's $2 poll tax.

The shift to a commission government had several effects. First, it reduced black voting and gradually eliminated blacks from elected and appointed public office. Second, it reduced political conflict by making blacks exclusively dependent on white decision makers. Third, business elites heavily influenced the initial commission governments, which tended toward a distinctly upper-class socioeconomic composition. Finally, eliminating blacks from public office and reducing their presence in the electorate freed business leaders to pursue the governmental efficiency that lay at the heart of the progressive political agenda. The resulting consensus, however, came at the expense of social and political representativeness.

The only major changes in Chattanooga politics and government over the next sixty years also served to reduce black political influence. A 1957 charter amendment, requiring commission candidates to run for specific posts effectively prevented African Americans from employing a "single shot" strategy to elect a black commissioner. When the percentage of blacks rose, in the late 1960s and early 1970s, the city offset these gains by annexing several mostly white suburban areas. Although voters eventually elected a relatively conciliatory African American as commissioner of health and education, in 1971, his election still left the black community disproportionately underrepresented.

The decision by blacks to file a lawsuit challenging Chattanooga's commission government reflected growing dissatisfaction with the city's political leadership. Efforts to rename a prominent thoroughfare in honor of Dr. Martin Luther King, Jr., met first with indifference and then with resistance and, finally, with unacceptably halfhearted measures. The shooting of three black women in downtown Chattanooga by members of the Ku Klux Klan angered the community. When the perpetrators received minimal sentences, residents in several black neighborhoods rioted. Then Mayor Pat Rose's appearance on the scene, with a revolver strapped to his hip, heightened tensions and generated nationwide media coverage. The questionable deaths of several blacks while in police custody added to the sense of frustration. Tensions were exacerbated during the 1980s as the local economy shifted away from a relatively high-wage industrial base to a low-wage service base.

A diverse group of activists, organizational leaders, and black professionals persuaded the Center for Constitutional Rights and the American Civil Liberties Union to file suit, challenging the structure of city government and the method of election. The suit contended that at-large commission elections violated Section 2 of the Voting Rights Act by diluting black voting strength and reducing the representativeness of local government. The plaintiffs also challenged an antiquated provision of the city charter that allowed nonresident owners of property in the city to vote in municipal elections.

The Federal District Court decided in favor of the plaintiffs and agreed that at-large elections had a discriminatory intent and effect. The court declared that property qualifications for nonresidents violated the Fourteenth Amendment to the United States Constitution and ordered the city and the plaintiffs to reach agreement on a new form of government, which would incorporate a system of district representation. The resulting plan called for a strong mayor-council government, with nonpartisan elections.

The change in government has transformed the character of Chattanooga politics. The inexperience of the new city council has helped the mayor dominate the policy-making process. Only the chair and the vice chair of the council have held previous elective office (city commissioner and school board member, respectively), and many observers believe that each of these individuals aspires to the mayor's office. Moreover, the increase in black representation, from 20 percent (one commissioner) to 44 percent (four councilmen), has brought a new dynamic to city politics. African American members of the council have boycotted government functions, questioned the mayor's commitment to affirmative action, persuaded their fellow council members to fund and attend a seminar on race relations, and voted against a resolution supporting local efforts to bring attention to child abuse because the organizers chose a white ribbon, representing "purity," as their symbol.

Although Chattanooga's government now represents the city's social composition more fully, it has yet to produce any fundamental changes in the distribution of city services or contracts. Nevertheless government officials clearly pay greater attention to questions of race in their deliberations and actions.

### Mayor Gene Roberts

Gene Roberts, the mayor of Chattanooga, has had a long career in public service. A native Chattanoogan, Mayor Roberts graduated from Chattanooga High School and the University of Chattanooga (now the University of Tennessee, Chattanooga). As a college student, he served as editor of the student newspaper. Roberts served with the Navy during the Korean War and played professional baseball after leaving the service. After graduating from college, Roberts became a special agent with the FBI. He later returned to Chattanooga as a reporter with both the *Chattanooga Times* and the *Chattanooga News-Free Press*. During his career with the *Times,* Roberts became associate editor.

As a public official, Roberts has held a variety of positions. He served as Chattanooga's fire and police commissioner from 1971 to 1979, when he accepted an appointed position as commissioner of the Tennessee Department of Public Safety, during the administration of Governor Lamar Alexander, a Republican. He was elected mayor in 1983 and has since been reelected twice. In the May 1990 election, held pursuant to the Federal District Court order, Roberts easily won election with 69 percent of the vote. Hence Roberts served as the last mayor under Chattanooga's commission form of government and as the first mayor under the new strong-mayor-council form.

## Methodology

The analysis presented here draws on data gathered from in-depth personal interviews with individuals who served in Chattanooga's old commission form of government and with officials serving in the new mayor-council government. The respondents considered a number of questions intended to assess their perceptions of the mayor's job responsibilities and leadership style under both forms of government. A content analysis served as the basis for categorizing responses and for describing the mayor's leadership style.

The panel of respondents included the mayor, the nine current members of the new city council, and incumbent administrators who also had served in the old government. In order to facilitate a comparison of the mayor's leadership style in the new mayor-council government with his leadership style during the two terms he served in the commission form, the panel included the seven individuals who had served on the city commission with the mayor. Blacks accounted for just over one-third of those interviewed (one former commissioner, three administrators, and four councilmen), and women made up just under 10 percent of the respondents (one administrator and one councilwoman).

## Gene Roberts's Leadership Style and Roles

Since Roberts was the mayor in office both before and after the change in the form of government in Chattanooga, it is possible to examine how the governmental structure and his individual characteristics have combined to affect his leadership style and roles.

### The Commission Form of Government

Previous studies of mayoral leadership style have focused on such diverse elements as political skills, approaches to problem solving, and relationships with the public and other political actors. Six such factors stand out as central elements of Gene Roberts's style: his proactive approach to problem solving; his willingness to try innovative solutions; his preference for addressing diverse problems through public-private partnerships; his reluctance to go to the public over the heads of other officeholders; his low-key, behind-the-scenes approach to consensus building; and his tolerance of other actors claiming credit for the policy successes that he has contributed to.

Chattanooga's efforts to bring the housing available to low-income residents up to code illustrate several elements of Gene Roberts's leadership style, especially his proactive approach to problems, his willingness to try innovative solutions, and his preference for public-private partnerships. The combined effects of urban renewal, downtown redevelopment, gentrification, changes in the federal tax code, and landlords' neglect had reduced the supply and quality of low-cost housing in the city, but the situation had not become critical. Nevertheless, the mayor offered behind-the-scenes political and financial support to the establishment of Chattanooga Neighborhood Enterprise (CNE), a not-for-profit organization, which would use public and private funds to make reduced-interest home-improvement loans available to low-income residents. After securing sufficient political support for the project, he made a public commitment of funds and pledged to support efforts to provide standard housing to all Chattanooga residents by the turn of the century. Toward this end, the mayor also supported, although to a limited extent, efforts to pass a local-option sales-tax referendum, which would provide additional funding for CNE's activities.

The formal position of mayor in Chattanooga's commission form of government more closely resembled the "chairman of the board" mayor that Svara (1987) has found in council-manager cities than the "chief executive" mayor found in strong-mayor–council governments. Chattanooga's old charter divided administrative authority among the five members of the city commission: the mayor and the commissioners of education, fire and police, public works, and public utilities. The five commission members shared responsibility for formulating policy, enacting ordinances, approving a budget, for hiring and firing city employees. Although the mayor had direct responsibility for such staff functions as finance and data processing, the personnel in these agencies depended on the other members of the commission, as well as on the mayor, for their appropriations and overall direction. The mayor also lacked the authority to interfere in the day-to-day operations of the line agencies under control of the other commissioners. Consequently, the commission form, as it evolved in Chattanooga, provided Gene Roberts with few of the formal resources available to mayors in strong-mayor–council cities. More important, the power-sharing characteristic of commission governments suggests an ability to build consensus among the members of the commission, a prerequisite of effective mayoral leadership.

Asked to describe his leadership style as mayor under the commission form of government, Roberts stressed his efforts to build consensus among his colleagues and to develop effective partnerships between government and the private sector. The data presented in Table 10.1 indicate that the other respondents, for the most part, agreed with the mayor's perception of his performance. Nearly three-fifths of the public officials who were questioned identified consensus building as a major role, while an additional 9 percent mentioned organizing relationships or roles among members of the commission. A number of factors affected the mayor's ability to forge a consensus. Positive factors included the mayor's skills as a listener, his reputation for integrity, his preference for working behind the scenes, and his willingness to let others publicly claim credit for accomplishments. Barriers to effective consensus building included such factors as complications arising from the use of intermediaries to avoid violating the open-meeting requirements of Tennessee's sunshine law, the mayor's inability to clearly articulate his positions, and the perception held by some that the mayor deliberately obscured his position on the issues at hand.

Although Gene Roberts was generally viewed as a consensus builder, several respondents indicated that the mayor frequently failed to develop a consensus before publicly announcing a new policy or program. In the words of a former commissioner, "He would surprise you with things . . . in open city commission meetings. . . . I think he went on the element of surprise as much as anything else." These comments appear to call into question the mayor's commitment to consensus building, but they speak more directly to the timing of his decisions.

A further examination of the data in Table 10.1 indicates that more than one-half of the sample mentioned the mayor's role as the city's chief financial officer. This finding comes as no surprise, in

Table 10.1. Mayoral Roles in the Commission Form of Government.

| Roles | Number of Respondents[a] | Percentage Responding[b] |
|---|---|---|
| Ceremonial and Presiding Duties | | |
| Performing ceremonial tasks | 2 | 9.1 |
| Being a spokesperson for the commission | 1 | 4.5 |
| Acting as presiding officer | 7 | 31.8 |
| Communication and Facilitation | | |
| Educating commission and public | 3 | 13.6 |
| Forming team, building consensus | 13 | 59.1 |
| Organization and Guidance | | |
| Setting goals, identifying problems | 2 | 9.1 |
| Organizing relationships and roles | 3 | 13.6 |
| Advocating policy | 2 | 9.1 |
| Promotion | | |
| Promoting city | 1 | 4.5 |
| Directing staff | 1 | 4.5 |
| Supervising financial operations | 12 | 54.5 |

[a]The total number of respondents was 22.
[b]The total far exceeds 100 percent because of multiple responses.

light of Chattanooga's recent history. During the early 1980s, Chattanooga, along with many of the nation's other cities, experienced severe financial distress, including inadequate revenues and a decline in the city's bond rating. A combination of factors, including substantial reductions in federal aid, continuing erosion of the city's industrial base (exacerbated by the nationwide recession), decline in sales-tax and property-tax revenues, and reluctance to raise tax rates in the face of a truculent electorate, contributed to the problem. Gene Roberts began his first term as mayor against this backdrop. He used his consensus-building skills and his formal authority to persuade his fellow commissioners to enact a series of measures that enabled the city first to weather the immediate crisis and then to gradually improve its financial health.

The collective leadership structure characteristic of a commission government tends to diffuse executive responsibility. Consequently, we expected relatively few respondents to single out problem identification, goal setting, and policy advocacy as significant components of Gene Roberts's role as mayor. The data shown in Table 10.1 confirm these expectations. Only four of the respondents characterized the mayor's job in terms of identifying problems, setting goals, and advocating solutions.

When analysis turns to a consideration of the ceremonial and presiding dimension of the mayor's responsibilities, the data provide several surprises. First, only one-third of the respondents identified the mayor's role as presiding officer at commission meetings as a significant element of his job. Second, very few respondents named such ceremonial tasks as presiding at groundbreakings or ribboncuttings as part of the mayor's job. Finally, only one respondent saw the mayor as a spokesperson or representative for the city of Chattanooga.

On balance, the data suggest that Mayor Roberts's personality interacted with the formal structure of the mayor's position in Chattanooga's commission form of government, to produce a leadership style that emphasized behind-the-scenes consensus building over highly visible policy entrepreneurship. Thus the mayor stressed the roles associated with communication and facilitation, rather than those related to promotion, organization, and presiding. This imbalance had several consequences. First, although the mayor persuaded his fellow commissioners to commit the city to a number of innovative and potentially significant projects, he rarely received credit for his role as the driving force behind them. Second, other local elected public officials, particularly the Hamilton County executive, dominated the policy agenda (at least the agenda presented by the media to the public). Third, and perhaps most important, the city's business leaders and members of the politically attentive public decried a perceived lack of vision and direction in city government, especially in the mayor's office. Indeed, the Chamber of Commerce emerged as a driving force behind efforts to replace the city commission with either metropolitan government or a strong-mayor–council government.

### The Mayor-Council Form of Government

Although the data indicate little change in Gene Roberts's leadership style, they do show substantial changes in perceptions of his job as mayor. Over four-fifths of the former and current municipal leaders who were interviewed singled out Gene Roberts's expanded administrative responsibilities as a central element of his job in the new strong-mayor–council government (see Table 10.2). Other frequently mentioned roles included organizing relationships and roles, advocating policy, and building consensus. Fewer respondents identified ceremonial roles, promoting the city, and setting goals as primary areas of activity.

### Structure and Leadership

The scholarly literature describing the relationship between institutional arrangements and mayoral leadership indicates that governmental structure powerfully affects an individual's leadership style and choices among alternative mayoral roles. The data graphically displayed in Figure 10.1, comparing respondents' perceptions of Gene Roberts's job in Chattanooga's strong-mayor–council government with their understanding of his job on the city commis-

Table 10.2. Mayoral Roles in the Mayor-Council Form of Government.

| Roles | Number of Respondents[a] | Percentage Responding[b] |
|---|---|---|
| Ceremonial and Presiding Duties | | |
| Performing ceremonial tasks | 2 | 9.1 |
| Being a spokesperson for the council | 2 | 9.1 |
| Acting as presiding officer | — | — |
| Communication and Facilitation | | |
| Educating council and public | 5 | 22.7 |
| Forming team, building consensus | 7 | 31.8 |
| Organization and Guidance | | |
| Setting goals, identifying problems | 1 | 4.5 |
| Organizing relationships and roles | 9 | 40.9 |
| Advocating policy | 7 | 36.4 |
| Promotion | | |
| Promoting city | 2 | 9.1 |
| Directing staff | 18 | 81.8 |
| Supervising financial operations | 3 | 13.6 |

[a]The total number of respondents was 22.
[b]The total far exceeds 100 percent because of multiple responses.

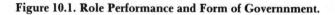

**Figure 10.1. Role Performance and Form of Governnment.**

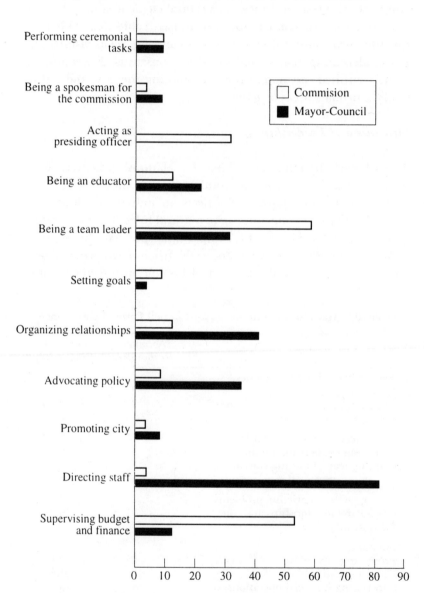

*Note:* The figure compares perceptions of the mayor's principal activities. The data are drawn from Tables 10.1 and 10.2.

sion, tend to confirm the hypothesized link between structure and leadership. An examination of Figure 10.1 reveals that the change in structure had little effect on the sample's perceptions of the cere- monial and spokesperson aspects of the mayor's job, but the imple- mentation of the mayor-council form did eliminate serving as presiding officer from the pool of roles that were identified. The change in form also altered the emphasis placed on the roles asso- ciated with communication and facilitation.

Seven of the nine new part-time city council members lack any prior governmental experience. Consequently, the respondents indicated, Mayor Roberts now spends a substantial proportion of his time trying to educate the novice council members about their responsibilities and those of the mayor, as well as about appropriate relationships between the two branches of city government. At the same time, the separation of powers built into the mayor-council government reduces opportunities for consensus building and raises the potential for conflict, a tendency exacerbated by the presence on the council of four African Americans, including one of the plain- tiffs in the federal court suit that resulted in Chattanooga's new form of government.

The new municipal structure upset a pattern of relationships developed over more than forty years. Administrators, who pre- viously had reported to one of the commissioners, now found them- selves directly accountable to the mayor. The mayor appointed two former commissioners as department heads. These individuals now had to relate to Gene Roberts as an administrative superior, rather than as a peer. More important, the court-ordered change in struc- ture added a city council with independent legislative and oversight responsibilities—a dramatic departure from the shared authority that had been characteristic of the city's commission government.

Thus members of the new government spent their first months in office developing an administrative structure, defining the responsibilities of the mayor and the council, and establishing relationships between the two. At the same time, the new govern- ment began to address a number of policy questions, including whether to seek federal funds for a fixed-rail trolley system through the downtown area and how best to deal with the need to reduce the volume of solid waste going to the city's landfill. The data displayed in Figure 10.1 indicate that these demands altered the extent of the mayor's involvement in the organizational and guidance roles. Specifically, the mayor now devoted substantially more effort to organizing relationships and to advocating preferred policy alternatives, and the mayor's involvement in directing staff increased substantially as he assumed responsibility for all administrative departments. A few respondents also specifically identified the mayor's continuing role as the city's chief financial officer.

### Mayoral Accomplishments: The Commission Era

During Gene Roberts's tenure as mayor in the commission era, Chattanooga undertook several major policy initiatives, including efforts to restore the city's fiscal health, continue downtown redevelopment, improve the quality of low-income housing, create an "incubator" to facilitate the growth of small businesses, expand the municipal airport, and develop the city's waterfront through construction of a major aquarium and restoration of the historically significant Walnut Street Bridge. With few exceptions (the Walnut Street Bridge restoration, the city's efforts to regain its financial health, and the airport expansion), these initiatives shared a number of characteristics. First, although many of these projects had their roots in private organizations, the mayor worked with these groups to develop additional private and governmental support. Second, the mayor's efforts generally took place behind the scenes, and he often received little or no credit for the projects once they had moved from the drawing board to the adoption and implementation phases of the policy-making process. Third, in most instances, the financial and administrative structures used in these projects involved some form of public-private partnership, ranging from Chattanooga Neighborhood Enterprise in the housing area to the River City Corporation for riverfront and downtown development. Finally, Mayor Roberts sought to build consensus for these projects among members of the city commission before going public. In cases where his efforts at consensus building failed, however, as they did in the case of the airport, the mayor demonstrated a willingness to push his plans through the commission in the face of intense opposition.

## *The Strong-Mayor–Council Era*

Chattanooga's mayor-council form of government is still in its infancy, but Mayor Roberts has several major accomplishments to his credit. Most important, he has fulfilled his responsibility to recommend an organizational plan and a budget for city government to the new council. When members of the council modified aspects of his plan in ways that potentially increased administrative accountability to the council, he accepted the proposed changes in a spirit of compromise. The mayor has also worked with the council to resolve the inevitable controversies regarding the division of responsibility and authority between the mayor and the council.

Despite the greater potential for conflict associated with the mayor-council form, the available evidence suggests that Gene Roberts has not really altered his leadership style. He still works to build consensus before presenting issues in a public forum. He has taken a more confrontational posture on some issues, however. For example, the city is considering a number of proposals for reducing its landfill requirements. Mayor Roberts generally favors curbside recycling; the chairman of the city council, a former commissioner, has advocated construction of a materials-recovery facility at the landfill. Both men have used the media and other public forums to advance their preferred alternatives and take potshots at each other.

## Leadership Type and Sources of Mayoral Leadership

Students of mayoral leadership have suggested a number of different schemes for classifying a municipal executive's leadership style. The preceding discussion of Gene Roberts's performance as mayor in the commission and strong-mayor–council forms of government suggests that his style incorporates several elements associated with the high-leadership type of executive but does not include others. On the one hand, his style includes a willingness to innovate; a high level of activism, characterized by networking at the local, state, and national levels; a basically conservative orientation in fiscal matters; a tendency to take liberal positions on some social issues; and a generally positive approach to his job as mayor. On the other hand, Gene Roberts prefers to work behind the scenes, eschews efforts to mobilize the public in support of his agenda, and avoids all but minimal steps toward the redistribution of political and economic resources. The commission form of government also denied the mayor the formal authority and strong political resources now available to him under the strong-mayor–council form.

## Leadership Resources

The case studies in this volume argue that mayoral leadership depends on a combination of structural and personal factors. Although most would agree with this conclusion, one still must question the relative importance of the different factors. Gene Roberts's performance as Chattanooga's mayor under both forms of government indicates that such personal factors as style, activity level, and vision powerfully affect the extent to which an individual executive takes advantage of the available institutional resources. Clearly, Gene Roberts has the personal qualities and political skills that made it possible for him to achieve a number of successes even with the limited resources associated with the mayor's position in the commission form of government. More important, his prior experiences seem to have shaped his performance as chief executive in the new strong-mayor–council government, where he has continued to emphasize consensus building rather than the executive leadership style usually associated with strong mayors.

## Conclusion

This case study has compared Gene Roberts's performance and leadership style as mayor in Chattanooga's new strong-mayor–council form of government with his performance and style as mayor in the old commission government. The study suggests several conclusions regarding mayoral leadership.

First, although students of mayoral performance tend to venerate the executive mayor found in mayor-council governments, the evidence from Chattanooga tends to support the conclusion that a facilitative leadership style may provide effective leadership in other forms of local government. Indeed, during his tenure as mayor in Chattanooga's commission government, Gene Roberts's accomplishments ranged from restoring the city's fiscal health to launching an innovative program to bring all housing in the city up to code by the turn of the century. Roberts managed to achieve these and other objectives even though he lacked many of the resources available to the chief executive in a mayor-council government. Instead, he used a facilitative style of leadership based on persuasion and consensus building—a style very similar to the one found in the council-manager cities and counties covered by the other case studies.

Second, comparison of the roles played by Gene Roberts in the strong-mayor–council government with those he played in the commission form indicates that while the structural aspects of the mayor's position may affect the relative importance of such individual activities as consensus building and policy advocacy, structural changes have minimal if any impact on leadership style. Indeed, leadership style seems more a function of personal qualities and preferences than of institutional resources—a conclusion suggested by Gene Roberts's continued preference for facilitative leadership, despite his having the additional resources provided by the strong-mayor–council form.

Finally, the results of the case study suggest that a full understanding of effective mayoral leadership will require more extensive empirical examination of leadership in commission governments.

## Reference

Svara, J. H. "Mayoral Leadership in Council-Manager Cities: Preconditions Versus Preconceptions." *Journal of Politics,* 1987, *49,* 207–227.

# 11

*James H. Svara*

# Key Leadership Issues and the Future of Council-Manager Government

Mayors and chairpersons can provide effective leadership in council-manager cities and counties; and in many (although not in most) cities and counties, they do. As the case studies in the preceding chapters demonstrate, the type of leadership provided matches a facilitative rather than a controlling, power-based model. This approach is well suited to the characteristics of the council-manager form of government and can work in the commission form. It is potentially useful in elected-executive forms as well. Knowledge and insights from the case studies encourage us to review and revise the ways we think about the office (see Chapter One) and permit us to refine our conceptualization of this position and of the facilitative leadership model.

    Changes in council-manager governments, however, and the special circumstances of very large cities raise questions about the relationship between political leadership and the future of council-manager government. In this regard, there are three issues to be explored.

The first issue concerns the style of the mayor or chairperson and the perception of leadership on the part of the media and the public. The type we have labeled the *comprehensive leader* or *director* receives recognition for leadership, whereas the *coordinator* does not necessarily get any more credit for leadership than a less effective mayor does. This is a problem that results partly from not defining leadership properly and from overlooking leadership of a facilitative nature. Nevertheless, it is also partly a reflection of the chief elected official's inability to communicate effectively with the public about where the city is headed. Insofar as it causes other officials or community leaders to bypass the chief elected officer, or even to recommend structural change to strengthen leadership, the failure to project a sense of purpose can limit the effectiveness of the chief elected official, produce distrust of the manager (who may appear to have more influence than is actually the case), and decrease the legitimacy of the government.

The second issue concerns whether structural change is needed to increase the leadership of elected officials—either modest adjustments in the mayor's position or changes that alter the form of government itself. Some take the position that only major structural change to expand the mayor's or chairperson's power over the manager will strengthen democratic leadership. The case studies have provided evidence that this approach is not necessary.

The third issue concerns whether changes in conditions in cities and in characteristics of city councils have altered the viability of the facilitative model of leadership. Once again, structural change is implicit in this issue. If the leadership style that is natural to the council-manager form is not viable, one must raise questions about the future of the form itself.

In dealing with all these issues, the argument will be made that it is a mistake to seek a quick structural "fix" by adding powers to the office of the chief elected official or changing the form of government. If structural change is not the answer to increased leadership, then alternative approaches are needed to enhance the leadership of the mayor or chairperson and make it more commonplace. Recommendations will be offered for strengthening mayors and chairpersons by increasing the likelihood and effectiveness of facilitative leadership in council-manager jurisdictions.

## Leadership of Chief Elected Officials in Council-Manager Jurisdictions: Evidence from Case Studies

The case studies presented in the previous chapters advance the conceptualization of the chief elected official's office and illuminate some aspects of the position not previously observed. These portraits of effective leaders in a variety of jurisdictions expand our repertoire of role models for council-manager jurisdictions and vividly depict how mayors and chairpersons can make unique contributions as political leaders in their governments. Observations and a summary of key points from the case studies are organized here in terms of the overall contributions, roles, types of leadership, relationships, and resources of effective leaders.

### Overall Contributions of Effective Leaders

What stands out most dramatically in the cases is the totality of positive effects that mayors and chairpersons can have on their communities. The parts of their leadership (their performance in specific roles) are important and will be sketched in the next section, but the whole of their leadership exceeds the sum of its parts. The activity of Mayor Mears of Decatur (Chapter Two) in the development of a hotel and convention center provides a good illustration of how specific roles are interwoven to provide general leadership on an important issue. He was a goal setter in developing support among community leaders for the project; a team leader in securing and holding on to the support of council members; a liaison with the city manager, whose activities complemented those of the mayor; a cheerleader in generating public support; a negotiator in dealings with property owners; and a representative of the city in contacts with various outside interests and agencies. Throughout, he coordinated his efforts with those of other key actors, who also made important contributions to the success of the effort, particularly the mayor pro tempore and the city manager. This example illustrates how effective mayors and chairpersons can take advantage of their strategic position and tap into the features of council-manager government to provide multifaceted leadership. In so doing, they expand the capacity of their governments to deal with the aspirations and needs of their communities.

The case studies demonstrate these broad contributions, more clearly than previous studies based on surveys. The contributions include the political and moral leadership that can be offered by the mayor or chairperson. As noted in the Preface, mayors and chairpersons as political leaders are operating at the interface between government and the community. Drawing on all their roles, they are engaged in shaping the governmental agenda (with varying mixtures of their own original ideas and ideas drawn from others), involving individuals and groups, mobilizing support, and establishing new relationships inside and outside the community. They can bring forth a commitment to the support of local governmental activities by convincing individuals and groups, as Mayor Taylor of Roanoke was adept at doing (Chapter Six), "what a difference it would make to the community." Other elected officials, the manager, and the staff also contribute to these activities. The potential for political leadership of mayors and chairpersons is unique, however, because they can weave communication channels together.

The mayor or chairperson, as the titular head of government, can also make a special contribution that bears on the legitimacy of the council-manager form, not simply by occupying the office but through actions that create widespread public recognition that the administrative structure is both an efficient mechanism for delivering services and a responsive and accountable part of a democratic local government.[1] Paula MacIlwaine (Chapter Three), as chairperson, helped reshape attitudes and promote acceptance of professionalism in a county government. Gary Halter, Jim Melvin, and Noel Taylor, among others, all gave explicit attention to monitoring and strengthening the values of the council-manager form of government and thereby strengthened the base of their own leadership in cooperative relationships with other officials.

## Leadership Roles

The cases contribute to a fuller understanding and an expanded definition of the roles that mayors and chairpersons can fill. Examples presented here correspond to the eleven roles listed in Chapter One.

Performing ceremonial tasks can be a tremendous asset if that role is used by the mayor to build public trust and support for other activities. Many of these officials were adept at linking ceremonial activities with substantive concerns and policy positions of the government. For example, Carla DuPuy (Chapter Five) dramatized the need for new approaches to solid waste and county recycling programs by climbing into a garbage can at a "pseudoevent." Betty Jo Rhea (Chapter Seven) was able to use these occasions to communicate on a personal level about what the city was doing. Michael Mears built his leadership partly by showing up and being highly visible as a representative of the city. Noel Taylor was adept at instilling civic pride by using ceremonial events for celebration. As Gary Halter (Chapter Eight) points out, however, ceremonial activities can also be a trap that consumes a lot of time and energy at the expense of other aspects of the job; mayors and chairpersons must be selective. Some mayors lessen the burden by actively involving other members of the council in ceremonial tasks and delegating many appearances to them.[2]

The spokesperson role is closely related to the ceremonial role, since the mayor or chairperson, in appearances before groups, is often disseminating information about the work of local government. The mayor personalizes communication about local government through contacts with a wide range of people. The cases clearly indicate that the mayor or chairperson is engaged in two-way communication, which the term *spokesperson* does not fully capture. Noel Taylor's accessibility affected the way people in the city related to government. Gary Halter saw himself as a "complaint center," receiving a large number of comments from citizens about their problems and concerns. (Halter also points out the importance of avoiding the dual trap of either inviting ever more complaints or becoming the person who tries to resolve them by channeling them directly to the manager or the appropriate staff member.) Mayors and chairpersons are a visible point of contact and represent an important link between government and citizens. Indeed, linkage is the essential aspect of this role. One means of formalizing the spokesperson role (and possibly the roles of educator and goal setter) is the "state of the city" address (see Chapters Six and Seven).

The mayor or chairperson, as presiding officer, is responsible for ensuring the orderly conduct of council meetings. Some, like Jim Melvin, are able to use this role to exert influence over the way issues are handled and how (and when) they are resolved. Carla DuPuy selected issues on which she would provide direction to the board. By extension, like Betty Jo Rhea, the mayor or chairperson may work with the manager in developing meeting agendas.

As educator, the mayor or chairperson can raise public consciousness about an issue. The ability to articulate issues is an important aid in education. Effective mayors have the ability to frame, explain, and communicate an issue in a way that it is recognized by other officials and the public; for example, consider John Crowley's articulation of the fiscal crisis in Pasadena, discussed in the Preface. Carla DuPuy viewed her job as one of raising the community's attention. Her approach demonstrates that active leaders merge educational efforts with efforts to build support for action. Articulation and mobilization, although conceptually distinct, are often blended. Mayors and chairpersons are key actors in generating support for public projects. They are often cheerleaders for their jurisdictions, as when they recruit new business.

The role of liaison with the manager is illuminated by all the cases. The nature of this relationship is important to the manager's performance because, as Wheeland (Chapter Seven) observes with regard to Mayor Rhea, the manager's effectiveness increases when the right mayor or chairperson is in place. A number of the cases demonstrate that the mayor or chairperson not only can improve communication between the council and the manager but also can engage in active partnership with the manager. For example, Mayor Mears and city manager Curtis Branscome had a complementary relationship. The mayor was the optimist, espousing arguments to support initiatives, whereas the manager was the pessimist, providing "reality checks" and making sure that plans were workable. In other situations, the roles might be reversed. Bob Herbert, city manager of Roanoke (Chapter Six) illustrates a more active role in initiating proposals, with the mayor determining by means of this support whether a project would be successful. Other chief elected officials, like Jim Melvin and Carla DuPuy, worked with their managers in a give-and-take manner.

Team building is advanced by explicit group-development measures (such as those used by Jim Melvin), by a general style that promotes a sense of cohesion and common purpose (compare Carla DuPuy, Betty Jo Rhea, and Noel Taylor, among others), and by an emphasis on collaborative decision making (see Michael Mears's style of settling disputes). One approach used by at least two officials (Carla DuPuy and Paula MacIlwaine) is the skillful use of questions to guide discussion toward agreement, as when DuPuy would ask, "What do we need to do to make this work?" Rhea recognized the importance of fairness to all council members in arranging compromises.

The cases make it clear that team building extends beyond working with the council, to building a broader network of support and interaction. Rhea made use of an extensive information network consisting of organizations at the local, state, and national levels. MacIlwaine broadened the boundaries of the team to include other elected county officials—the county engineer, the auditor, the county prosecutor, and the sheriff—and incorporated them into planning and decision making. She also built a network of support among business and labor leaders, party officials, local governmental officials, nonprofit service and cultural organizations, and other citizens by including them in a strategic planning process.

Goal setting was accomplished by some leaders through attention to matters that required action (Melvin), retreats for the council (Halter), or the fostering of community-based strategic planning (Rhea, Taylor, MacIlwaine.) The chief elected official may focus on specific goals or foster a general orientation: a climate for positive change (Taylor), a sense of direction (Rhea), or a common commitment to problem solving (DuPuy). For the facilitative mayor, goal setting is a collaborative process. Mears helped other council members get things accomplished. DuPuy would draw on information and ideas from a variety of sources inside and outside of government, until a plan was developed that most participants could claim parts of as their own. Taylor used his annual "state of the city" address to make recommendations derived from the public, the city staff, and his own ideas about what would move the city ahead.

Delegating or organizing involves assigning tasks, to ensure that coordination is maintained. The chief elected official monitors the governmental process and makes adjustments, as necessary. For example, Carla DuPuy selected the issues to which she would pay attention partly on the basis of what was left over. By so doing, she empowered other commissioners to pursue their areas of interest and avoided competition over who would take the lead. She also ensured that important concerns, like solid-waste disposal, were not neglected.

The mayor or chairperson can also take steps to reinforce the values and division of functions in a council-manager government, by instituting an evaluation process for the manager, setting goals for improved staff productivity, and seeking to improve the sensitivity of staff to citizens, as Jim Melvin did. This role involves active support for the council-manager form, including acting as a political buffer between the manager and unwarranted outside attacks (see Chapter Eight).

As policy advocate, the mayor or chairperson initiates programs and policies to address problems in the community. Examples include creating a foundation for industrial development (Halter), a hotel and convention center (Mears), a regional waste-treatment facility (Melvin), and welfare reforms (MacIlwaine). If active in this role, the chief elected official is instrumental in shaping the policy agenda. The agenda can have the clear stamp of the mayor or chairperson but still be drawn from the council and other sources (Mears, Melvin), or it can be derived primarily from the mayor or the chairperson's personal preferences (Halter, MacIlwaine).

Mayors and chairpersons are usually actively engaged in external relations. The activities that fall into this category are diverse and cover many of the roles already discussed. Promotion of the city is closely linked with the ceremonial role (Betty Jo Rhea). In the council-manager form, mayors and chairpersons are uniquely situated to take the initiative in relations with other governments because they act as official representatives. Building working relationships with other governments involves networking (Rhea). Some policy initiatives (such as the countywide tax-sharing program promoted by MacIlwaine, or the founding of a new megaregional organization by DuPuy) involve intergovernmental relations. Rather than separate external relations into a separate role, it is more useful to add an external-relations aspect to other roles, where this aspect would be relevant. These points also suggest that the activity of the mayor or chairperson, as official representative and promoter, should be recognized as a distinct role.

### Revision of Roles

The evidence from the case studies greatly enriches our description of the eleven roles already identified in Chapter One. The cases also point to some shortcomings and limitations in the list of roles. Here is a revised list:

#### Traditional and "Automatic" Roles

1. Ceremonial figure: giving speeches, offering greetings, cutting ribbons
2. Link to the public: acting as spokesperson for the council; announcing and explaining positions taken by the council; receiving comments and complaints from citizens; making government more accessible to citizens; conducting media relations
3. Presiding officer: facilitating discussion and resolution of business in council meetings; helping determine agenda for meetings
4. Representative and promoter: acting as liaison with local, state, and federal governments; promoting intergovernmental cooperation; acting as a representative of the council before outside agencies; promoting the city or county; creating a positive image; attracting development

#### Active Coordinating and Communicating Roles

5. Articulator and mobilizer: educating the council, manager, and/or public; articulating issues; promoting understanding of problems; instilling awareness of the need for action; building support for projects

6. Liaison and partner with the manager: being the council's liaison with the city manager; increasing communication and understanding between the council and the manager; building teamwork and sharing tasks with the manager in a complementary way
7. Team relations and network builder: unifying the council; establishing a positive tone for the council; developing a network of communication and support inside and outside government; helping others accomplish their goals; actively involving the community in governmental affairs

*Policy and Organizing Roles*

8. Goal setter: setting goals and objectives; identifying problems; lining up majorities on the council; building consensus; creating a sense of direction and a climate for change
9. Delegator/organizer: assigning tasks for coordinated effort; helping the council and the manager maintain their roles; helping council members recognize their responsibilities; defining and adjusting the relationship between the council and the manager; defending the values of council-manager government
10. Policy initiator: developing programs and policies to address problems; shaping the policy agenda

The first four roles have been labeled *traditional* or *"automatic."* These roles are built into the office; all mayors and chairpersons play them unless they make an effort to avoid them. Obviously, mayors (and chairpersons, perhaps to a slightly lesser extent) are asked to perform ceremonial tasks. As noted earlier, these may be either an opportunity or (if accepted with no constraints) a curse. The second role has been broadened from "spokesperson," to recognize the general role played by the mayor or chairperson as a link to the public. Beyond announcing and explaining positions taken by the council, the chief elected official, by virtue of the nature of the office, receives a large volume of comments and complaints from citizens and has extensive dealings with the media. Thus this official makes government more accessible to citizens. As presiding officer, the mayor or chairpersons foster discussion and resolution of business in council meetings and may help develop meeting agendas. A new role added to this set is that of representative and promoter. This role builds on the other traditional ones and includes those contacts that the chief elected official, as titular head, has with other local governments and with state and federal government agencies. Contacts with external agencies are closely related to the general activity of promoting the jurisdiction and creating a positive image.

The next three roles involved active coordination and communication—active in the sense that the mayor or chairperson must recognize and choose to fill them; these roles are not built into the position.[3] In this set of roles, we are likely to see the differences between the approach and effectiveness of an activist mayor or chairperson and a passive one. The first role in this set, formerly the educator role, has been expanded and renamed the role of articulator and mobilizer. As already noted, it is difficult in practice to distinguish between efforts to educate and efforts to convince or win support. A key aspect of this role is raising awareness by articulating issues and promoting understanding of problems, but these activities are also usually undertaken with the intent of prompting action. The role of liaison with the manager continues to be very important in this conceptual framework but has been broadened to recognize the active partnership that may exist between the mayor or chairperson and the manager. The role of team leader has also expanded and now includes networking; thus the role is now that of team relations and network builder. Effective mayors not only unify the council and establish a positive tone but are also likely to develop networks of communication and support that extend outside government. These mayors actively involve the community in governmental affairs as well. One aspect of this role is helping others accomplish their goals.

The final three roles are essentially the same as before, but each has been broadened somewhat. In the role of goal setter, there is general as well as specific leadership, as when the mayor or chairperson creates a sense of direction or a climate for change. Consensus building is connected with this role, too, since consensus appears to be reached in terms of common goals. The role of delegator and organizer is the same, with the addition of defending the values of council-manager government. The mayor or chairperson who is effective in this role adjusts relationships not only internally but also externally. He or she can then provide a buffer between governmental officials and the public and help orient staff to citizens in a more positive way. The final role is that of policy initiator (formerly advocate). This change distinguishes the mayor or chairperson who develops programs and policies to address problems. Advocacy of policies shaped by others (including the mayor or chairperson) is included in the role of articulator and mobilizer; the policy initiator has a substantial impact on the shaping of the governmental policy agenda.

In sum, the case studies in this volume have clarified the roles, as originally described in Chapter One, and offer a wider range of activities to illustrate them. The revised list of roles now includes only ten and eliminates external relations as a separate role category. Virtually all the roles have been broadened to capture a wider range of interactions and more active involvement of other officials and persons, organizations, and agencies outside of government. Of course, these roles are mutually reinforcing. Success in one enhances success in the others. Furthermore, they are played concurrently.

## Types of Leadership

There is variation in the nature and scope of leadership even among the effective mayors who are the subjects of the preceding cases. The distinction between the coordinator and the director, based on previous research, is further substantiated by most of the cases. Both types create an atmosphere that promotes cohesion and communication among officials and strengthens the capacity of the council to identify problems and make decisions. The coordinators—Rhea, DuPuy, Taylor, and possibly Gene Roberts of Chattanooga (Chapter Ten)—are not strongly associated with a policy agenda of their own, even though they contribute to fashioning and acting on agendas. The directors—Halter, MacIlwaine, Mears, and Melvin—do have their "own" policy agendas, although these reflect to a greater or lesser extent, the views of other officials. This is a subtle distinction in the sense that neither type is a solitary leader, and both types

have broad goals for their cities. The coordinators are also associated with selected policy initiatives, as pointed out in the Preface.
The distinction is captured, however, by Winner's observation
(Chapter Six) that Mayor Taylor believed that he knew what was
best for Roanoke and did want to be progressive, but without any
specific agenda. Wheeland (Chapter Seven) points out Mayor
Rhea's concern about policies, but he also says that Rhea does not
attempt to develop them and have them adopted by public officials
and community leaders. Rhea's policy leadership is more general,
according to Wheeland. Mead, in Chapter Five, notes that Carla
DuPuy espoused no particular issues and had no preestablished
agenda.

It is difficult to classify Gene Roberts as a commission
mayor. He was viewed as proactive and innovative, and yet he received low marks as goal setter and policy advocate. (Only 9 percent
of the respondents saw these as major roles that he filled.) His
strongest area of performance was in forming consensus as a team
builder.

The chairpersons and mayors who are coordinators have
been highly effective at developing a sense of cohesion and purpose
in their cities or counties. The spirit of cooperation they have
helped instill did not exist before they took office. Part of their
leadership has been to shape the policy-making process. They are
not themselves active policy initiators, however. They have raised
issues, and they have advanced policies, but they are more process-
oriented than policy-oriented.

The directorial mayors and chairpersons have created agendas
in the sense that they have originated agendas (at least in part) and
put their imprint on them, and they are recognized by other officials
and by the public for this contribution. These officials have fully
developed all aspects of the office. They provide traditional, coordinative, organizing, and policy leadership. Because of the scope and
extent of their activity, they are perceived as leaders by the public and
the media. This becomes an important resource in itself. By incorporating policy and organizing in their facilitative leadership, these
officials provide a focal point for their governments.

Differences between the coordinators and the directors in
these case studies are somewhat muted because the coordinators

engage in some of the policy and organizing roles. They are strong at goal setting, and they promote understanding of roles and a constructive division of labor between the council and the manager. They also have been responsible for some policy initiatives and are seen as contributors to policy formation. Rhea is probably typical of this group: among all the roles she performs, she received the lowest rating from other officials for developing programs and policies, but that rating was moderately good, rather than below average or poor.

### Relationships

The cases illuminate the mayor's or chairperson's key relationships with the council, the manager, and the community. With regard to the council, a mayor may fill a vacuum by proposing policy ideas, and the council may then be receptive to the mayor's lead. In other situations, the mayor or chairperson works to fashion an agenda from a fragmented council or helps the council develop its own agenda. It would appear that the latter condition is becoming more common. The San Diego case (Chapter Nine) raises a question: Should the mayor be given power over the council, in order to bring the council into line with his or her agenda? The other case studies indicate that with team building, active involvement, and patient listening, it is possible for the mayor or chairperson to pull council members together into a functioning group, not necessarily agreeing with each other on all substantive matters but agreeing to support a process of making decisions. If no one on the council is able to promote sufficient cohesion, then the local government is hamstrung, and the remedies recommended by Sparrow in Chapter Nine may be necessary.

In relationships with the manager, the case studies indicate (again with the exception of San Diego) that strength and effectiveness in the mayor's or chairperson's office support rather than weaken the manager. The chief elected official helps promote communication between the council and the manager and shields the manager from interference. As noted in the discussion of the liaison role, mayors or chairpersons and managers, in many cases, have developed partnerships in which each side complemented the other in active joint leadership.

In relationships with the community, the mayor or chairperson helps link citizens with local government. Several leaders featured in the case studies took active steps to involve citizens in decision making. By such actions, a chief elected official makes government more accessible and increases citizens' input. With strong moral leadership, the mayor or chairperson contributes to the legitimacy of the council-manager form and strengthens the position of the manager. Some mayors used analogies, such as "parish" or "family," to suggest the close relationship between citizens and government.

Effective mayors and chairpersons extended external relations to key community groups, economic interests, governmental officials, and other organizations, agencies, and governments from which the local government needed support or resources. The ability to establish and broaden networks was a key attribute of these chief elected officials. Again, there is no clear distinction between the coordinators and the directors in their adeptness at handling these relationships.

## Resources

The resources needed to fill the mayor's office, as suggested in previous research, fall into the categories of formal and informal resources that determine the *nature of* the office and resources that define *performance in* the office. The cases indicate that facilitative leadership does not depend on a position of superior power. There are resources available in the council-manager form, and within the incumbent as a person, to develop leadership in the areas of coordination and policy guidance. The strategic location occupied by the chief elected official provides the foundation for effective leadership. Mayors and chairpersons with a clear conception of the job—its possibilities, interdependencies, and limitations—are more likely to be able to take advantage of this resource.

Willingness and ability to commit time can give the mayor or chairperson a relative advantage over other officials (examples include DuPuy, Mears, Melvin, Rhea, and Taylor), but this does not mean that the amount of time per se determines effectiveness. Halter contrasts the way he used his own time with the approach of the mayor in the neighboring city of Bryan. That mayor also spent a substantial amount of time on the job, but it was largely taken up by the time-consuming traps that Halter sought to avoid.[4] Jonathan Howes, former mayor of Chapel Hill, North Carolina, has observed that over his years in office, a number of council members began spending more time in their positions than he did as mayor.[5] Highly active council members may increase the difficulty the mayor has in coordinating their efforts. Mayors cannot become leaders by dint of the time spent on the job alone, yet a minimal commitment appears to constitute the *sine qua non* of success. It is not the amount of time per se that is important but what use is made of it and how it is converted to other resources, like knowledge or networks.

The importance of personal qualities in determining the inclination of individuals to seek leadership and their ability to exercise it is confirmed by the cases. Energy, resourcefulness, contacts, connections, the ability to communicate, a clear sense of purpose, and the ability to keep sight of broad goals while making specific choices are important for leadership in any setting. Effective leaders have a positive attitude and are able to convey that orientation to others. These qualities must be channeled into appropriate role behavior, however. In council-manager governments, the foundational roles—performing ceremonial tasks, presiding, linking the government to the public, representating, promoting, articulating, mobilizing, serving as a liaison, and building teams and networks— support goal setting, organizing, and policy initiation. A highly committed, assertive, impatient mayor or chairperson can jump into the higher-level roles without developing the others, but he or she runs the risk of having only short-term success or being isolated from the council.

Information is a key resource. Through self-education, the chief elected official stays on top of issues. A high level of knowledge strengthens the mayor or chairperson in interactions with the rest of the council, staff, and citizens and is a source of influence in working with others. Mayor Rhea made good use of her trips to other cities, learning about practices that could be considered at home.

The cases illustrate the importance of the strategic location of the chief elected official. He or she is in a favorable position to secure and channel information and build relationships. A resource most clearly manifested by Carla DuPuy and Paula MacIlwaine was close contact with staff. Knowing staff personally and communicating with them informally were assets, in terms of information and sympathetic responses to ideas. The chief elected official must clearly show that these ties to staff will not lead to any bypassing of the manager or to any attempts to take individual action to remedy problems; doing so will jeopardize working relationships with the manager and/or the council.

Another resource is integrity. It undergirds the trust that other officials have in the mayor or chairperson. One of Mayor Taylor's assets was that he was considered to be both above reproach and clearly concerned about the public interest, rather than about self-interest. Similarly, Mayor Rhea was viewed as an "honest broker" who could be counted on for fairness in working out compromises with the council.

To be effective as a coordinator or director, the mayor or chairperson needs certain interpersonal skills for leadership. The mayor or chairperson must be effective at working with others and must accept certain responsibilities to them. Inclusiveness, sharing of information, facilitation of the expression of divergent views, and ability to resolve differences are important traits for the mayor or chairperson to have in his or her dealings with the council. The relationship with the manager requires tact, respect, the ability to share authority, and trust in the manager's commitment to advancing the goals of the city and achieving the highest performance from government as a whole.

Finally, mayors and chairpersons need to be flexible and capable of shifting the emphases they place on their different roles. The chief elected official acts as a stabilizer who attends to those areas where contributions are needed at a given time. As a consequence, the mayor or chairperson may shift in the extent to which he or she is central to decisions, visible to the public, and assertive of his or her own point of view, depending on conditions. Despite this flexibility, however, one constant should be a clear sense of purpose, which is conveyed by the mayor or chairperson to all participants in the governmental process.

Here is a summary of the factors that contribute to the effective performance of a mayor or chairperson:

### Resources Derived from Position

- Strategic location for securing and channeling information and building relationships
- Access to information
- Support of and interaction with the city or county manager
- Staff support necessary for filling demands of the ceremonial role
- Powers and duties that enhance visibility and support the delegator role of the mayor or chairperson but do not isolate him or her from other members of the governing board, as such powers as veto or staff-appointment authority would do

### Informal Resources

- Support of key groups in the community
- Contacts and connections; desire to expand network
- Media attention and support

### Personal Resources, Attributes, and Characteristics

- Clear conception of the office
- Understanding of how to fill roles appropriately and of how to use traditional and coordinating/communicating roles as the foundation for goal setting, organizing, and policy initiation
- Clear sense of purpose
- Time to devote to the office (with efficient use of time, avoidance of traps, and conversion of time to other resources, such as knowledge and network building)
- Energy
- Positive attitude
- Resourcefulness
- Integrity and fairness
- Commitment to full involvement of members of the governing

board through inclusiveness, sharing of information, support for the expression of divergent views, and acceptance of the initiative of other members

- Respect for authority and prerogatives of the city or county manager

*Skills*

- Ability to communicate (particularly active listening and effective speaking)
- Ability to set goals and priorities and keep sight of broad goals while making specific choices
- Ability to enlist and motivate others
- Ability to resolve conflicts and differences
- Flexibility (ability to shift the emphasis placed on different roles)

There is considerable interaction among these factors. As we have seen, the position itself, with no unilateral powers over other officials, permits the mayor or chairperson to establish positive relationships with those officials—but only if he or she has a good appreciation of the potential of the office and possesses skills of facilitative leadership. This array of factors indicates that personal attributes and skills are more numerous and important than either formal or informal resources.

### Constraints

Mayors and chairpersons depend on internal and external support to be effective. Inside the government, the council's response is critical. Externally, the chief elected official needs to be able to draw on the support of key groups, sources of influence, and shapers of values. Durning (Chapter Two) points out that although Mayor Mears benefited from the backing of the council and influential groups, internal and external support, by their very nature, may become constraints on the mayor's leadership. Clearly, the permission of the council is needed in order for mayors and chairpersons to work on their own agendas. The check of the council also compels the mayor to act in a facilitative way and adopt roles that stress teamwork. The chief elected official cannot act alone or compel the council's support, and so there must be reciprocity between him or her and the council, both in goals and in style. Furthermore, the issues and policies pursued by the mayor or chairperson are likely to be limited to those that have the support of the governing coalition in the community. It is a powerful asset for the chief elected official to be able to tap into support for consensus goals in the community. Moreover, the effective mayor or chairperson can be more successful in accomplishing these goals than the governing coalition can be, acting on its own or through a poorly led council. The reverse side, however, is that the chief elected official will have difficulty seeking to move beyond or to change those goals.

Durning suggests that more attention be given to the relationship between the roles and resources of mayors and chairpersons and the context in which certain values, goals, and leadership roles and styles are permitted, required, or constrained. This is an important area for further inquiry. It is clear that all the directorial chief elected officials were drawn from or represented the views of the most influential groups in the community, although it would appear that some (for example, MacIlwaine) helped shape or reconfigure the governing coalition. They not only acted on but also helped identify goals. For example, Halter appeared to give the council a sense of purpose, to a greater extent than he received permission from it, partly because he discreetly helped get supporters elected to the council. Melvin, by contrast with his predecessors and successors, defined his relationship with the council, rather than simply accepting a definition from the council, as did Mears. The cases suggest that the *interaction* between the chief elected official and the internal and external sources of support should be examined, and that researchers should be open to the possibility that the influences run in both directions.

### Recap: The Facilitative Model of Leadership

The mayors and chairpersons profiled in the case studies are practitioners of facilitative leadership. The leadership they provide, the roles they fill, the relationships they establish, the resources they use, and the constraints under which they operate are grounded in a facilitative model. Their experience indicates that one can conceive of leadership in government as collaborative and as focused on the accomplishment of common goals. In the alternative innovative-entrepreneurial model, leadership is competitive and focused on individual goals. The former model presumes that relationships among officials are essentially cooperative—a condition commonly produced by the integrated authority of the council-manager form. The latter is appropriate to a setting in which relationships are conflictual—a condition typically produced by the separation of powers in the mayor-council or county executive forms of government.[6]

From the case studies, the facilitative model in local government can be elaborated more fully than before. The characteristics of the facilitative leader can be divided into three categories: the leader's attitude toward other officials, the kinds of interaction the leader fosters, and the leader's approach to goal setting:

### Attitude Toward Other Officials

- The leader does not attempt to control or diminish the contributions of other officials.
- The leader empowers others by drawing out their contributions and helping them accomplish their goals.
- The leader values and maintains mutual respect and trust.

### Kinds of Interaction Fostered

- The leader promotes open and honest communication among officials.
- The leader seeks to manage conflict and resolve differences in a way that advances the mutual interests of all officials.
- The leader is willing to share leadership and form partnerships.
- The leader fosters understanding of distinct roles and coordinated effort among officials.

### Approach to Goal Setting

- The leader fosters the creation of a shared vision, incorporating his or her own goals and the goals of others.
- The leader promotes commitment to the shared vision.

- The leader focuses the attention and efforts of officials on accomplishing the shared vision.

This kind of leader is committed to helping other officials accomplish their goals. He or she promotes open communication among officials. His or her approach to managing conflict stresses collaboration, in which the interests of the leader and others are mutually satisfied, as opposed to competition (assertion of one's own preferences over those of others), accommodation (sacrificing of one's own interests to those of others), compromising (splitting the difference among interests), or avoiding (ignoring conflict) (see Thomas and Kilmann, 1974). The leader shares leadership and seeks to coordinate efforts among officials. Finally, the leader seeks to create a shared vision that incorporates his or her own goals and the goals of others, promoting commitment to the vision and focusing everyone's effort on accomplishing it.

Described in this way, the practice of facilitative leadership is not confined to a particular official. Other members of the council and the manager can and frequently do use the same style in their own behavior. The connection of this style with the chief elected official is stressed here for two reasons: first, it is the approach to leadership that best suits the nature of the office in the council-manager form of government; and second, without effective facilitative leadership from the mayor or chairperson, it is more difficult for other officials to sustain a collaborative approach to achieving goals on their own. Consequently, the facilitative model is integrally (but not exclusively) linked to the chief elected official.

### Issues: Leadership Type and the Visibility of the Mayor

The distinction between the coordinator and the director may have a bearing on public perception of the mayor's or chairperson's effectiveness. If the key coordinator roles of team builder, liaison, and broker of information are stressed, with little initiation of policy, leadership may be relatively invisible.[7] The assessment of Gene Roberts's leadership appears to have been lowered by his working behind the scenes and allowing others to take credit for ideas that he initiated. A low profile and, in the council-manager governments, a harmonious working relationship with the manager may be interpreted to mean that the mayor or chairperson makes no particular contribution.

Similarly, if members of the council are highly independent, the mayor or chairperson may appear to be insignificant. The chief elected official will have difficulty countering this perception if the council members often move in separate directions. The mayor's or chairperson's job can become a lot like herding cats. Helping the council members move in the same direction and function effectively as a group is an accomplishment, but one that may not be recognized by the media and citizens.

In the four case studies of coordinative leaders presented in this volume, there appears to be broad appreciation of the chief elected official's leadership contributions. If the mayor or chairperson is not associated with an agenda, however, there is a greater chance that he or she may be perceived as weak and ineffective. Take the example of the mayor of Sacramento who served in from 1984–1992. A newspaper review of the positive and negative assessments of her performance captures the difficulty of pinning down what constitutes leadership (DeBare, 1991, p. A6): "Complaints about her leadership ability have plagued Mayor Rubin since she first took office. The mayor has always retorted that it is a question of style, not ability. As a feminist. . . , she would rather work quietly and cooperatively with her colleagues than twist arms or pound tables."[8] This could be an example of a coordinator mayor who is not being recognized for her contributions; as one critic put it, the agenda was set by others, not by the mayor. As we have seen, however, coordinative mayors and chairpersons are not the primary initiators of local governmental agendas. But other information in the article raises questions about whether the mayor has in fact been an effective coordinator: the mayor "failed to emerge as a consensus-builder and leader," and the council had difficulty handling some decisions and was characterized by some as "floundering." Critics also charged that the city missed opportunities because the mayor failed to take the lead and often played a sideline role. Simply on the basis of this analysis, it would appear that the mayor does not have all the attributes or accomplishments of a coordinator, much less those of a director. The failure to build consensus and the inability to strengthen the council as a decision-making body would indicate that the mayor is not an effective coordinator, despite whatever her intentions might have been. Anyway, even a coordinator should have the ability to fill the vacuum and take the lead when other members of the council do not. A basic part of the problem with this mayor's performance appears to be that her critics did not identify a coherent overall agenda during her tenure. This does not mean that a mayor or chairperson should be expected to come up with all the initiatives, or that the chief elected official should be incapable of supporting the ideas of others and letting them take the lead. Still, the mayor or chairperson should be able to communicate what goals the local government is pursuing and how they all fit together. Doing so will not guarantee that the chief elected official will be recognized as a leader by the media, but failing to do so invites the justifiable charge of a leadership void.

Weak leadership becomes an *issue*, as opposed to a public relations problem for the mayor or chairperson, when it creates dissatisfaction with local government and causes persons or groups to bypass the mayor or chairperson because of his or her perceived ineffectiveness. Lack of an agenda—the chief elected official's and/or the council's—impedes the council's ability to act decisively and coherently. It can even fuel efforts to change the form of government, in order to "strengthen" leadership. Coordinator mayors and chairpersons, who help to shape a consensus incorporating the ideas of the council and the community, need to be certain that they are communicating underlying purposes and strategies to the public.

### Structure and Leadership

In most cities (over 60 percent) and some counties, the method of selecting the chief elected official has been changed from selection by the governing board to direct election by voters. The primary reason is to make the mayor or chairperson a more effective leader and to strengthen the link between voters and local government. In some places, proposals have been considered to make more substantial changes and give the mayor or chairperson special powers. In San Jose, for example, the mayor develops the budget to be presented to the city council. Some mayors have proposed changing the city charter to permit the mayor to nominate the city manager to the council. The possibility of changing to the mayor-council or county executive form is being given more attention in some large jurisdictions. Change in the form of government is rare, but it happened in 1993 in St. Petersburg and West Palm Beach, Florida.

## Modest Changes in the Mayor's or Chairperson's Position

In the council-manager form, the most common revision affecting the chief elected official is direct election of the mayor or chairperson. Expanded power to make appointments, as well as other new responsibilities, have also been considered. These changes are modest, but they generated considerable debate among present-day urban reformers who were involved in the most recent revision of the model city and county charters, completed in 1989 by the National Civic League. Starting in 1899, the model charter has expressed the current thinking of municipal reformers about what constitutes the best provisions for local governmental charters. In a departure from previous model charters, the seventh revision (National Civic League, 1989) provides for direct election of the mayor as an option equal to election from within the council and specifies additional responsibilities for the mayor. The introduction to the seventh revision indicates that each community should consider which method would be "most conducive to the development of strong political leadership" (pp. xvi–xvii). The commentary notes, however, that "in many cities, particularly the larger ones, it is believed that this method [direct election] increases the potential for mayoral leadership by giving the mayor a city-wide popular support base" (p. 25). Protasel (1988) offers indirect evidence that this is the case by showing that abandonment of the council-manager form is less common in cities with direct election of the mayor.

The mayor's or chairperson's role is further enhanced over that prescribed in earlier revisions by the chief elected official's being given authority or responsibilities in three areas: the mayor or chairperson should (1) appoint members of citizen advisory boards and commissions with the consent of the council, (2) represent the city or county in intergovernmental relationships, and (3) present an annual "state of the city (or county)" message (for counties, see National Civic League, 1990). These expanded responsibilities are recommended for mayors and chairpersons in all cities and counties, regardless of how they are selected. The new charter attempts to crystallize a new leadership position in the council-manager form of government. The authority to appoint members of advisory boards, and the responsibilities of representing the city in external relations and preparing a summary statement of the city's conditions, needs, and direction, are designed to enhance the mayor's leadership role without diminishing the authority of the council or the manager. There is the clear intent to make the office a source of coordination among officials in city government and a guiding force in policy development. The recommendation that the mayor or chairperson be directly elected when the council is elected from districts reflects the hope that the mayor will exert a centralizing and coalescing impact on council members with diverse perspectives.

The case studies presented in this volume do not resolve the debate over the superiority of direct election versus selection from within the council, but they do shed some light on this structural question, on which reformers have differed. It is reasonable to assume that direct election enhances the leadership potential of the mayor or chairperson. A chief elected official would not have to so literally secure the permission of the council for a style or program, since he or she would be chosen independently of the council. Furthermore, by directly mobilizing popular support through the electoral process, the mayor or chairperson may have somewhat greater freedom to develop goals that go beyond the prevailing consensus. Moreover, when the mayor or chairperson uses the electoral process to demonstrate broad popularity that cuts across racial, economic, and political lines (consider Mayor Taylor of Roanoke), the chief elected official has a unique source of influence. Still, among the three directorial mayors featured here, two were initially chosen by their councils, rather than by voters, as was the chairperson categorized as a director. By contrast, two of the three coordinative leaders were elected. The relationship between method of selection and mayoral leadership is a complex one; direct election will not in itself make the chief elected official an effective policy initiator.

The cases also offer insights into two other recommendations of the National Civic League. First, several mayors have made good use of an annual "state of the city" address, including Mayor Rhea, who initiated the practice in her city in 1987. It provides a vehicle for education and goal setting and for reinforcing team building by giving expression to the goals of the council. Second, the activity of the mayor or chairperson in intergovernmental relations (Crowley's efforts in the California legislature, DuPuy's formation of the Carolinas Counties Coalition, MacIlwaine's plan for revenue sharing) or interorganizational relations (Mears's negotiations with MARTA) has been an important element in the strong leadership provided by many of the facilitative mayors and chairpersons.

There is no direct information from the case studies on the impact of giving appointment power to the mayor or chairperson, but it seems unlikely that this power in itself would substantially alter the influence of the chief elected official. What is important is whether the mayor or chairperson uses the responsibilities of the office in a facilitative leadership style, to engage all officials in effective decision making.

The case studies do not offer any information about the impact of giving the mayor or chairperson veto power. Melvin opposed the idea because he felt it would divide the mayor from the council; Protasel (1989) offers a similar argument.

The voting status of the mayor is emphasized by Wheeland, in Chapter Seven. In his opinion, the fact that Mayor Rhea could both preside at council meetings and vote as a regular member contributed to her acceptance by other council members.[9] All the other mayors and chairpersons featured in the case studies (including Roberts, under the commission form) were voting members of their governing board.

## Substantial Changes in the Mayor's or Chairperson's Position

Sparrow's study of San Diego (Chapter Nine) questions whether there is an outer limit of change beyond which facilitative leadership is no longer appropriate as the dominant model of leadership. He feels that this limit has been reached in San Diego. Part of the reason is the emergence, during Wilson's tenure, of full-time council members with independent staffs. The council is now fragmented, with each member operating as an "independent department head." The mayor cannot reclaim control over other elected officials. Charter change, in Sparrow's opinion, is now required; for officials and voters to know what they can expect from the mayor, the powers of the mayor's office need to be institutionalized.

The claim that council-manager government cannot work in very large, complex cities (and counties) is not a new one (see Banfield and Wilson, 1963). The emergence, in many of the other case-study cities, of mayors who use a collaborative style to overcome dissension and drift suggests that the facilitative model can be effective in very large cities if the right kind of leader appears. Furthermore, structural change is not necessarily a more likely path to increased governmental effectiveness.

The creation of executive mayors (or executive chairpersons) in this form is likely to produce other changes, which may have negative consequences. If the powers assigned to the mayor separate the mayor from the council and subordinate the manager to the chief elected official, then separation of powers enters the governmental process. The emergence of mayor-centered systems of governance in council-manager cities is likely to produce greater conflict between the council and the mayor and to create ambiguity in the lines of authority between each set of elected officials and the manager. The advantages of cooperative relationships between elected and professional leaders are jeopardized. The professional independence of the manager may be compromised, and the potential for more independent leadership from the mayor is likely to be offset by increased resistance from the council. Strengthening the powers of the mayor with respect to the council could also have the effect of diminishing the influence of more representative, district-based councils that include larger numbers of minority-group members (Blodgett, 1994). It is certainly more difficult to achieve consensus in socially and ethnically diverse councils, but decreasing the significance of the council in local government is not the only answer.

There could well be a net loss in leadership if the council is weakened and the professionalism of the manager is constrained in favor of formal powers for the mayor or chairperson or a change in the form of government. Since these case studies indicate that the chief elected official can be effective even when the council is divided, one could argue that it is more productive to promote the facilitative leadership of the mayor or chairperson than to change the structure substantially and make it more difficult for such leadership to emerge.

A recent assessment of the contributions of Mayor Emanuel Cleaver of Kansas City provides support for this argument (Enos, 1993). Cleaver has been identified in that assessment as a policy leader with an "aggressive economic-development agenda." In addition, he has "taken on a healing role" and "mend[ed] fences" on the city council. The mayor has been able to foster "cooperation on a panel once plagued by infighting." In the words of a community leader, "The council is a team now, and the mayor is the quarterback." Finding a facilitative leader to bring cohesion and a sense of purpose to a council-manager city may be easier and more efficacious than changing the powers of the mayor's office or changing the form of government.

### Facilitative Leadership in Mayor-Council Cities

The Chattanooga case (Chapter Ten) indicates that the facilitative style practiced in the commission form can be sustained by the same mayor after a charter change to adopt the mayor-council form. Gene Roberts was still seen as a team leader by one-third of the officials interviewed and was seen as an educator more often than he had been under the commission form. The dynamics of interaction in governments with separation of powers can easily push the chief elected official into adopting a power-oriented leadership style, but Roberts managed to maintain a facilitative style.

Indeed, the facilitative approach may have relevance to both the mayor-council form and the county executive form. Obviously, mayors and county executives do not have direct control over a wide range of participants in the political process (members of governing boards, citizens, interest groups, officials in other local governments). Even their own organizations are likely to include some staff with independent authority (especially in counties), and the literature on leadership in the private sector argues for the facilitative model, rather than for reliance on formal power, even though the chief executive officer in a corporation does have formal power on which to draw.

There is evidence that Roberts's experience is neither unique nor simply due to his having begun his tenure under the commission form. For example, Mayor Ed Rendell of Philadelphia has been called "one of the more adept facilitators in office at the moment" (Gurwitt, 1993, p. 40). He has been able to overcome a long period of dissension "by carefully sharing both the spotlight and his thinking" with other elected officials and by sharing his power to achieve consensus. Another example appears to be Edward H. McNamara, elected in 1986 as county executive in Wayne County, Michigan. Emphasizing a team approach, he reorganized county government, made management changes, took measures to control health and child-care costs for indigents, and fostered economic development (Shubart, 1992). Recognized in 1992 by *City & State* as one of the top local government executives, he credited the team approach in county government for the accomplishments that had been achieved. Of course, both these strong executives have formal powers as well. An observer in Philadelphia comments that Rendell has used the powers of his office to offset the resistance of employee unions to budget cuts; if the power of the mayor were fragmented, "there would be too many discordant voices without anyone in charge" (Gurwitt, 1993, p. 41).

Nevertheless, recognizing the value of the facilitative approach and avoiding the divisive consequences of attempts to impose control are positive alternatives for "strong" mayors and county executives. One mayor in a strong mayor-council city has concluded that mayors like himself may be more effective if they stress cooperation with other participants in local government. Michael B. Keys (1990), mayor of Elyria, Ohio, interviewed six other strong mayors and reports these findings:[10]

- Effective city government is characterized more by cooperation than by conflict.
- The mayor should serve a team-building function, working to build consensus in the council.

- The mayor should blend direction to the council in some areas with facilitation of the council's decision making in other areas.

Keys's conclusion is that an executive mayor both wishes and is able to be a facilitator with the council in certain areas. To do so, an elected chief executive needs to understand this alternative approach to leadership and to have training in the necessary skills.

## Change and the Viability of Facilitative Leadership

The College Station case (Chapter Eight) raises questions about the impact of change on the viability of facilitative leadership, even in small cities. The council in College Station has become more diverse and contentious as narrowly focused neighborhood advocates and business representatives have replaced the university employees who had dominated the council. A strong leadership role for the mayor had previously been expected, but meeting this expectation was simplified by the fact that the mayor was giving expression to values shared by most members of the council. A collaborative style of leadership, which had been "natural" for working with a homogeneous council, no longer worked as well.

Similar changes are occurring throughout the country. Council members are more diverse in their characteristics and seek to speak for a wider range of interests (Svara, 1991). More activist in their orientation, they are more frequently inclined to pursue independent political agendas. More are inclined to see council membership as the start of a political career (Ehrenhalt, 1991). By contrast with more homogeneous councils, made up of people who view council membership as community service, councils today include larger numbers of independent members from diverse backgrounds, with varied and sometimes narrow agendas. Such councils are not likely to accept the leadership of the mayor or chairperson passively.

Facilitative leadership is still appropriate in these situations, but a mayor or chairperson, to be effective, will have to find new ways to foster stronger working relationships and fashion a common sense of purpose and direction. The mayors and chairpersons in many of these case studies provided leadership that transformed relationships in precisely this kind of situation. This was certainly true of DuPuy, Mears, and MacIlwaine. Mayors Rhea and Taylor helped establish a new level of communication among officials and with the public. Such contributions are particularly important in periods when a city and its political climate are changing.

Changes that are occurring on councils and in communities where the diversity of the population is increasing do not undermine the viability of facilitative leadership, although they certainly strain it. Chief elected officials probably face greater difficulty in getting the "permission" of councils to be effective leaders. Mayors and chairpersons must rise to this new challenge by raising the level of their performance as facilitative leaders. Gurwitt (1993) concludes his assessment of whether governmental structure can produce effective political leaders with this advice: "The most important challenge isn't to write charters for them; it is to nurture them in the first place" (p. 41).

## Recommendations for Strengthening Leadership

Efforts to improve performance should start with the campaign for office—among the electorate, or within the council. A newly elected chief should also pay attention to the way he or she moves into the position during the transition process. All mayors and chairpersons need to examine key aspects of the council process: promoting trust and cooperation, goal setting, council procedures, and working relationships.

### Selection of Mayors and Chairpersons

When a mayor or chairperson is directly elected, the campaign and the coverage in the media will typically highlight some but not all of the information that voters need in order to choose an effective facilitative leader. Campaign activities are akin to the ceremonial and promotional aspects of the job; platforms and proposals offer insights into the extent to which the candidate will bring policy initiative to the office. It is important to determine what the candidate wants to accomplish and what kind of agenda the candidate has. Two evaluative questions about the policy agenda are the following: How well does the agenda match the needs of the community and the local government? How realistic is it, in terms of the nature of the mayor's or chairperson's office?

The interpersonal qualities of the candidate are likely to be less evident, unless voters and reporters specifically look for them. How will the candidate work with other officials to accomplish goals? How well is the candidate listening to other candidates and to incumbent members of the council as they talk about their own ideas for local government? What is the nature and extent of the candidate's networks? What is his or her record in working with others on collaborative efforts? Candidates often receive support for projecting themselves as solitary leaders, singlehandedly tackling problems and charting a new course for the future, but facilitative leadership will be strengthened by people who can work with and through others.

The task of assessing the less obvious personal qualities of the candidate will be easier for the members of a governing body who choose the mayor or chairperson from within their own ranks, particularly if they have had experience in working with the prospective chief elected official.[11] Nevertheless, a mayor or chairperson selected from within the council does not have the opportunity to generate popular support for policy initiatives in an election. Consequently, he or she may have greater difficulty securing support for an agenda from other officials.

### Transition to Office

Our common view of the transition process is that the newly elected official must take charge, hit the ground running, and do as much as possible to put his or her stamp on government before opponents regroup and obstruct the new official's plans. This advice, although applicable to conflict situations and the transition of an elected executive, is typically inappropriate for council-manager governments. The key goal of the new mayor or chairperson is to strengthen teamwork and develop a common sense of direction and purpose. In other words, the new mayor or chairperson seeks to put facilitative leadership into practice *as soon as the election is over.*

The government has a direction, set by the previous council, and the administrative organization continues to operate under the city or county manager. This is still an important time, however, for taking stock and setting in motion actions that will lead to change. Rapid change—for its own sake, or to take advantage of a closing "window of opportunity"—is not required. Since the mayor or chairperson and the council can initiate shifts in policy or direct the manager to alter administrative practice at any time, they can concentrate initially on establishing goals and assessing the need for change.

On occasion, the mayor or chairperson comes into office with the feeling that the manager should be changed. Of course, removing the manager is an action taken by the entire council, not just by the mayor or chairperson. But, unless there is evidence of wrongdoing that cannot be ignored, there are two major reasons why the mayor or chairperson should not move quickly to line up a majority of the council for terminating the manager's tenure.[12] First, the new mayor or chairperson should realize that he or she has not been in a good position to judge the competence or responsiveness of the manager. Those with no experience on the council may feel that the manager is "in charge" and therefore must be removed in order for them to change priorities or programs. This perception from a distance is usually erroneous; the manager has probably been doing what the council wanted. A mayor or chairperson who served on the council may be concerned that the manager was so close to the former chief elected official that an effective working relationship with the new mayor or chairperson will be impossible. An incumbent may even have been able to manipulate events, to make it appear that the manager was supporting him or her in the campaign. This apparent closeness may be the impression that the former mayor or chairperson wanted to create, rather than excessive loyalty to the previous incumbent on the manager's part. Second, as several of the cases demonstrate, the performance of the manager is affected by the abilities of the mayor or chairperson. Shortcomings could have been produced in part by the weakness of the previous incumbent in promoting effective teamwork. Stronger leadership by the mayor or chairperson, as we have seen, can enhance the performance of both the manager and the council.

The mayor or chairperson and new council members should

assume that the manager will perform in a professionally responsible way, to assist them in taking office and to help them achieve their goals in office. In most cities and counties, this assumption is warranted. In the atypical situation, in which the manager is perceived to be wedded to the previous mayor or council and hostile to newcomers, the reality usually is that the manager is just as intent on working for the new council and will demonstrate that, if given the chance. Therefore, making a change would be unnecessary, costly, and disruptive of a smooth transition. When the manager's performance is objectively judged to be unsatisfactory, after a period of joint work the council can make a change, with neither the appearance nor the reality of claiming the spoils of electoral victory.[13]

### Promoting Trust and Cooperation

The foundation for building effective relationships is a clear understanding of the mayor or chairperson's role in the governmental process. Although it is the exception rather than the rule, some mayors and chairpersons—both new and experienced—produce tension with the other members of the council or the manager because of a poor understanding of their own role. For example, the mayor who says, "I'm in charge" and seeks to make unilateral changes in policy or practice (outside his or her own office) is going to strain relationships. The manager is put into a difficult position, since he or she is obligated to defend two principles: that the whole council makes policy, and that the manager is the chief executive officer. The support of the council may also be jeopardized.

The mayor or chairperson should lead the council and the manager in a collective effort to determine how they can all work together effectively and ensure a high level of performance in the government. The chief elected official should pay attention to process and promote awareness of the need for change when it is warranted. This will often entail the use of special kinds of meetings, at which the council is not addressing an agenda of specific actions. These may take the form of periodic work sessions, a retreat, or a combination of the two.

If the groundwork is properly laid, a council retreat can be a useful vehicle for accomplishing a number of tasks (Jenne, 1988). It is important that the entire council accept the idea of having a retreat and agree to participate. The council does not need to leave town, but the retreat should be so structured as to make it different from a normal council meeting. There should be sufficient time, usually one or two days, to discuss a range of issues fully. Arrangements should be made to have an outside facilitator guide the council through its discussion. This is an open meeting, but media representatives, if they attend, should be encouraged to respect the spirit of the session. The purpose is an open-ended exploration of where the city is going and how officials work together, and officials are encouraged to try out ideas. Comments should not be reported in the detail that would be expected of debate that precedes an official action of the council at a regular meeting, nor should they be taken out of context. Whatever method is used to organize the discussion, attention should be given to goal setting and to relations between and among the mayor or chairperson, the council, and the manager.

### Goal and Priority Setting

The goal-setting process starts with a review of conditions and trends in the city or county, drawing on information prepared by the manager and staff. This background information is helpful for ensuring that goals address real conditions, rather than superficial symptoms of deeper problems. This information may also reveal problems that have not been recognized. Goals are the long-term improvements that the council would like to accomplish. When agreement is reached, goals provide a framework for identifying the policies and programs that should be undertaken in the short term (the next year or two). It is important to establish priorities among these policies and projects, as a guide to the manager and staff about where to place emphasis and how to allocate scarce resources.

As we have seen, effective mayors and chairpersons differ in the degree to which they seek to have their own policy agendas accepted by their councils. Some place more emphasis on creating a common commitment to goal setting and help all officials work through the process of generating and sorting out proposals, including their own. Others advocate a comprehensive set of initiatives. These officials can provide important policy leadership, as long as they recognize that they cannot impose their ideas on the council or exclude council members from policy development. Either approach can work well if the mayor or chairperson pays close attention to whether other members of the council are coming forth with ideas of their own.

In addition to policy initiatives, the council should consider whether improvements in administration (service delivery) or management (productivity) are needed. If so, council members should confer with the manager to set clear goals and expectations about the nature of change, and they should review the manager's proposed timetable for accomplishing it.

### Council Procedures

It is useful for officials to examine the council's work methods and procedures periodically. Are the timing and frequency of meetings appropriate? Is there dissatisfaction with the length of meetings or with how smoothly they run? As presiding officer, the chief elected official will guide the council in the conduct of its business and should look at how well the process is organized. The mayor or chairperson and the manager should review how well prepared the chief elected official is to handle items that will be covered in a meeting, and whether more careful briefing is required. With more careful preparation, meetings may become shorter and more productive. The mayor or chairperson should encourage the council to discuss mutual expectations of the mayor, council members, and the manager and staff regarding preparation and the conduct of meetings. (It is useful to cover these topics, along with policy goals, at the council retreat.) Other matters that should be addressed include appointment of board and commission members, committee assignments, and the council's relations with the public.

### Working Relationships

In addition to procedures, the working relationship between the mayor or chairperson and the manager and between the council and the manager should be examined. How the mayor or chairperson and the manager will work together should be clearly understood and accepted. The council's and the chief elected official's mutual expectations should be reviewed. It is important for everyone to recognize that the mayor or chairperson monitors and adjusts relationships to ensure effective interaction. For example, this may entail talking to an individual council member who is getting involved in dealing with the staff. If council members are dissatisfied with the amount and kind of information that is being provided to them in advance of meetings, the mayor can work with the manager to adjust it. It is particularly important to ensure that a regular process has been established for the council's appraisal of the performance of the city or county manager.

In sum, the mayor or chairperson must take responsibility for carefully examining how the city or county does its business (the *process* of government) and where the city or county is going (the *purpose* of government). Using extensive consultation with the council and the manager, and in regular contact with a wide range of groups in the community, the mayor or chairperson can guide officials through a process of constructive change.

### Conclusion

Mayors and chairpersons can be important leaders in council-manager communities, and there are many who are because they use a facilitative style of leadership. The material presented here offers a description of the roles these officials fill, the resources they use, and the impact they have. The case studies provide detailed portraits of a select group of successful chief elected officials. From these studies, it has been possible to refine the conceptualization of the job of the mayor or chairperson and to fully elaborate a facilitative leadership model for the public sector. Although this leadership approach is not confined to council-manager governments or to the chief elected official, it is particularly well suited to the office of mayor or chairperson in this form of government.

Cities and counties are at a critical juncture in the choice of methods to enhance the leadership of the chief elected official. They can seek to increase the ability of this official to be a facilitative leader, who will operate within the normal confines of the council-manager form, or they can separate the mayor or chairperson from the council by giving this official some formal power in policy making, administration, and/or management. The experience in mayor-council cities (the experience of Chattanooga notwithstanding) is for the mayor to seek ever more formal power in order to exert greater control over the council.

Effective mayors and chairpersons do not need to overshadow the rest of the council or supplant the city manager. The cases illustrate how the mayor or chairperson can have a positive impact on the level of the council's involvement in goal setting and policy making. Evidence from a survey of cities in North Carolina and Ohio indicates that high mayoral leadership increases the council's attention to long-range concerns, makes the council more proactive, and improves the council's ability to make decisions. Furthermore, the council is more actively engaged in the formation of mission and the setting of policy as the mayor's leadership expands. The leadership of the mayor or chairperson offsets a tendency for the council to be essentially reactive and restricted to simply reviewing proposals that come from the manager.

The manager's involvement is not negatively affected by the level of the mayor's leadership. Referring again to the survey of cities, we can see that there is a higher level of positive interaction when elected leaders are stronger. Strong facilitative leadership can be provided, along with that of the city manager. The working relationship is strengthened as leadership by the mayor or chairperson expands, particularly the relationship between the chief elected official and the manager. As noted in Chapter One, survey data indicate that mayors who are ranked lower in leadership are also perceived to be too involved in administrative activities. It appears that effective leaders instill a sense of purpose and set broad goals, whereas mayors or chairpersons with limited horizons are preoccupied with the here-and-now and inclined to meddle in administrative details.

Therefore, there is no evidence to support the presumption that a high level of leadership necessarily causes the mayor to take over executive functions or leads to conflict with the manager, nor is structural change to expand the powers of the chief elected official the only path to strengthening elected leadership. The combination of political and professional leadership is a unique strength of the council-manager form of government. A key to ensuring that the council and the manager will work together effectively and move in a positive direction is facilitative leadership by the mayor or chairperson. The case studies indicate that the mayor or chairperson can focus the council's attention on important goals and lead the council and the manager to accomplish them. With increasing diversity on governing boards and in American communities, strong facilitative leadership may be the prerequisite of effective governmental performance in the 1990s and beyond.

## Notes

1.  Professor Larry Keller of Cleveland State University stressed this point in his paper on the "moral leadership" of Mayor Murray Seasongood of Cincinnati, presented at the 1991 conference on facilitative leadership for which the papers that became the chapters in this volume were prepared.
2.  For example, Mayor James Eason of Hampton, Virginia, whose leadership was described in a paper for the conference (see note 1) by Assistant City Manager Elizabeth A. Walker, takes the position that the mayor should share this task with all other members of the council and should not take on a much heavier burden of commitment than other members do.
3.  There is room for confusion here, since the first four roles also involve communication, coordination, or both, and can be filled more or less actively. For example, one mayor may actively seek out the media and be forthcoming with information, whereas another may avoid the media as much as possible. The roles are essentially built into the position, and the mayor or chairperson is prompted to fill them by general expectations, demands, and charter provisions.
4.  Mayor Eason of Hampton refuses to spend inordinately more time than other council members and seeks to delegate ceremonial tasks to other members of the council whenever possible.
5.  Jonathan Howes, director of the Center for Urban and Re-

gional Studies at the University of North Carolina, Chapel Hill, made these comments at the conference where the cases were originally presented.

6. This is not a pejorative statement. Separation of powers is supposed to lead to conflict as one official checks the power of another, and we ought not to be surprised when it does.

7. According to Mead, however, DuPuy quickly earned a reputation for effectiveness.

8. There is no independent confirmation of these assessments. The example is useful, however, because it illustrates how one might identify a true coordinator.

9. See C. M. Wheeland, "The Mayor in Small Council-Manager Municipalities: Are Mayors to Be Seen and Not Heard?" *National Civic Review*, 1990, *79*, 337–349. Wheeland concludes that the absence of regular voting status limits a mayor's leadership.

10. These points are from an unpublished paper by Keys. He prepared it in conjunction with the Council Collaboration Program conducted by the Public Services Institute, under the direction of James Kunde, who at that time was on the staff of Lorain Community College, in cooperation with the National League of Cities.

11. It should be noted, however, that a sizable proportion of mayors and chairpersons selected by the council is in fact determined by formal or informal conventions. For example, among the subjects in the case studies, Mayor Melvin was first selected mayor because he was the highest overall vote getter in an at-large election, and Chairperson DuPuy had the highest vote total among the Republican majority.

12. In addition to the factors discussed, it is also important to preserve the principle that the manager's office is a nonpolitical one, which does not change with a new mayor or a new majority on the council. Precipitous action could create the political expectation that a new mayor should pick his or her own manager. The reputation of the city or the county as a good place for managers to work will also be tarnished, and the best candidates may avoid the city or county government in the future. Moreover, the valuable assistance that the man-

ager provides during the transition period will be lost or diminished if the new chief elected officer clearly wants the manager to be removed.

13.    Three atypical situations will alter the normal transition process: if the manager is patently unsuitable for office, if the manager resigns for whatever reason after the election, or if the lame-duck council fires the manager even though newly elected members of the council would have preferred to have the manager continue. In any of these situations, a greater burden will fall on the mayor or the chairperson-elect to organize the transition.

## References

Banfield, E. C., and Wilson, J. Q. *City Politics.* New York: Vintage Books, 1963.

Blodgett, T. "Beware the Lure of the 'Strong Mayor.' " *Public Management,* 1994, *76,* 6–11.

DeBare, I. "After 20 Years, Question Lingers: Can Rubin Lead?" *Sacramento Bee,* Apr. 8, 1991, pp. A1, A6.

Ehrenhalt, A. *The United States of Ambition.* New York: Random House, 1991.

Enos, G. "Cleaver Making Good Use of the Bully Pulpit." *City & State,* May 10, 1993, pp. 3, 23.

Gurwitt, R. "The Lure of the Strong Mayor." *Governing,* 1993, *8,* 36–41.

Jenne, K. "Governing Board Retreats." *Popular Government,* 1988, *53,* 20–26.

Keys, M. B. "Facilitation: Next Stop—City Hall?" Unpublished paper, Elyria, Ohio, 1990.

National Civic League. *Model City Charter.* (7th rev.) Denver, Colo.: National Civic League Press, 1989.

National Civic League. *Model County Charter.* (Rev. ed.) Denver, Colo.: National Civic League Press, 1990.

Protasel, G. J. "Abandonments of the Council-Manager Plan: A New Institutionalist Perspective." *Public Administration Review,* 1988, *48,* 807–812.

Protasel, G. J. "Leadership in Council-Manager Cities: The Institutional Implications." In H. G. Frederickson (ed.), *Ideal and Practice in City Management*. Washington, D.C.: International City Management Association, 1989.

Shubart, E. "Call Him Mr. Ideas." *City & State*, Aug. 24, 1992, pp. 9, 22.

Svara, J. H. *Continuity and Change in American City Councils, 1979–1989*. Washington, D.C.: National League of Cities, 1991.

Thomas, K. W., and Kilmann, R. H. *Conflict Mode Instrument*. Tuxedo, N.Y.: Xicom, 1974.

# *Index*